Iowa
Assessments
SUCCESS STRATEGIES
Math

IA Test Review
for the Iowa
Assessments

Dear Future Exam Success Story

First of all, **THANK YOU** for purchasing Mometrix study materials!

Second, congratulations! You are one of the few determined test-takers who are committed to doing whatever it takes to excel on your exam. **You have come to the right place.** We developed these study materials with one goal in mind: to deliver you the information you need in a format that's concise and easy to use.

In addition to optimizing your guide for the content of the test, we've outlined our recommended steps for breaking down the preparation process into small, attainable goals so you can make sure you stay on track.

We've also analyzed the entire test-taking process, identifying the most common pitfalls and showing how you can overcome them and be ready for any curveball the test throws you.

Standardized testing is one of the biggest obstacles on your road to success, which only increases the importance of doing well in the high-pressure, high-stakes environment of test day. Your results on this test could have a significant impact on your future, and this guide provides the information and practical advice to help you achieve your full potential on test day.

Your success is our success

We would love to hear from you! If you would like to share the story of your exam success or if you have any questions or comments in regard to our products, please contact us at **800-673-8175** or **support@mometrix.com**.

Thanks again for your business and we wish you continued success!

Sincerely,
The Mometrix Test Preparation Team

> **Need more help? Check out our flashcards at:**
> **http://MometrixFlashcards.com/Iowa**

TABLE OF CONTENTS

Introduction

Thank you for purchasing this resource! You have made the choice to prepare yourself for a test that could have a huge impact on your future, and this guide is designed to help you be fully ready for test day. Obviously, it's important to have a solid understanding of the test material, but you also need to be prepared for the unique environment and stressors of the test, so that you can perform to the best of your abilities.

For this purpose, the first section that appears in this guide is the **Success Strategies**. We've devoted countless hours to meticulously researching what works and what doesn't, and we've boiled down our findings to the five most impactful steps you can take to improve your performance on the test. We start at the beginning with study planning and move through the preparation process, all the way to the testing strategies that will help you get the most out of what you know when you're finally sitting in front of the test.

We recommend that you start preparing for your test as far in advance as possible. However, if you've bought this guide as a last-minute study resource and only have a few days before your test, we recommend that you skip over the first two Success Strategies since they address a long-term study plan.

If you struggle with **test anxiety**, we strongly encourage you to check out our recommendations for how you can overcome it. Test anxiety is a formidable foe, but it can be beaten, and we want to make sure you have the tools you need to defeat it.

Success Strategy #1 – Plan Big, Study Small

There's a lot riding on your performance. If you want to ace this test, you're going to need to keep your skills sharp and the material fresh in your mind. You need a plan that lets you review everything you need to know while still fitting in your schedule. We'll break this strategy down into three categories.

Information Organization

Start with the information you already have: the official test outline. From this, you can make a complete list of all the concepts you need to cover before the test. Organize these concepts into groups that can be studied together, and create a list of any related vocabulary you need to learn so you can brush up on any difficult terms. You'll want to keep this vocabulary list handy once you actually start studying since you may need to add to it along the way.

Time Management

Once you have your set of study concepts, decide how to spread them out over the time you have left before the test. Break your study plan into small, clear goals so you have a manageable task for each day and know exactly what you're doing. Then, just focus on one small step at a time. When you manage your time this way, you don't need to spend hours at a time studying. Studying a small block of content for a short period each day helps you retain information better and avoid stressing over how much you have left to do. You can relax knowing that you have a plan to cover everything in time. In order for this strategy to be effective though, you have to start studying early and stick to your schedule. Avoid the exhaustion and futility that comes from last-minute cramming!

Study Environment

The environment you study in has a big impact on your learning. Studying in a coffee shop, while probably more enjoyable, is not likely to be as fruitful as studying in a quiet room. It's important to keep distractions to a minimum. You're only planning to study for a short block of time, so make the most of it. Don't pause to check your phone or get up to find a snack. It's also important to **avoid multitasking**. Research has consistently shown that multitasking will make your studying dramatically less effective. Your study area should also be comfortable and well-lit so you don't have the distraction of straining your eyes or sitting on an uncomfortable chair.

The time of day you study is also important. You want to be rested and alert. Don't wait until just before bedtime. Study when you'll be most likely to comprehend and remember. Even better, if you know what time of day your test will be, set that time aside for study. That way your brain will be used to working on that subject at that specific time and you'll have a better chance of recalling information.

Finally, it can be helpful to team up with others who are studying for the same test. Your actual studying should be done in as isolated an environment as possible, but the work of organizing the information and setting up the study plan can be divided up. In between study sessions, you can discuss with your teammates the concepts that you're all studying and quiz each other on the

2

details. Just be sure that your teammates are as serious about the test as you are. If you find that your study time is being replaced with social time, you might need to find a new team.

Success Strategy #2 – Make Your Studying Count

You're devoting a lot of time and effort to preparing for this test, so you want to be absolutely certain it will pay off. This means doing more than just reading the content and hoping you can remember it on test day. It's important to make every minute of study count. There are two main areas you can focus on to make your studying count:

Retention

It doesn't matter how much time you study if you can't remember the material. You need to make sure you are retaining the concepts. To check your retention of the information you're learning, try recalling it at later times with minimal prompting. Try carrying around flashcards and glance at one or two from time to time or ask a friend who's also studying for the test to quiz you.

To enhance your retention, look for ways to put the information into practice so that you can apply it rather than simply recalling it. If you're using the information in practical ways, it will be much easier to remember. Similarly, it helps to solidify a concept in your mind if you're not only reading it to yourself but also explaining it to someone else. Ask a friend to let you teach them about a concept you're a little shaky on (or speak aloud to an imaginary audience if necessary). As you try to summarize, define, give examples, and answer your friend's questions, you'll understand the concepts better and they will stay with you longer. Finally, step back for a big picture view and ask yourself how each piece of information fits with the whole subject. When you link the different concepts together and see them working together as a whole, it's easier to remember the individual components.

Finally, practice showing your work on any multi-step problems, even if you're just studying. Writing out each step you take to solve a problem will help solidify the process in your mind, and you'll be more likely to remember it during the test.

Modality

Modality simply refers to the means or method by which you study. Choosing a study modality that fits your own individual learning style is crucial. No two people learn best in exactly the same way, so it's important to know your strengths and use them to your advantage.

For example, if you learn best by visualization, focus on visualizing a concept in your mind and draw an image or a diagram. Try color-coding your notes, illustrating them, or creating symbols that will trigger your mind to recall a learned concept. If you learn best by hearing or discussing information, find a study partner who learns the same way or read aloud to yourself. Think about how to put the information in your own words. Imagine that you are giving a lecture on the topic and record yourself so you can listen to it later.

For any learning style, flashcards can be helpful. Organize the information so you can take advantage of spare moments to review. Underline key words or phrases. Use different colors for different categories. Mnemonic devices (such as creating a short list in which every item starts with the same letter) can also help with retention. Find what works best for you and use it to store the information in your mind most effectively and easily.

4

Success Strategy #3 – Practice the Right Way

Your success on test day depends not only on how many hours you put into preparing, but also on whether you prepared the right way. It's good to check along the way to see if your studying is paying off. One of the most effective ways to do this is by taking practice tests to evaluate your progress. Practice tests are useful because they show exactly where you need to improve. Every time you take a practice test, pay special attention to these three groups of questions:

- The questions you got wrong
- The questions you had to guess on, even if you guessed right
- The questions you found difficult or slow to work through

This will show you exactly what your weak areas are, and where you need to devote more study time. Ask yourself why each of these questions gave you trouble. Was it because you didn't understand the material? Was it because you didn't remember the vocabulary? Do you need more repetitions on this type of question to build speed and confidence? Dig into those questions and figure out how you can strengthen your weak areas as you go back to review the material.

Additionally, many practice tests have a section explaining the answer choices. It can be tempting to read the explanation and think that you now have a good understanding of the concept. However, an explanation likely only covers part of the question's broader context. Even if the explanation makes sense, **go back and investigate** every concept related to the question until you're positive you have a thorough understanding.

As you go along, keep in mind that the practice test is just that: practice. Memorizing these questions and answers will not be very helpful on the actual test because it is unlikely to have any of the same exact questions. If you only know the right answers to the sample questions, you won't be prepared for the real thing. **Study the concepts** until you understand them fully, and then you'll be able to answer any question that shows up on the test.

It's important to wait on the practice tests until you're ready. If you take a test on your first day of study, you may be overwhelmed by the amount of material covered and how much you need to learn. Work up to it gradually.

On test day, you'll need to be prepared for answering questions, managing your time, and using the test-taking strategies you've learned. It's a lot to balance, like a mental marathon that will have a big impact on your future. Like training for a marathon, you'll need to start slowly and work your way up. When test day arrives, you'll be ready.

Start with what you've read in the first two Success Strategies—plan your course and study in the way that works best for you. If you have time, consider using multiple study resources to get different approaches to the same concepts. It can be helpful to see difficult concepts from more than one angle. Then find a good source for practice tests. Many times, the test website will suggest potential study resources or provide sample tests.

Practice Test Strategy

If you're able to find at least three practice tests, we recommend this strategy:

UNTIMED AND OPEN-BOOK PRACTICE

Take the first test with no time constraints and with your notes and study guide handy. Take your time and focus on applying the strategies you've learned.

TIMED AND OPEN-BOOK PRACTICE

Take the second practice test open-book as well, but set a timer and practice pacing yourself to finish in time.

TIMED AND CLOSED-BOOK PRACTICE

Take any other practice tests as if it were test day. Set a timer and put away your study materials. Sit at a table or desk in a quiet room, imagine yourself at the testing center, and answer questions as quickly and accurately as possible.

Keep repeating timed and closed-book tests on a regular basis until you run out of practice tests or it's time for the actual test. Your mind will be ready for the schedule and stress of test day, and you'll be able to focus on recalling the material you've learned.

Success Strategy #4 – Pace Yourself

Once you're fully prepared for the material on the test, your biggest challenge on test day will be managing your time. Just knowing that the clock is ticking can make you panic even if you have plenty of time left. Work on pacing yourself so you can build confidence against the time constraints of the exam. Pacing is a difficult skill to master, especially in a high-pressure environment, so **practice is vital**.

Set time expectations for your pace based on how much time is available. For example, if a section has 60 questions and the time limit is 30 minutes, you know you have to average 30 seconds or less per question in order to answer them all. Although 30 seconds is the hard limit, set 25 seconds per question as your goal, so you reserve extra time to spend on harder questions. When you budget extra time for the harder questions, you no longer have any reason to stress when those questions take longer to answer.

Don't let this time expectation distract you from working through the test at a calm, steady pace, but keep it in mind so you don't spend too much time on any one question. Recognize that taking extra time on one question you don't understand may keep you from answering two that you do understand later in the test. If your time limit for a question is up and you're still not sure of the answer, mark it and move on, and come back to it later if the time and the test format allow. If the testing format doesn't allow you to return to earlier questions, just make an educated guess; then put it out of your mind and move on.

On the easier questions, be careful not to rush. It may seem wise to hurry through them so you have more time for the challenging ones, but it's not worth missing one if you know the concept and just didn't take the time to read the question fully. Work efficiently but make sure you understand the question and have looked at all of the answer choices, since more than one may seem right at first.

Even if you're paying attention to the time, you may find yourself a little behind at some point. You should speed up to get back on track, but do so wisely. Don't panic; just take a few seconds less on each question until you're caught up. Don't guess without thinking, but do look through the answer choices and eliminate any you know are wrong. If you can get down to two choices, it is often worthwhile to guess from those. Once you've chosen an answer, move on and don't dwell on any that you skipped or had to hurry through. If a question was taking too long, chances are it was one of the harder ones, so you weren't as likely to get it right anyway.

On the other hand, if you find yourself getting ahead of schedule, it may be beneficial to slow down a little. The more quickly you work, the more likely you are to make a careless mistake that will affect your score. You've budgeted time for each question, so don't be afraid to spend that time. Practice an efficient but careful pace to get the most out of the time you have.

Test-Taking Strategies

This section contains a list of test-taking strategies that you may find helpful as you work through the test. By taking what you know and applying logical thought, you can maximize your chances of answering any question correctly!

It is very important to realize that every question is different and every person is different: no single strategy will work on every question, and no single strategy will work for every person. That's why we've included all of them here, so you can try them out and determine which ones work best for different types of questions and which ones work best for you.

Question Strategies

READ CAREFULLY

Read the question and answer choices carefully. Don't miss the question because you misread the terms. You have plenty of time to read each question thoroughly and make sure you understand what is being asked. Yet a happy medium must be attained, so don't waste too much time. You must read carefully, but efficiently.

CONTEXTUAL CLUES

Look for contextual clues. If the question includes a word you are not familiar with, look at the immediate context for some indication of what the word might mean. Contextual clues can often give you all the information you need to decipher the meaning of an unfamiliar word. Even if you can't determine the meaning, you may be able to narrow down the possibilities enough to make a solid guess at the answer to the question.

PREFIXES

If you're having trouble with a word in the question or answer choices, try dissecting it. Take advantage of every clue that the word might include. Prefixes and suffixes can be a huge help. Usually they allow you to determine a basic meaning. Pre- means before, post- means after, pro - is positive, de- is negative. From prefixes and suffixes, you can get an idea of the general meaning of the word and try to put it into context.

HEDGE WORDS

Watch out for critical hedge words, such as *likely, may, can, sometimes, often, almost, mostly, usually, generally, rarely,* and *sometimes.* Question writers insert these hedge phrases to cover every possibility. Often an answer choice will be wrong simply because it leaves no room for exception. Be on guard for answer choices that have definitive words such as *exactly* and *always.*

SWITCHBACK WORDS

Stay alert for *switchbacks.* These are the words and phrases frequently used to alert you to shifts in thought. The most common switchback words are *but, although,* and *however.* Others include *nevertheless, on the other hand, even though, while, in spite of, despite, regardless of.* Switchback words are important to catch because they can change the direction of the question or an answer choice.

8

FACE VALUE

When in doubt, use common sense. Accept the situation in the problem at face value. Don't read too much into it. These problems will not require you to make wild assumptions. If you have to go beyond creativity and warp time or space in order to have an answer choice fit the question, then you should move on and consider the other answer choices. These are normal problems rooted in reality. The applicable relationship or explanation may not be readily apparent, but it is there for you to figure out. Use your common sense to interpret anything that isn't clear.

Answer Choice Strategies

ANSWER SELECTION

The most thorough way to pick an answer choice is to identify and eliminate wrong answers until only one is left, then confirm it is the correct answer. Sometimes an answer choice may immediately seem right, but be careful. The test writers will usually put more than one reasonable answer choice on each question, so take a second to read all of them and make sure that the other choices are not equally obvious. As long as you have time left, it is better to read every answer choice than to pick the first one that looks right without checking the others.

ANSWER CHOICE FAMILIES

An answer choice family consists of two (in rare cases, three) answer choices that are very similar in construction and cannot all be true at the same time. If you see two answer choices that are direct opposites or parallels, one of them is usually the correct answer. For instance, if one answer choice says that quantity x increases and another either says that quantity x decreases (opposite) or says that quantity y increases (parallel), then those answer choices would fall into the same family. An answer choice that doesn't match the construction of the answer choice family is more likely to be incorrect. Most questions will not have answer choice families, but when they do appear, you should be prepared to recognize them.

ELIMINATE ANSWERS

Eliminate answer choices as soon as you realize they are wrong, but make sure you consider all possibilities. If you are eliminating answer choices and realize that the last one you are left with is also wrong, don't panic. Start over and consider each choice again. There may be something you missed the first time that you will realize on the second pass.

AVOID FACT TRAPS

Don't be distracted by an answer choice that is factually true but doesn't answer the question. You are looking for the choice that answers the question. Stay focused on what the question is asking for so you don't accidentally pick an answer that is true but incorrect. Always go back to the question and make sure the answer choice you've selected actually answers the question and is not merely a true statement.

EXTREME STATEMENTS

In general, you should avoid answers that put forth extreme actions as standard practice or proclaim controversial ideas as established fact. An answer choice that states the "process should be used in certain situations, if..." is much more likely to be correct than one that states the "process should be discontinued completely." The first is a calm rational statement and doesn't even make a definitive, uncompromising stance, using a hedge word *if* to provide wiggle room, whereas the second choice is a radical idea and far more extreme.

9

BENCHMARK

As you read through the answer choices and you come across one that seems to answer the question well, mentally select that answer choice. This is not your final answer, but it's the one that will help you evaluate the other answer choices. The one that you selected is your benchmark or standard for judging each of the other answer choices. Every other answer choice must be compared to your benchmark. That choice is correct until proven otherwise by another answer choice beating it. If you find a better answer, then that one becomes your new benchmark. Once you've decided that no other choice answers the question as well as your benchmark, you have your final answer.

PREDICT THE ANSWER

Before you even start looking at the answer choices, it is often best to try to predict the answer. When you come up with the answer on your own, it is easier to avoid distractions and traps because you will know exactly what to look for. The right answer choice is unlikely to be word-for-word what you came up with, but it should be a close match. Even if you are confident that you have the right answer, you should still take the time to read each option before moving on.

General Strategies

TOUGH QUESTIONS

If you are stumped on a problem or it appears too hard or too difficult, don't waste time. Move on! Remember though, if you can quickly check for obviously incorrect answer choices, your chances of guessing correctly are greatly improved. Before you completely give up, at least try to knock out a couple of possible answers. Eliminate what you can and then guess at the remaining answer choices before moving on.

CHECK YOUR WORK

Since you will probably not know every term listed and the answer to every question, it is important that you get credit for the ones that you do know. Don't miss any questions through careless mistakes. If at all possible, try to take a second to look back over your answer selection and make sure you've selected the correct answer choice and haven't made a costly careless mistake (such as marking an answer choice that you didn't mean to mark). This quick double check should more than pay for itself in caught mistakes for the time it costs.

PACE YOURSELF

It's easy to be overwhelmed when you're looking at a page full of questions; your mind is confused and full of random thoughts, and the clock is ticking down faster than you would like. Calm down and maintain the pace that you have set for yourself. Especially as you get down to the last few minutes of the test, don't let the small numbers on the clock make you panic. As long as you are on track by monitoring your pace, you are guaranteed to have time for each question.

DON'T RUSH

It is very easy to make errors when you are in a hurry. Maintaining a fast pace in answering questions is pointless if it makes you miss questions that you would have gotten right otherwise. Test writers like to include distracting information and wrong answers that seem right. Taking a little extra time to avoid careless mistakes can make all the difference in your test score. Find a pace that allows you to be confident in the answers that you select.

KEEP MOVING

Panicking will not help you pass the test, so do your best to stay calm and keep moving. Taking deep breaths and going through the answer elimination steps you practiced can help to break through a stress barrier and keep your pace.

Final Notes

The combination of a solid foundation of content knowledge and the confidence that comes from practicing your plan for applying that knowledge is the key to maximizing your performance on test day. As your foundation of content knowledge is built up and strengthened, you'll find that the strategies included in this chapter become more and more effective in helping you quickly sift through the distractions and traps of the test to isolate the correct answer.

Now it's time to move on to the test content chapters of this book, but be sure to keep your goal in mind. As you read, think about how you will be able to apply this information on the test. If you've already seen sample questions for the test and you have an idea of the question format and style, try to come up with questions of your own that you can answer based on what you're reading. This will give you valuable practice applying your knowledge in the same ways you can expect to on test day.

Good luck and good studying!

Number and Quantities

Numbers

CLASSIFICATIONS OF NUMBERS

Numbers are the basic building blocks of mathematics. Specific features of numbers are identified by the following terms:

Integer – any positive or negative whole number, including zero. Integers do not include fractions $\left(\frac{1}{3}\right)$, decimals (0.56), or mixed numbers $\left(7\frac{3}{4}\right)$.

Prime number – any whole number greater than 1 that has only two factors, itself and 1; that is, a number that can be divided evenly only by 1 and itself.

Composite number – any whole number greater than 1 that has more than two different factors; in other words, any whole number that is not a prime number. For example: The composite number 8 has the factors of 1, 2, 4, and 8.

Even number – any integer that can be divided by 2 without leaving a remainder. For example: 2, 4, 6, 8, and so on.

Odd number – any integer that cannot be divided evenly by 2. For example: 3, 5, 7, 9, and so on.

Decimal number – any number that uses a decimal point to show the part of the number that is less than one. Example: 1.234.

Decimal point – a symbol used to separate the ones place from the tenths place in decimals or dollars from cents in currency.

Decimal place – the position of a number to the right of the decimal point. In the decimal 0.123, the 1 is in the first place to the right of the decimal point, indicating tenths; the 2 is in the second place, indicating hundredths; and the 3 is in the third place, indicating thousandths.

The **decimal**, or base 10, system is a number system that uses ten different digits (0, 1, 2, 3, 4, 5, 6, 7, 8, 9). An example of a number system that uses something other than ten digits is the **binary**, or base 2, number system, used by computers, which uses only the numbers 0 and 1. It is thought that the decimal system originated because people had only their 10 fingers for counting.

Rational numbers include all integers, decimals, and fractions. Any terminating or repeating decimal number is a rational number.

Irrational numbers cannot be written as fractions or decimals because the number of decimal places is infinite and there is no recurring pattern of digits within the number. For example, pi (π) begins with 3.141592 and continues without terminating or repeating, so pi is an irrational number.

13

Real numbers are the set of all rational and irrational numbers.

THE NUMBER LINE

A number line is a graph to see the distance between numbers. Basically, this graph shows the relationship between numbers. So a number line may have a point for zero and may show negative numbers on the left side of the line. Also, any positive numbers are placed on the right side of the line. For example, consider the points labeled on the following number line:

We can use the dashed lines on the number line to identify each point. Each dashed line between two whole numbers is $\frac{1}{4}$. The line halfway between two numbers is $\frac{1}{2}$.

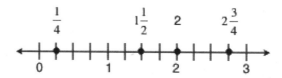

NUMBERS IN WORD FORM AND PLACE VALUE

When writing numbers out in word form or translating word form to numbers, it is essential to understand how a place value system works. In the decimal or base-10 system, each digit of a number represents how many of the corresponding place value – a specific factor of 10 – are contained in the number being represented. To make reading numbers easier, every three digits to the left of the decimal place is preceded by a comma. The following table demonstrates some of the place values:

Power of 10	10^3	10^2	10^1	10^0	10^{-1}	10^{-2}	10^{-3}
Value	1,000	100	10	1	0.1	0.01	0.001
Place	thousands	hundreds	tens	ones	tenths	hundredths	thousandths

For example, consider the number 4,546.09, which can be separated into each place value like this:

4: thousands
5: hundreds
4: tens
6: ones
0: tenths
9: hundredths

This number in word form would be *four thousand five hundred forty-six and nine hundredths*.

> **Review Video: Number Place Value**
> Visit mometrix.com/academy and enter code: 205433

ABSOLUTE VALUE

A precursor to working with negative numbers is understanding what **absolute values** are. A number's absolute value is simply the distance away from zero a number is on the number line. The absolute value of a number is always positive and is written $|x|$. For example, the absolute value of 3, written as $|3|$, is 3 because the distance between 0 and 3 on a number line is three units. Likewise, the absolute value of –3, written as $|-3|$, is 3 because the distance between 0 and –3 on a number line is three units. So $|3| = |-3|$.

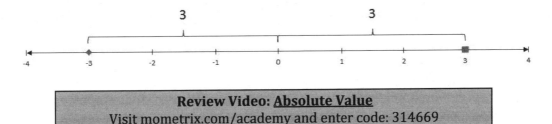

> **Review Video: Absolute Value**
> Visit mometrix.com/academy and enter code: 314669

Operations

OPERATIONS

An **operation** is simply a mathematical process that takes some value(s) as input(s) and produces an output. Elementary operations are often written in the following form: *value operation value*. For instance, in the expression $1 + 2$ the values are 1 and 2 and the operation is addition. Performing the operation gives the output of 3. In this way we can say that $1 + 2$ and 3 are equal, or $1 + 2 = 3$.

ADDITION

Addition increases the value of one quantity by the value of another quantity (both called **addends**). For example, $2 + 4 = 6; 8 + 9 = 17$. The result is called the **sum**. With addition, the order does not matter, $4 + 2 = 2 + 4$.

When adding signed numbers, if the signs are the same simply add the absolute values of the addends and apply the original sign to the sum. For example, $(+4) + (+8) = +12$ and $(-4) + (-8) = -12$. When the original signs are different, take the absolute values of the addends and subtract the smaller value from the larger value, then apply the original sign of the larger value to the difference. For instance, $(+4) + (-8) = -4$ and $(-4) + (+8) = +4$.

15

SUBTRACTION

Subtraction is the opposite operation to addition; it decreases the value of one quantity (the **minuend**) by the value of another quantity (the **subtrahend**). For example, $6 - 4 = 2; 17 - 8 = 9$. The result is called the **difference**. Note that with subtraction, the order does matter, $6 - 4 \neq 4 - 6$.

For subtracting signed numbers, change the sign of the subtrahend and then follow the same rules used for addition. For example, $(+4) - (+8) = (+4) + (-8) = -4$.

> **Review Video: Addition and Subtraction**
> Visit mometrix.com/academy and enter code: 521157

MULTIPLICATION

Multiplication can be thought of as repeated addition. One number (the **multiplier**) indicates how many times to add the other number (the **multiplicand**) to itself. For example, 3×2 (three times two) $= 2 + 2 + 2 = 6$. With multiplication, the order does not matter: $2 \times 3 = 3 \times 2$ or $3 + 3 = 2 + 2 + 2$, either way the result (the **product**) is the same.

If the signs are the same, the product is positive when multiplying signed numbers. For example, $(+4) \times (+8) = +32$ and $(-4) \times (-8) = +32$. If the signs are opposite, the product is negative. For example, $(+4) \times (-8) = -32$ and $(-4) \times (+8) = -32$. When more than two factors are multiplied together, the sign of the product is determined by how many negative factors are present. If there are an odd number of negative factors then the product is negative, whereas an even number of negative factors indicates a positive product. For instance, $(+4) \times (-8) \times (-2) = +64$ and $(-4) \times (-8) \times (-2) = -64$.

DIVISION

Division is the opposite operation to multiplication; one number (the **divisor**) tells us how many parts to divide the other number (the **dividend**) into. The result of division is called the **quotient**. For example, $20 \div 4 = 5$; if 20 is split into 4 equal parts, each part is 5. With division, the order of the numbers does matter, $20 \div 4 \neq 4 \div 20$.

The rules for dividing signed numbers are similar to multiplying signed numbers. If the dividend and divisor have the same sign, the quotient is positive. If the dividend and divisor have opposite signs, the quotient is negative. For example, $(-4) \div (+8) = -0.5$.

> **Review Video: Multiplication and Division**
> Visit mometrix.com/academy and enter code: 643326

PARENTHESES

Parentheses are used to designate which operations should be done first when there are multiple operations. Example: $4 - (2 + 1) = 1$; the parentheses tell us that we must add 2 and 1, and then subtract the sum from 4, rather than subtracting 2 from 4 and then adding 1 (this would give us an answer of 3).

> **Review Video: Mathematical Parentheses**
> Visit mometrix.com/academy and enter code: 978600

EXPONENTS

An **exponent** is a superscript number placed next to another number at the top right. It indicates how many times the base number is to be multiplied by itself. Exponents provide a shorthand way to write what would be a longer mathematical expression, for example: $2^4 = 2 \times 2 \times 2 \times 2$. A number with an exponent of 2 is said to be "squared," while a number with an exponent of 3 is said to be "cubed." The value of a number raised to an exponent is called its power. So 8^4 is read as "8 to the 4th power," or "8 raised to the power of 4."

The properties of exponents are as follows:

Property	Description
$a^1 = a$	Any number to the power of 1 is equal to itself
$1^n = 1$	The number 1 raised to any power is equal to 1
$a^0 = 1$	Any number raised to the power of 0 is equal to 1
$a^n \times a^m = a^{n+m}$	Add exponents to multiply powers of the same base number
$a^n \div a^m = a^{n-m}$	Subtract exponents to divide powers of the same base number
$(a^n)^m = a^{n \times m}$	When a power is raised to a power, the exponents are multiplied
$(a \times b)^n = a^n \times b^n$ $(a \div b)^n = a^n \div b^n$	Multiplication and division operations inside parentheses can be raised to a power. This is the same as each term being raised to that power.
$a^{-n} = \dfrac{1}{a^n}$	A negative exponent is the same as the reciprocal of a positive exponent

Note that exponents do not have to be integers. Fractional or decimal exponents follow all the rules above as well. Example: $5^{\frac{1}{4}} \times 5^{\frac{3}{4}} = 5^{\frac{1}{4}+\frac{3}{4}} = 5^1 = 5$.

> **Review Video: Exponents**
> Visit mometrix.com/academy and enter code: 600998
>
> **Review Video: Laws of Exponents**
> Visit mometrix.com/academy and enter code: 532558

ROOTS

A **root**, such as a square root, is another way of writing a fractional exponent. Instead of using a superscript, roots use the radical symbol ($\sqrt{}$) to indicate the operation. A radical will have a number underneath the bar, and may sometimes have a number in the upper left: $\sqrt[n]{a}$, read as "the nth root of a." The relationship between radical notation and exponent notation can be described by this equation: $\sqrt[n]{a} = a^{\frac{1}{n}}$. The two special cases of $n = 2$ and $n = 3$ are called square roots and cube roots. If there is no number to the upper left, the radical is understood to be a square root ($n = 2$). Nearly all of the roots you encounter will be square roots. A square root is the same as a number raised to the one-half power. When we say that a is the square root of b ($a = \sqrt{b}$), we mean that a multiplied by itself equals b: ($a \times a = b$).

A **perfect square** is a number that has an integer for its square root. There are 10 perfect squares from 1 to 100: 1, 4, 9, 16, 25, 36, 49, 64, 81, 100 (the squares of integers 1 through 10).

> **Review Video: Roots**
> Visit mometrix.com/academy and enter code: 795655
>
> **Review Video: Square Root and Perfect Square**
> Visit mometrix.com/academy and enter code: 648063

ORDER OF OPERATIONS

Order of operations is a set of rules that dictates the order in which we must perform each operation in an expression so that we will evaluate it accurately. If we have an expression that includes multiple different operations, order of operations tells us which operations to do first. The most common mnemonic for order of operations is **PEMDAS**, or "Please Excuse My Dear Aunt Sally." PEMDAS stands for parentheses, exponents, multiplication, division, addition, and subtraction. It is important to understand that multiplication and division have equal precedence, as do addition and subtraction, so those pairs of operations are simply worked from left to right in order.

For example, evaluating the expression $5 + 20 \div 4 \times (2 + 3) - 6$ using the correct order of operations would be done like this:

- **P:** Perform the operations inside the parentheses: $(2 + 3) = 5$
- **E:** Simplify the exponents.
  - The equation now looks like this: $5 + 20 \div 4 \times 5 - 6$
- **MD:** Perform multiplication and division from left to right: $20 \div 4 = 5$; then $5 \times 5 = 25$
  - The equation now looks like this: $5 + 25 - 6$
- **AS:** Perform addition and subtraction from left to right: $5 + 25 = 30$; then $30 - 6 = 24$

> **Review Video: Order of Operations**
> Visit mometrix.com/academy and enter code: 259675

SUBTRACTION WITH REGROUPING

A great way to make use of some of the features built into the decimal system would be regrouping when attempting longform subtraction operations. When subtracting within a place value, sometimes the minuend is smaller than the subtrahend, **regrouping** enables you to 'borrow' a unit from a place value to the left in order to get a positive difference. For example, consider subtracting 189 from 525 with regrouping.

> **Review Video: Subtracting Large Numbers**
> Visit mometrix.com/academy and enter code: 603350

First, set up the subtraction problem in vertical form:

```
  525
- 189
```

Notice that the numbers in the ones and tens columns of 525 are smaller than the numbers in the ones and tens columns of 189. This means you will need to use regrouping to perform subtraction:

```
  5  2  5
- 1  8  9
```

To subtract 9 from 5 in the ones column you will need to borrow from the 2 in the ten's columns:

```
  5  1  15
- 1  8   9
         6
```

Next, to subtract 8 from 1 in the tens column you will need to borrow from the 5 in the hundred's column:

```
    4   11   15
 -  1    8    9
         3    6
```

Last, subtract the 1 from the 4 in the hundred's column:

```
    4   11   15
 -  1    8    9
    3    3    6
```

Factoring

FACTORS AND GREATEST COMMON FACTOR

Factors are numbers that are multiplied together to obtain a **product**. For example, in the equation $2 \times 3 = 6$, the numbers 2 and 3 are factors. A **prime number** has only two factors (1 and itself), but other numbers can have many factors.

A **common factor** is a number that divides exactly into two or more other numbers. For example, the factors of 12 are 1, 2, 3, 4, 6, and 12, while the factors of 15 are 1, 3, 5, and 15. The common factors of 12 and 15 are 1 and 3.

A **prime factor** is also a prime number. Therefore, the prime factors of 12 are 2 and 3. For 15, the prime factors are 3 and 5.

The **greatest common factor (GCF)** is the largest number that is a factor of two or more numbers. For example, the factors of 15 are 1, 3, 5, and 15; the factors of 35 are 1, 5, 7, and 35. Therefore, the greatest common factor of 15 and 35 is 5.

> **Review Video: Factors**
> Visit mometrix.com/academy and enter code: 920086
>
> **Review Video: Greatest Common Factor (GCF)**
> Visit mometrix.com/academy and enter code: 838699

MULTIPLES AND LEAST COMMON MULTIPLE

Often listed out in multiplication tables, **multiples** are integer increments of a given factor. In other words, dividing a multiple by the factor will result in an integer. For example, the multiples of 7 include: $1 \times 7 = 7$, $2 \times 7 = 14$, $3 \times 7 = 21$, $4 \times 7 = 28$, $5 \times 7 = 35$. Dividing 7, 14, 21, 28, or 35 by 7 will result in the integers 1, 2, 3, 4, and 5, respectively.

The least common multiple (**LCM**) is the smallest number that is a multiple of two or more numbers. For example, the multiples of 3 include 3, 6, 9, 12, 15, etc.; the multiples of 5 include 5, 10, 15, 20, etc. Therefore, the least common multiple of 3 and 5 is 15.

> **Review Video: Multiples**
> Visit mometrix.com/academy and enter code: 626738

Rational Numbers

FRACTIONS

A **fraction** is a number that is expressed as one integer written above another integer, with a dividing line between them $\left(\frac{x}{y}\right)$. It represents the **quotient** of the two numbers "x divided by y." It can also be thought of as x out of y equal parts.

The top number of a fraction is called the **numerator**, and it represents the number of parts under consideration. The 1 in $\frac{1}{4}$ means that 1 part out of the whole is being considered in the calculation. The bottom number of a fraction is called the **denominator**, and it represents the total number of equal parts. The 4 in $\frac{1}{4}$ means that the whole consists of 4 equal parts. A fraction cannot have a denominator of zero; this is referred to as "*undefined.*"

Fractions can be manipulated, without changing the value of the fraction, by multiplying or dividing (but not adding or subtracting) both the numerator and denominator by the same number. If you divide both numbers by a common factor, you are **reducing** or simplifying the fraction. Two fractions that have the same value but are expressed differently are known as **equivalent fractions**. For example, $\frac{2}{10}$, $\frac{3}{15}$, $\frac{4}{20}$, and $\frac{5}{25}$ are all equivalent fractions. They can also all be reduced or simplified to $\frac{1}{5}$.

When two fractions are manipulated so that they have the same denominator, this is known as finding a **common denominator**. The number chosen to be that common denominator should be the least common multiple of the two original denominators. Example: $\frac{3}{4}$ and $\frac{5}{6}$; the least common multiple of 4 and 6 is 12. Manipulating to achieve the common denominator: $\frac{3}{4} = \frac{9}{12}$; $\frac{5}{6} = \frac{10}{12}$.

PROPER FRACTIONS AND MIXED NUMBERS

A fraction whose denominator is greater than its numerator is known as a **proper fraction**, while a fraction whose numerator is greater than its denominator is known as an **improper fraction**. Proper fractions have values *less than one* and improper fractions have values *greater than one*.

A **mixed number** is a number that contains both an integer and a fraction. Any improper fraction can be rewritten as a mixed number. Example: $\frac{8}{3} = \frac{6}{3} + \frac{2}{3} = 2 + \frac{2}{3} = 2\frac{2}{3}$. Similarly, any mixed number can be rewritten as an improper fraction. Example: $1\frac{3}{5} = 1 + \frac{3}{5} = \frac{5}{5} + \frac{3}{5} = \frac{8}{5}$.

> **Review Video: Proper and Improper Fractions and Mixed Numbers**
> Visit mometrix.com/academy and enter code: 211077
>
> **Review Video: Fractions**
> Visit mometrix.com/academy and enter code: 262335

ADDING AND SUBTRACTING FRACTIONS

If two fractions have a common denominator, they can be added or subtracted simply by adding or subtracting the two numerators and retaining the same denominator. If the two fractions do not already have the same denominator, one or both of them must be manipulated to achieve a common denominator before they can be added or subtracted. Example: $\frac{1}{2} + \frac{1}{4} = \frac{2}{4} + \frac{1}{4} = \frac{3}{4}$.

> **Review Video: Adding and Subtracting Fractions**
> Visit mometrix.com/academy and enter code: 378080

MULTIPLYING FRACTIONS

Two fractions can be multiplied by multiplying the two numerators to find the new numerator and the two denominators to find the new denominator. Example: $\frac{1}{3} \times \frac{2}{3} = \frac{1\times2}{3\times3} = \frac{2}{9}$.

> **Review Video: Multiplying Fractions**
> Visit mometrix.com/academy and enter code: 638849

DIVIDING FRACTIONS

Two fractions can be divided by flipping the numerator and denominator of the second fraction and then proceeding as though it were a multiplication problem. Example: $\frac{2}{3} \div \frac{3}{4} = \frac{2}{3} \times \frac{4}{3} = \frac{8}{9}$.

> **Review Video: Dividing Fractions**
> Visit mometrix.com/academy and enter code: 300874

MULTIPLYING A MIXED NUMBER BY A WHOLE NUMBER OR A DECIMAL

When multiplying a mixed number by something, it is usually best to convert it to an improper fraction first. Additionally, if the multiplicand is a decimal, it is most often simplest to convert it to a fraction. For instance, to multiply $4\frac{3}{8}$ by 3.5, begin by rewriting each quantity as a whole number plus a proper fraction. Remember, a mixed number is a fraction added to a whole number and a decimal is a representation of the sum of fractions, specifically tenths, hundredths, thousandths, and so on:

$$4\frac{3}{8} \times 3.5 = \left(4 + \frac{3}{8}\right) \times \left(3 + \frac{1}{2}\right)$$

Next, the quantities being added need to be expressed with the same denominator. This is achieved by multiplying and dividing the whole number by the denominator of the fraction. Recall that a whole number is equivalent to that number divided by 1:

$$= \left(\frac{4}{1} \times \frac{8}{8} + \frac{3}{8}\right) \times \left(\frac{3}{1} \times \frac{2}{2} + \frac{1}{2}\right)$$

When multiplying fractions, remember to multiply the numerators and denominators separately:

$$= \left(\frac{4 \times 8}{1 \times 8} + \frac{3}{8}\right) \times \left(\frac{3 \times 2}{1 \times 2} + \frac{1}{2}\right)$$
$$= \left(\frac{32}{8} + \frac{3}{8}\right) \times \left(\frac{6}{2} + \frac{1}{2}\right)$$

Now that the fractions have the same denominators, they can be added:

$$= \frac{35}{8} \times \frac{7}{2}$$

Finally, perform the last multiplication and then simplify:

$$= \frac{35 \times 7}{8 \times 2} = \frac{245}{16} = \frac{240}{16} + \frac{5}{16} = 15\frac{5}{16}$$

DECIMALS

Decimals are one way to represent parts of a whole. Using the place value system, each digit to the right of a decimal point denotes the number of units of a corresponding *negative* power of ten. For example, consider the decimal 0.24. We can use a model to represent the decimal. Since a dime is worth one-tenth of a dollar and a penny is worth one-hundredth of a dollar, one possible model to represent this fraction is to have 2 dimes representing the 2 in the tenths place and 4 pennies representing the 4 in the hundredths place:

To write the decimal as a fraction, put the decimal in the numerator with 1 in the denominator. Multiply the numerator and denominator by tens until there are no more decimal places. Then simplify the fraction to lowest terms. For example, converting 0.24 to a fraction:

$$0.24 = \frac{0.24}{1} = \frac{0.24 \times 100}{1 \times 100} = \frac{24}{100} = \frac{6}{25}$$

Review Video: Decimals
Visit mometrix.com/academy and enter code: 837268

22

OPERATIONS WITH DECIMALS
ADDING AND SUBTRACTING DECIMALS

When adding and subtracting decimals, the decimal points must always be aligned. Adding decimals is just like adding regular whole numbers. Example: $4.5 + 2.0 = 6.5$.

If the problem-solver does not properly align the decimal points, an incorrect answer of 4.7 may result. An easy way to add decimals is to align all of the decimal points in a vertical column visually. This will allow one to see exactly where the decimal should be placed in the final answer. Begin adding from right to left. Add each column in turn, making sure to carry the number to the left if a column adds up to more than 9. The same rules apply to the subtraction of decimals.

> **Review Video: Adding and Subtracting Decimals**
> Visit mometrix.com/academy and enter code: 381101

MULTIPLYING DECIMALS

A simple multiplication problem has two components: a **multiplicand** and a **multiplier**. When multiplying decimals, work as though the numbers were whole rather than decimals. Once the final product is calculated, count the number of places to the right of the decimal in both the multiplicand and the multiplier. Then, count that number of places from the right of the product and place the decimal in that position.

For example, 12.3×2.56 has a total of three places to the right of the respective decimals. Multiply 123×256 to get 31,488. Now, beginning on the right, count three places to the left and insert the decimal. The final product will be 31.488.

> **Review Video: Multiplying Decimals**
> Visit mometrix.com/academy and enter code: 731574

DIVIDING DECIMALS

Every division problem has a **divisor** and a **dividend**. The dividend is the number that is being divided. In the problem $14 \div 7$, 14 is the dividend and 7 is the divisor. In a division problem with decimals, the divisor must be converted into a whole number. Begin by moving the decimal in the divisor to the right until a whole number is created. Next, move the decimal in the dividend the same number of spaces to the right. For example, 4.9 into 24.5 would become 49 into 245. The decimal was moved one space to the right to create a whole number in the divisor, and then the same was done for the dividend. Once the whole numbers are created, the problem is carried out normally: $245 \div 49 = 5$.

> **Review Video: Dividing Decimals**
> Visit mometrix.com/academy and enter code: 560690

PERCENTAGES

Percentages can be thought of as fractions that are based on a whole of 100; that is, one whole is equal to 100%. The word **percent** means "per hundred." Percentage problems are often presented in three main ways:

- Find what percentage of some number another number is.
  - Example: What percentage of 40 is 8?
- Find what number is some percentage of a given number.

23

o Example: What number is 20% of 40?
- Find what number another number is a given percentage of.
  o Example: What number is 8 20% of?

There are three components in each of these cases: a **whole** (W), a **part** (P), and a **percentage** (%). These are related by the equation: $P = W \times \%$. This can easily be rearranged into other forms that may suit different questions better: $\% = \frac{P}{W}$ and $W = \frac{P}{\%}$. Percentage problems are often also word problems. As such, a large part of solving them is figuring out which quantities are what. For example, consider the following word problem:

In a school cafeteria, 7 students choose pizza, 9 choose hamburgers, and 4 choose tacos. What percentage of student choose tacos?

To find the whole, you must first add all of the parts: $7 + 9 + 4 = 20$. The percentage can then be found by dividing the part by the whole ($\% = \frac{P}{W}$): $\frac{4}{20} = \frac{20}{100} = 20\%$.

> **Review Video: Percentages**
> Visit mometrix.com/academy and enter code: 141911

CONVERTING BETWEEN PERCENTAGES, FRACTIONS, AND DECIMALS

Converting decimals to percentages and percentages to decimals is as simple as moving the decimal point. To *convert from a decimal to a percentage*, move the decimal point **two places to the right**. To *convert from a percentage to a decimal*, move it **two places to the left**. It may be helpful to remember that the percentage number will always be larger than the equivalent decimal number. For example:

$$0.23 = 23\% \quad 5.34 = 534\% \quad 0.007 = 0.7\%$$
$$700\% = 7.00 \quad 86\% = 0.86 \quad 0.15\% = 0.0015$$

To convert a fraction to a decimal, simply divide the numerator by the denominator in the fraction. To convert a decimal to a fraction, put the decimal in the numerator with 1 in the denominator. Multiply the numerator and denominator by tens until there are no more decimal places. Then simplify the fraction to lowest terms. For example, converting 0.24 to a fraction:

$$0.24 = \frac{0.24}{1} = \frac{0.24 \times 100}{1 \times 100} = \frac{24}{100} = \frac{6}{25}$$

Fractions can be converted to a percentage by finding equivalent fractions with a denominator of 100. For example,

$$\frac{7}{10} = \frac{70}{100} = 70\% \quad \frac{1}{4} = \frac{25}{100} = 25\%$$

To convert a percentage to a fraction, divide the percentage number by 100 and reduce the fraction to its simplest possible terms. For example,

$$60\% = \frac{60}{100} = \frac{3}{5} \quad 96\% = \frac{96}{100} = \frac{24}{25}$$

Review Video: Converting Decimals to Fractions and Percentages
Visit mometrix.com/academy and enter code: 986765

Review Video: Converting Fractions to Percentages and Decimals
Visit mometrix.com/academy and enter code: 306233

Review Video: Converting Percentages to Decimals and Fractions
Visit mometrix.com/academy and enter code: 287297

RATIONAL NUMBERS

The term **rational** means that the number can be expressed as a ratio or fraction. That is, a number, r, is rational if and only if it can be represented by a fraction $\frac{a}{b}$ where a and b are integers and b does not equal 0. The set of rational numbers includes integers and decimals. If there is no finite way to represent a value with a fraction of integers, then the number is **irrational**. Common examples of irrational numbers include: $\sqrt{5}, (1 + \sqrt{2})$, and π.

Review Video: Rational Numbers
Visit mometrix.com/academy and enter code: 280645

Proportions and Ratios

PROPORTIONS

A proportion is a relationship between two quantities that dictates how one changes when the other changes. A **direct proportion** describes a relationship in which a quantity increases by a set amount for every increase in the other quantity, or decreases by that same amount for every decrease in the other quantity. Example: Assuming a constant driving speed, the time required for a car trip increases as the distance of the trip increases. The distance to be traveled and the time required to travel are directly proportional.

Inverse proportion is a relationship in which an increase in one quantity is accompanied by a decrease in the other, or vice versa. Example: the time required for a car trip decreases as the speed increases and increases as the speed decreases, so the time required is inversely proportional to the speed of the car.

Review Video: Proportions
Visit mometrix.com/academy and enter code: 505355

RATIOS

A **ratio** is a comparison of two quantities in a particular order. Example: If there are 14 computers in a lab, and the class has 20 students, there is a student to computer ratio of 20 to 14, commonly written as 20:14. Ratios are normally reduced to their smallest whole number representation, so 20:14 would be reduced to 10:7 by dividing both sides by 2.

CONSTANT OF PROPORTIONALITY

When two quantities have a proportional relationship, there exists a **constant of proportionality** between the quantities; the product of this constant and one of the quantities is equal to the other quantity. For example, if one lemon costs $0.25, two lemons cost $0.50, and three lemons cost $0.75, there is a proportional relationship between the total cost of lemons and the number of lemons purchased. The constant of proportionality is the **unit price**, namely $0.25/lemon. Notice that the total price of lemons, t, can be found by multiplying the unit price of lemons, p, and the number of lemons, n: $t = pn$.

WORK/UNIT RATE

Unit rate expresses a quantity of one thing in terms of one unit of another. For example, if you travel 30 miles every two hours, a unit rate expresses this comparison in terms of one hour: in one hour you travel 15 miles, so your unit rate is 15 miles per hour. Other examples are how much one ounce of food costs (price per ounce) or figuring out how much one egg costs out of the dozen (price per 1 egg, instead of price per 12 eggs). The denominator of a unit rate is always 1. Unit rates are used to compare different situations to solve problems. For example, to make sure you get the best deal when deciding which kind of soda to buy, you can find the unit rate of each. If soda #1 costs $1.50 for a 1-liter bottle, and soda #2 costs $2.75 for a 2-liter bottle, it would be a better deal to buy soda #2, because its unit rate is only $1.375 per 1-liter, which is cheaper than soda #1. Unit rates can also help determine the length of time a given event will take. For example, if you can paint 2 rooms in 4.5 hours, you can determine how long it will take you to paint 5 rooms by solving for the unit rate per room and then multiplying that by 5.

SLOPE

On a graph with two points, (x_1, y_1) and (x_2, y_2), the **slope** is found with the formula $m = \frac{y_2 - y_1}{x_2 - x_1}$; where $x_1 \neq x_2$ and m stands for slope. If the value of the slope is **positive**, the line has an *upward direction* from left to right. If the value of the slope is **negative**, the line has a *downward direction* from left to right. Consider the following example:

A new book goes on sale in bookstores and online stores. In the first month, 5,000 copies of the book are sold. Over time, the book continues to grow in popularity. The data for the number of copies sold is in the table below.

# of Months on Sale	1	2	3	4	5
# of Copies Sold (In Thousands)	5	10	15	20	25

So, the number of copies that are sold and the time that the book is on sale is a proportional relationship. In this example, an equation can be used to show the data: $y = 5x$, where x is the number of months that the book is on sale. Also, y is the number of copies sold. So the slope of the corresponding line is $\frac{\text{rise}}{\text{run}} = \frac{5}{1} = 5$.

FINDING AN UNKNOWN IN EQUIVALENT EXPRESSIONS

It is often necessary to apply information given about a rate or proportion to a new scenario. For example, if you know that Jedha can run a marathon (26 miles) in 3 hours, how long would it take her to run 10 miles at the same pace? Start by setting up equivalent expressions:

$$\frac{26 \text{ mi}}{3 \text{ hr}} = \frac{10 \text{ mi}}{x \text{ hr}}$$

Now, cross multiply and solve for x:

$$26x = 30$$
$$x = \frac{30}{26} = \frac{15}{13}$$
$$x \cong 1.15 \text{ hrs } or \text{ 1 hr 9 min}$$

So, at this pace, Jedha could run 10 miles in about 1.15 hours or about 1 hour and 9 minutes.

Algebra

Expressions

TERMS AND COEFFICIENTS

Mathematical expressions consist of a combination of one or more values arranged in terms that are added together. As such, an expression could be just a single number, including zero. A **variable term** is the product of a real number, also called a **coefficient**, and one or more variables, each of which may be raised to an exponent. Expressions may also include numbers without a variable, called **constants** or **constant terms**. The expression $6s^2$, for example, is a single term where the coefficient is the real number 6 and the variable is s^2. Note that if a term is written as simply a variable to some exponent, like t^2, then the coefficient is 1, because $t^2 = 1t^2$.

LINEAR EXPRESSIONS

A **single variable linear expression** is the sum of a single variable term, where the variable has no exponent, and a constant, which may be zero. For instance, the expression $2w + 7$ has $2w$ as the variable term and 7 as the constant term. It is important to realize that terms are separated by addition or subtraction. Since an expression is a sum of terms, expressions such as $5x - 3$ can be written as $5x + (-3)$ to emphasize that the constant term is negative. A real-world example of a single variable linear expression is the perimeter of a square, four times the side length, often expressed: $4s$.

In general, a **linear expression** is the sum of any number of variable terms so long as none of the variables have an exponent. For example, $3m + 8n - \frac{1}{4}p + 5.5q - 1$ is a linear expression, but $3y^3$ is not. In the same way, the expression for the perimeter of a general triangle, the sum of the side lengths $(a + b + c)$ is considered to be linear, but the expression for the area of a square, the side length squared (s^2) is not.

Equations

LINEAR EQUATIONS

Equations that can be written as $ax + b = 0$, where $a \neq 0$, are referred to as **one variable linear equations**. A solution to such an equation is called a **root**. In the case where we have the equation $5x + 10 = 0$, if we solve for x we get a solution of $x = -2$. In other words, the root of the equation is -2. This is found by first subtracting 10 from both sides, which gives $5x = -10$. Next, simply divide both sides by the coefficient of the variable, in this case 5, to get $x = -2$. This can be checked by plugging -2 back into the original equation $(5)(-2) + 10 = -10 + 10 = 0$.

The **solution set** is the set of all solutions of an equation. In our example, the solution set would simply be -2. If there were more solutions (there usually are in multivariable equations) then they would also be included in the solution set. When an equation has no true solutions, it is referred to as an **empty set**. Equations with identical solution sets are **equivalent equations**. An **identity** is a term whose value or determinant is equal to 1.

28

Linear equations can be written many ways. Below is a list of some forms linear equations can take:

- **Standard Form**: $Ax + By = C$; the slope is $\frac{-A}{B}$ and the y-intercept is $\frac{C}{B}$
- **Slope Intercept Form**: $y = mx + b$, where m is the slope and b is the y-intercept
- **Point-Slope Form**: $y - y_1 = m(x - x_1)$, where m is the slope and (x_1, y_1) is a point on the line
- **Two-Point Form**: $\frac{y-y_1}{x-x_1} = \frac{y_2-y_1}{x_2-x_1}$, where (x_1, y_1) and (x_2, y_2) are two points on the given line
- **Intercept Form**: $\frac{x}{x_1} + \frac{y}{y_1} = 1$, where $(x_1, 0)$ is the point at which a line intersects the x-axis, and $(0, y_1)$ is the point at which the same line intersects the y-axis

> **Review Video: Slope-Intercept and Point-Slope Forms**
> Visit mometrix.com/academy and enter code: 113216

SOLVING ONE-VARIABLE LINEAR EQUATIONS

Multiply all terms by the lowest common denominator to eliminate any fractions. Look for addition or subtraction to undo so you can isolate the variable on one side of the equal sign. Divide both sides by the coefficient of the variable. When you have a value for the variable, substitute this value into the original equation to make sure you have a true equation. Consider the following example:

Kim's savings are represented by the table below. Represent her savings, using an equation.

X (Months)	Y (Total Savings)
2	$1300
5	$2050
9	$3050
11	$3550
16	$4800

The table shows a function with a constant rate of change, or slope, of 250. Given the points on the table, the slopes can be calculated as $(2050 - 1300)/(5 - 2)$, $(3050 - 2050)/(9 - 5)$, $(3550 - 3050)/(11 - 9)$, and $(4800 - 3550)/(16 - 11)$, each of which equals 250. Thus, the table shows a constant rate of change, indicating a linear function. The slope-intercept form of a linear equation is written as $y = mx + b$, where m represents the slope and b represents the y-intercept. Substituting the slope into this form gives $y = 250x + b$. Substituting corresponding x- and y-values from any point into this equation will give the y-intercept, or b. Using the point, (2, 1300), gives $1300 = 250(2) + b$, which simplifies as b = 800. Thus, her savings may be represented by the equation, $y = 250x + 800$.

RULES FOR MANIPULATING EQUATIONS

LIKE TERMS

Like terms are terms in an equation that have the same variable, regardless of whether or not they also have the same coefficient. This includes terms that *lack* a variable; all constants (i.e. numbers without variables) are considered like terms. If the equation involves terms with a variable raised to different powers, the like terms are those that have the variable raised to the same power.

For example, consider the equation $x^2 + 3x + 2 = 2x^2 + x - 7 + 2x$. In this equation, 2 and −7 are like terms; they are both constants. $3x$, x, and $2x$ are like terms, they all include the variable x raised to the first power. x^2 and $2x^2$ are like terms, they both include the variable x, raised to the second power. $2x$ and $2x^2$ are not like terms; although they both involve the variable x, the variable

29

is not raised to the same power in both terms. The fact that they have the same coefficient, 2, is not relevant.

CARRYING OUT THE SAME OPERATION ON BOTH SIDES OF AN EQUATION

When solving an equation, the general procedure is to carry out a series of operations on both sides of an equation, choosing operations that will tend to simplify the equation when doing so. The reason why the same operation must be carried out on both sides of the equation is because that leaves the meaning of the equation unchanged, and yields a result that is equivalent to the original equation. This would not be the case if we carried out an operation on one side of an equation and not the other. Consider what an equation means: it is a statement that two values or expressions are equal. If we carry out the same operation on both sides of the equation—add 3 to both sides, for example—then the two sides of the equation are changed in the same way, and so remain equal. If we do that to only one side of the equation—add 3 to one side but not the other—then that wouldn't be true; if we change one side of the equation but not the other then the two sides are no longer equal.

ADVANTAGE OF COMBINING LIKE TERMS

Combining like terms refers to adding or subtracting like terms—terms with the same variable—and therefore reducing sets of like terms to a single term. The main advantage of doing this is that it simplifies the equation. Often, combining like terms can be done as the first step in solving an equation, though it can also be done later, such as after distributing terms in a product.

For example, consider the equation $2(x + 3) + 3(2 + x + 3) = -4$. The 2 and the 3 in the second set of parentheses are like terms, and we can combine them, yielding $2(x + 3) + 3(x + 5) = -4$. Now we can carry out the multiplications implied by the parentheses, distributing the outer 2 and 3 accordingly: $2x + 6 + 3x + 15 = -4$. The $2x$ and the $3x$ are like terms, and we can add them together: $5x + 6 + 15 = -4$. Now, the constants 6, 15, and –4 are also like terms, and we can combine them as well: subtracting 6 and 15 from both sides of the equation, we get $5x = -4 - 6 - 15$, or $5x = -25$, which simplifies further to $x = -5$.

CANCELING TERMS ON OPPOSITE SIDES OF AN EQUATION

Two terms on opposite sides of an equation can be canceled if and only if they *exactly* match each other. They must have the same variable raised to the same power and the same coefficient. For example, in the equation $3x + 2x^2 + 6 = 2x^2 - 6$, $2x^2$ appears on both sides of the equation and can be canceled, leaving $3x + 6 = -6$. The 6 on each side of the equation *cannot* be canceled, because it is added on one side of the equation and subtracted on the other. While they cannot be canceled, however, the 6 and –6 are like terms and can be combined, yielding $3x = -12$, which simplifies further to $x = -4$.

It's also important to note that the terms to be canceled must be independent terms and cannot be part of a larger term. For example, consider the equation $2(x + 6) = 3(x + 4) + 1$. We cannot cancel the x's, because even though they match each other they are part of the larger terms $2(x + 6)$ and $3(x + 4)$. We must first distribute the 2 and 3, yielding $2x + 12 = 3x + 12 + 1$. Now we see that the terms with the x's do not match, but the 12s do, and can be canceled, leaving $2x = 3x + 1$, which simplifies to $x = -1$.

PROCESS FOR MANIPULATING EQUATIONS
ISOLATING VARIABLES

To **isolate a variable** means to manipulate the equation so that the variable appears by itself on one side of the equation, and does not appear at all on the other side. Generally, an equation or inequality is considered to be solved once the variable is isolated and the other side of the equation or inequality is simplified as much as possible. In the case of a two-variable equation or inequality, only one variable needs to be isolated; it will not usually be possible to simultaneously isolate both variables.

For a linear equation—an equation in which the variable only appears raised to the first power—isolating a variable can be done by first moving all the terms with the variable to one side of the equation and all other terms to the other side. (*Moving* a term really means adding the inverse of the term to both sides; when a term is *moved* to the other side of the equation its sign is flipped.) Then combine like terms on each side. Finally, divide both sides by the coefficient of the variable, if applicable. The steps need not necessarily be done in this order, but this order will always work.

EQUATIONS WITH MORE THAN ONE SOLUTION

Some types of non-linear equations, such as equations involving squares of variables, may have more than one solution. For example, the equation $x^2 = 4$ has two solutions: 2 and –2. Equations with absolute values can also have multiple solutions: $|x| = 1$ has the solutions $x = 1$ and $x = -1$.

It is also possible for a linear equation to have more than one solution, but only if the equation is true regardless of the value of the variable. In this case, the equation is considered to have infinitely many solutions, because any possible value of the variable is a solution. We know a linear equation has infinitely many solutions if when we combine like terms the variables cancel, leaving a true statement. For example, consider the equation $2(3x + 5) = x + 5(x + 2)$. Distributing, we get $6x + 10 = x + 5x + 10$; combining like terms gives $6x + 10 = 6x + 10$, and the $6x$ terms cancel to leave $10 = 10$. This is clearly true, so the original equation is true for any value of x. We could also have canceled the 10s leaving $0 = 0$, but again this is clearly true—in general if both sides of the equation match exactly, it has infinitely many solutions.

EQUATIONS WITH NO SOLUTION

Some types of non-linear equations, such as equations involving squares of variables, may have no solution. For example, the equation $x^2 = -2$ has no solutions in the real numbers, because the square of any real number must be positive. Similarly, $|x| = -1$ has no solution, because the absolute value of a number is always positive.

It is also possible for an equation to have no solution even if does not involve any powers greater than one, absolute values, or other special functions. For example, the equation $2(x + 3) + x = 3x$ has no solution. We can see that if we try to solve it. First, we distribute, leaving $2x + 6 + x = 3x$. But now if we try to combine all the terms with the variable, we find that they cancel: we have $3x$ on the left and $3x$ on the right, canceling to leave us with $6 = 0$. This is clearly false. In general, whenever the variable terms in an equation cancel leaving different constants on both sides, it means that the equation has no solution. (If we are left with the *same* constant on both sides, the equation has infinitely many solutions instead.)

FEATURES OF EQUATIONS THAT REQUIRE SPECIAL TREATMENT
LINEAR EQUATIONS

A linear equation is an equation in which variables only appear by themselves; they are not multiplied together, not with exponents other than one, and not inside absolute value signs or any other functions. For example, the equation $x + 1 - 3x = 5 - x$ is a linear equation; while x appears multiple times, it never appears with an exponent other than one, or inside any function. The two-variable equation $2x - 3y = 5 + 2x$ is also a linear equation. In contrast, the equation $x^2 - 5 = 3x$ is *not* a linear equation, because it involves the term x^2. $\sqrt{x} = 5$ is not a linear equation, because it involves a square root. $(x - 1)^2 = 4$ is not a linear equation because even though there's no exponent on the x directly, it appears as part of an expression that is squared. The two-variable equation $x + xy - y = 5$ is not a linear equation because it includes the term xy, where two variables are multiplied together.

Linear equations can always be solved (or shown to have no solution) by combining like terms and performing simple operations on both sides of the equation. Some non-linear equations can be solved by similar methods, but others may require more advanced methods of solution, if they can be solved analytically at all.

SOLVING EQUATIONS INVOLVING ROOTS

In an equation involving roots, the first step is to isolate the term with the root, if possible, and then raise both sides of the equation to the appropriate power to eliminate it. Consider an example equation, $2\sqrt{x + 1} - 1 = 3$. In this case, begin by adding 1 to both sides, yielding $2\sqrt{x + 1} = 4$, and then dividing both sides by 2, yielding $\sqrt{x + 1} = 2$. Now square both sides, yielding $x + 1 = 4$. Finally, subtracting 1 from both sides yields $x = 3$.

Squaring both sides of an equation may, however, yield a spurious solution—a solution to the squared equation that is *not* a solution of the original equation. It's therefore necessary to plug the solution back into the original equation to make sure it works. In this case, it does: $2\sqrt{3 + 1} - 1 = 2\sqrt{4} - 1 = 2(2) - 1 = 4 - 1 = 3$.

The same procedure applies for other roots as well. For example, given the equation $3 + \sqrt[3]{2x} = 5$, we can first subtract 3 from both sides, yielding $\sqrt[3]{2x} = 2$ and isolating the root. Raising both sides to the third power yields $2x = 2^3$, i.e. $2x = 8$. We can now divide both sides by 2 to get $x = 4$.

SOLVING EQUATIONS WITH EXPONENTS

To solve an equation involving an exponent, the first step is to isolate the variable with the exponent. We can then take the appropriate root of both sides to eliminate the exponent. For instance, for the equation $2x^3 + 17 = 5x^3 - 7$, we can subtract $5x^3$ from both sides to get $-3x^3 + 17 = -7$, and then subtract 17 from both sides to get $-3x^3 = -24$. Finally, we can divide both sides by –3 to get $x^3 = 8$. Finally, we can take the cube root of both sides to get $x = \sqrt[3]{8} = 2$.

One important but often overlooked point is that equations with an exponent greater than 1 may have more than one answer. The solution to $x^2 = 9$ isn't simply $x = 3$; it's $x = \pm 3$ (that is, $x = 3$ or $x = -3$). For a slightly more complicated example, consider the equation $(x - 1)^2 - 1 = 3$. Adding 1 to both sides yields $(x - 1)^2 = 4$; taking the square root of both sides yields $x - 1 = 2$. We can then add 1 to both sides to get $x = 3$. However, there's a second solution. We also have the possibility that $x - 1 = -2$, in which case $x = -1$. Both $x = 3$ and $x = -1$ are valid solutions, as can be verified by substituting them both into the original equation.

SOLVING EQUATIONS WITH ABSOLUTE VALUES

When solving an equation with an absolute value, the first step is to isolate the absolute value term. We then consider two possibilities: when the expression inside the absolute value is positive or when it is negative. In the former case, the expression in the absolute value equals the expression on the other side of the equation; in the latter, it equals the additive inverse of that expression—the expression times negative one. We consider each case separately and finally check for spurious solutions.

For instance, consider solving $|2x - 1| + x = 5$ for x. We can first isolate the absolute value by moving the x to the other side: $|2x - 1| = -x + 5$. Now, we have two possibilities. First, that $2x - 1$ is positive, and hence $2x - 1 = -x + 5$. Rearranging and combining like terms yields $3x = 6$, and hence $x = 2$. The other possibility is that $2x - 1$ is negative, and hence $2x - 1 = -(-x + 5) = x - 5$. In this case, rearranging and combining like terms yields $x = -4$. Substituting $x = 2$ and $x = -4$ back into the original equation, we see that they are both valid solutions.

Note that the absolute value of a sum or difference applies to the sum or difference as a whole, not to the individual terms; in general, $|2x - 1|$ is not equal to $|2x + 1|$ or to $|2x| - 1$.

> **Review Video: Solving Absolute Value Inequalities**
> Visit mometrix.com/academy and enter code: 997008

SPURIOUS SOLUTIONS

A **spurious solution** may arise when we square both sides of an equation as a step in solving it or under certain other operations on the equation. It is a solution to the squared or otherwise modified equation that is *not* a solution of the original equation. To identify a spurious solution, it's useful when you solve an equation involving roots or absolute values to plug the solution back into the original equation to make sure it's valid.

CHOOSING WHICH VARIABLE TO ISOLATE IN TWO-VARIABLE EQUATIONS

Similar to methods for a one-variable equation, solving a two-variable equation involves isolating a variable: manipulating the equation so that a variable appears by itself on one side of the equation, and not at all on the other side. However, in a two-variable equation, you will usually only be able to isolate one of the variables; the other variable may appear on the other side along with constant terms, or with exponents or other functions.

Often one variable will be much more easily isolated than the other, and therefore that's the variable you should choose. If one variable appears with various exponents, and the other is only raised to the first power, the latter variable is the one to isolate: given the equation $a^2 + 2b = a^3 + b + 3$, the b only appears to the first power, whereas a appears squared and cubed, so b is the variable that can be solved for: combining like terms and isolating the b on the left side of the equation, we get $b = a^3 - a^2 + 3$. If both variables are equally easy to isolate, then it's best to isolate the independent variable, if one is defined; if the two variables are x and y, the convention is that y is the independent variable.

Inequalities

WORKING WITH INEQUALITIES

Commonly in algebra and other upper-level fields of math you find yourself working with mathematical expressions that do not equal each other. The statement comparing such expressions with symbols such as < (less than) or > (greater than) is called an *inequality*. An example of an inequality is $7x > 5$. To solve for x, simply divide both sides by 7 and the solution is shown to be $x > \frac{5}{7}$. Graphs of the solution set of inequalities are represented on a number line. Open circles are used to show that an expression approaches a number but is never quite equal to that number.

> **Review Video: Inequalities**
> Visit mometrix.com/academy and enter code: 347842

Conditional inequalities are those with certain values for the variable that will make the condition true and other values for the variable where the condition will be false. **Absolute inequalities** can have any real number as the value for the variable to make the condition true, while there is no real number value for the variable that will make the condition false. Solving inequalities is done by following the same rules for solving equations with the exception that when multiplying or dividing by a negative number the direction of the inequality sign must be flipped or reversed. **Double inequalities** are situations where two inequality statements apply to the same variable expression. An example of this is $-c < ax + b < c$.

DETERMINING SOLUTIONS TO INEQUALITIES

To determine whether a coordinate is a solution of an inequality, you can substitute the values of the coordinate into the inequality, simplify, and check whether the resulting statement holds true. For instance, to determine whether $(-2,4)$ is a solution of the inequality $y \geq -2x + 3$, substitute the values into the inequality, $4 \geq -2(-2) + 3$. Simplify the right side of the inequality and the result is $4 \geq 7$, which is a false statement. Therefore, the coordinate is not a solution of the inequality. You can also use this method to determine which part of the graph of an inequality is shaded. The graph of $y \geq -2x + 3$ includes the solid line $y = -2x + 3$ and, since it excludes the point $(-2,4)$ to the left of the line, it is shaded to the right of the line.

FLIPPING INEQUALITY SIGNS

When given an inequality, we can always turn the entire inequality around, swapping the two sides of the inequality and changing the inequality sign. For instance, $x + 2 > 2x - 3$ is equivalent to $2x - 3 < x + 2$. Aside from that, normally the inequality does not change if we carry out the same operation on both sides of the inequality. There is, however, one principal exception: if we *multiply* or *divide* both sides of the inequality by a *negative number*, the inequality is flipped. For example, if we take the inequality $-2x < 6$ and divide both sides by -2, the inequality flips and we are left with $x > -3$. This *only* applies to multiplication and division, and only with negative numbers. Multiplying or dividing both sides by a positive number, or adding or subtracting any number regardless of sign, does not flip the inequality.

COMPOUND INEQUALITIES

A **compound inequality** is an equality that consists of two inequalities combined with *and* or *or*. The two components of a proper compound inequality must be of opposite type: that is, one must be greater than (or greater than or equal to), the other less than (or less than or equal to). For instance, "$x + 1 < 2$ or $x + 1 > 3$" is a compound inequality, as is "$2x \geq 4$ and $2x \leq 6$." An *and* inequality can be written more compactly by having one inequality on each side of the common part: "$2x \geq 1$ and $2x \leq 6$," can also be written as $1 \leq 2x \leq 6$.

In order for the compound inequality to be meaningful, the two parts of an *and* inequality must overlap; otherwise no numbers satisfy the inequality. On the other hand, if the two parts of an *or* inequality overlap, then *all* numbers satisfy the inequality and as such the inequality is usually not meaningful.

Solving a compound inequality requires solving each part separately. For example, given the compound inequality "$x + 1 < 2$ or $x + 1 > 3$," the first inequality, $x + 1 < 2$, reduces to $x < 1$, and the second part, $x + 1 > 3$, reduces to $x > 2$, so the whole compound inequality can be written as "$x < 1$ or $x > 2$." Similarly, $1 \leq 2x \leq 6$ can be solved by dividing each term by 2, yielding $\frac{1}{2} \leq x \leq 3$.

SOLVING INEQUALITIES INVOLVING ABSOLUTE VALUES

To solve an inequality involving an absolute value, first isolate the term with the absolute value. Then proceed to treat the two cases separately as with an absolute value equation, but flipping the inequality in the case where the expression in the absolute value is negative (since that essentially involves multiplying both sides by -1.) The two cases are then combined into a compound inequality; if the absolute value is on the greater side of the inequality, then it is an *or* compound inequality, if on the lesser side, then it's an *and*.

Consider the inequality $2 + |x - 1| \geq 3$. We can isolate the absolute value term by subtracting 2 from both sides: $|x - 1| \geq 1$. Now, we're left with the two cases $x - 1 \geq 1$ or $x - 1 \leq -1$: note that in the latter, negative case, the inequality is flipped. $x - 1 \geq 1$ reduces to $x \geq 2$, and $x - 1 \leq -1$ reduces to $x \leq 0$. Since in the inequality $|x - 1| \geq 1$ the absolute value is on the greater side, the two cases combine into an *or* compound inequality, so the final, solved inequality is "$x \leq 0$ or $x \geq 2$."

> **Review Video: Solving Absolute Value Inequalities**
> Visit mometrix.com/academy and enter code: 997008

SOLVING INEQUALITIES INVOLVING SQUARE ROOTS

Solving an inequality with a square root involves two parts. First, we solve the inequality as if it were an equation, isolating the square root and then squaring both sides of the equation. Second, we restrict the solution to the set of values of x for which the value inside the square root sign is non-negative.

For example, in the inequality, $\sqrt{x - 2} + 1 < 5$, we can isolate the square root by subtracting 1 from both sides, yielding $\sqrt{x - 2} < 4$. Squaring both sides of the inequality yields $x - 2 < 16$, so $x < 18$. Since we can't take the square root of a negative number, we also require the part inside the square root to be non-negative. In this case, that means $x - 2 \geq 0$. Adding 2 to both sides of the inequality yields $x \geq 2$. Our final answer is a compound inequality combining the two simple inequalities: $x \geq 2$ and $x < 18$, or $2 \leq x < 18$.

Note that we only get a compound inequality if the two simple inequalities are in opposite directions; otherwise we take the one that is more restrictive.

The same technique can be used for other even roots, such as fourth roots. It is *not*, however, used for cube roots or other odd roots—negative numbers *do* have cube roots, so the condition that the quantity inside the root sign cannot be negative does not apply.

SPECIAL CIRCUMSTANCES

Sometimes an inequality involving an absolute value or an even exponent is true for all values of x, and we don't need to do any further work to solve it. This is true if the inequality, once the absolute value or exponent term is isolated, says that term is greater than a negative number (or greater than or equal to zero). Since an absolute value or a number raised to an even exponent is *always* non-negative, this inequality is always true.

GRAPHICAL SOLUTIONS TO EQUATIONS AND INEQUALITIES

When equations are shown graphically, they are usually shown on a **Cartesian coordinate plane**. The Cartesian coordinate plane consists of two number lines placed perpendicular to each other and intersecting at the zero point, also known as the origin. The horizontal number line is known as the x-axis, with positive values to the right of the origin, and negative values to the left of the origin.

The vertical number line is known as the *y*-axis, with positive values above the origin, and negative values below the origin. Any point on the plane can be identified by an ordered pair in the form (x, y), called coordinates. The *x*-value of the coordinate is called the abscissa, and the *y*-value of the coordinate is called the ordinate. The two number lines divide the plane into **four quadrants**: I, II, III, and IV.

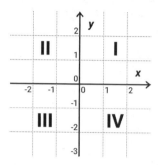

Note that in quadrant I $x > 0$ and $y > 0$, in quadrant II $x < 0$ and $y > 0$, in quadrant III $x < 0$ and $y < 0$, and in quadrant IV $x > 0$ and $y < 0$.

Recall that if the value of the slope of a line is positive, the line slopes upward from left to right. If the value of the slope is negative, the line slopes downward from left to right. If the *y*-coordinates are the same for two points on a line, the slope is 0 and the line is a **horizontal line**. If the *x*-coordinates are the same for two points on a line, there is no slope and the line is a **vertical line**. Two or more lines that have equivalent slopes are **parallel lines**. **Perpendicular lines** have slopes that are negative reciprocals of each other, such as $\frac{a}{b}$ and $\frac{-b}{a}$.

GRAPHING SIMPLE INEQUALITIES

To graph a simple inequality, we first mark on the number line the value that signifies the end point of the inequality. If the inequality is strict (involves a less than or greater than), we use a hollow circle; if it is not strict (less than or equal to or greater than or equal to), we use a solid circle. We then fill in the part of the number line that satisfies the inequality: to the left of the marked point for less than (or less than or equal to), to the right for greater than (or greater than or equal to).

For example, we would graph the inequality $x < 5$ by putting a hollow circle at 5 and filling in the part of the line to the left:

GRAPHING COMPOUND INEQUALITIES

To graph a compound inequality, we fill in both parts of the inequality for an *or* inequality, or the overlap between them for an *and* inequality. More specifically, we start by plotting the endpoints of each inequality on the number line. For an *or* inequality, we then fill in the appropriate side of the line for each inequality. Typically, the two component inequalities do not overlap, which means the shaded part is *outside* the two points. For an *and* inequality, we instead fill in the part of the line that meets both inequalities.

For the inequality "$x \leq -3$ or $x > 4$," we first put a solid circle at –3 and a hollow circle at 4. We then fill the parts of the line *outside* these circles:

GRAPHING INEQUALITIES INCLUDING ABSOLUTE VALUES

An inequality with an absolute value can be converted to a compound inequality. To graph the inequality, first convert it to a compound inequality, and then graph that normally. If the absolute value is on the greater side of the inequality, we end up with an *or* inequality; we plot the endpoints of the inequality on the number line and fill in the part of the line *outside* those points. If the absolute value is on the smaller side of the inequality, we end up with an *and* inequality; we plot the endpoints of the inequality on the number line and fill in the part of the line *between* those points.

For example, the inequality $|x + 1| \geq 4$ can be rewritten as $x \geq 3$ or $x \leq -5$. We place solid circles at the points 3 and -5 and fill in the part of the line *outside* them:

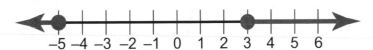

GRAPHING EQUATIONS IN TWO VARIABLES

One way of graphing an equation in two variables is to plot enough points to get an idea for its shape and then draw the appropriate curve through those points. A point can be plotted by substituting in a value for one variable and solving for the other. If the equation is linear, we only need two points and can then draw a straight line between them.

For example, consider the equation $y = 2x - 1$. This is a linear equation—both variables only appear raised to the first power—so we only need two points. When $x = 0, y = 2(0) - 1 = -1$. When $x = 2, y = 2(2) - 1 = 3$. We can therefore choose the points $(0, -1)$ and $(2, 3)$, and draw a line between them:

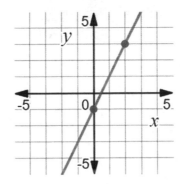

GRAPHING INEQUALITIES IN TWO VARIABLES

To graph an inequality in two variables, we first graph the border of the inequality. This means graphing the equation that we get if we replace the inequality sign with an equals sign. If the inequality is strict (> or <), we graph the border with a dashed or dotted line; if it is not strict (≥ or ≤), we use a solid line. We can then test any point not on the border to see if it satisfies the inequality. If it does, we shade in that side of the border; if not, we shade in the other side. As an example, consider $y > 2x + 2$. To graph this inequality, we first graph the border, $y = 2x + 2$. Since it is a strict inequality, we use a dashed line. Then, we choose a test point. This can be any point not on the border; in this case, we will choose the origin, (0,0). (This makes the calculation easy and is generally a good choice unless the border passes through the origin.) Putting this into the original inequality, we get $0 > 2(0) + 2$, i.e. $0 > 2$. This is *not* true, so we shade in the side of the border that does *not* include the point (0,0):

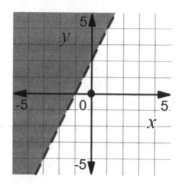

GRAPHING COMPOUND INEQUALITIES IN TWO VARIABLES

One way to graph a compound inequality in two variables is to first graph each of the component inequalities. For an *and* inequality, we then shade in only the parts where the two graphs overlap; for an *or* inequality, we shade in any region that pertains to either of the individual inequalities.

Consider the graph of "$y \geq x - 1$ *and* $y \leq -x$":

We first shade in the individual inequalities:

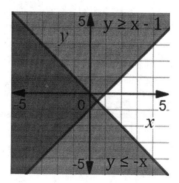

Now, since the compound inequality has an *and*, we only leave shaded the overlap—the part that pertains to *both* inequalities:

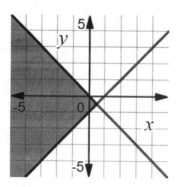

38

If instead the inequality had been "$y \geq x - 1$ *or* $y \leq -x$," our final graph would involve the *total* shaded area:

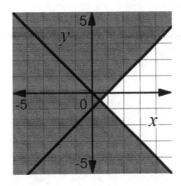

Systems of Equations

SOLVING SYSTEMS OF EQUATIONS

A **system of equations** is a set of simultaneous equations that all use the same variables. A solution to a system of equations must be true for each equation in the system. **Consistent systems** are those with at least one solution. **Inconsistent systems** are systems of equations that have no solution.

> **Review Video: Systems of Equations**
> Visit mometrix.com/academy and enter code: 658153

SUBSTITUTION

To solve a system of linear equations by **substitution**, start with the easier equation and solve for one of the variables. Express this variable in terms of the other variable. Substitute this expression in the other equation and solve for the other variable. The solution should be expressed in the form (x, y). Substitute the values into both of the original equations to check your answer. Consider the following system of equations:

$$x + 6y = 15$$
$$3x - 12y = 18$$

Solving the first equation for x: $x = 15 - 6y$

Substitute this value in place of x in the second equation, and solve for y:

$$3(15 - 6y) - 12y = 18$$
$$45 - 18y - 12y = 18$$
$$30y = 27$$
$$y = \frac{27}{30} = \frac{9}{10} = 0.9$$

Plug this value for y back into the first equation to solve for x:

$$x = 15 - 6(0.9) = 15 - 5.4 = 9.6$$

Check both equations if you have time:

$$9.6 + 6(0.9) = 15 \qquad 3(9.6) - 12(0.9) = 18$$
$$9.6 + 5.4 = 15 \qquad 28.8 - 10.8 = 18$$
$$15 = 15 \qquad\qquad 18 = 18$$

Therefore, the solution is (9.6, 0.9).

ELIMINATION

To solve a system of equations using **elimination**, begin by rewriting both equations in standard form $Ax + By = C$. Check to see if the coefficients of one pair of like variables add to zero. If not, multiply one or both of the equations by a non-zero number to make one set of like variables add to zero. Add the two equations to solve for one of the variables. Substitute this value into one of the original equations to solve for the other variable. Check your work by substituting into the other equation. Now, let's look at solving the following system using the elimination method:

$$5x + 6y = 4$$
$$x + 2y = 4$$

If we multiply the second equation by -3, we can eliminate the y terms:

$$5x + 6y = 4$$
$$-3x - 6y = -12$$

Add the equations together and solve for x:

$$2x = -8$$
$$x = \frac{-8}{2} = -4$$

Plug the value for x back in to either of the original equations and solve for y:

$$-4 + 2y = 4$$
$$y = \frac{4 + 4}{2} = 4$$

Check both equations if you have time:

$$5(-4) + 6(4) = 4 \qquad -4 + 2(4) = 4$$
$$-20 + 24 = 4 \qquad -4 + 8 = 4$$
$$4 = 4 \qquad\qquad 4 = 4$$

Therefore, the solution is (-4,4).

> **Review Video: Substitution and Elimination for Solving Linear Systems**
> Visit mometrix.com/academy and enter code: 958611

GRAPHICALLY

To solve a system of linear equations **graphically**, plot both equations on the same graph. The solution of the equations is the point where both lines cross. If the lines do not cross (are parallel), then there is **no solution**.

For example, consider the following system of equations:

$$y = 2x + 7$$
$$y = -x + 1$$

Since these equations are given in slope-intercept form, they are easy to graph; the y intercepts of the lines are $(0,7)$ and $(0,1)$. The respective slopes are 2 and –1, thus the graphs look like this:

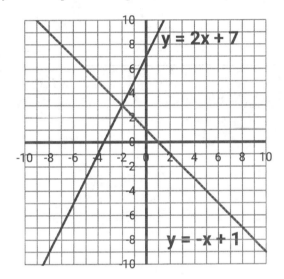

The two lines intersect at the point $(-2,3)$, thus this is the solution to the system of equations.

Solving a system graphically is generally only practical if both coordinates of the solution are integers; otherwise the intersection will lie between gridlines on the graph and the coordinates will be difficult or impossible to determine exactly. It also helps if, as in this example, the equations are in slope-intercept form or some other form that makes them easy to graph. Otherwise, another method of solution (by substitution or elimination) is likely to be more useful.

SOLVING SYSTEMS OF EQUATIONS USING THE TRACE FEATURE

Using the trace feature on a calculator requires that you rewrite each equation, isolating the y-variable on one side of the equal sign. Enter both equations in the graphing calculator and plot the graphs simultaneously. Use the trace cursor to find where the two lines cross. Use the zoom feature if necessary to obtain more accurate results. Always check your answer by substituting into the original equations. The trace method is likely to be less accurate than other methods due to the resolution of graphing calculators but is a useful tool to provide an approximate answer.

CALCULATIONS USING POINTS

Sometimes you need to perform calculations using only points on a graph as input data. Using points, you can determine what the **midpoint** and **distance** are. If you know the equation for a line, you can calculate the distance between the line and the point.

To find the **midpoint** of two points (x_1, y_1) and (x_2, y_2), average the x-coordinates to get the x-coordinate of the midpoint, and average the y-coordinates to get the y-coordinate of the midpoint. The formula is: $\left(\frac{x_1+x_2}{2}, \frac{y_1+y_2}{2}\right)$.

The **distance** between two points is the same as the length of the hypotenuse of a right triangle with the two given points as endpoints, and the two sides of the right triangle parallel to the x-axis and y-axis, respectively. The length of the segment parallel to the x-axis is the difference between the x-coordinates of the two points. The length of the segment parallel to the y-axis is the difference between the y-coordinates of the two points. Use the Pythagorean theorem $a^2 + b^2 = c^2$ or $c = \sqrt{a^2 + b^2}$ to find the distance. The formula is $d = \sqrt{(x_2 - x_1)^2 + (y_2 - y_1)^2}$.

When a line is in the format $Ax + By + C = 0$, where A, B, and C are coefficients, you can use a point (x_1, y_1) not on the line and apply the formula $d = \frac{|Ax_1 + By_1 + C|}{\sqrt{A^2 + B^2}}$ to find the distance between the line and the point (x_1, y_1).

> **Review Video: Calculations Using Points on a Graph**
> Visit mometrix.com/academy and enter code: 883228

Polynomial Algebra

MONOMIALS AND POLYNOMIALS

A **monomial** is a single variable or product of constants and variables, such as x, $2x$, or $\frac{2}{x}$. There will never be addition or subtraction symbols in a monomial. Like monomials have like variables, but they may have different coefficients. **Polynomials** are algebraic expressions that use addition and subtraction to combine two or more monomials. Two terms make a **binomial**, three terms make a **trinomial**, etc. The **degree of a monomial** is the sum of the exponents of the variables. The **degree of a polynomial** is the highest degree of any individual term.

> **Review Video: Polynomials**
> Visit mometrix.com/academy and enter code: 305005

SIMPLIFYING POLYNOMIALS

Simplifying polynomials requires combining like terms. The like terms in a polynomial expression are those that have the same variable raised to the same power. It is often helpful to connect the like terms with arrows or lines in order to separate them from the other monomials. Once you have determined the like terms, you can rearrange the polynomial by placing them together. Remember to include the sign that is in front of each term. Once the like terms are placed together, you can apply each operation and simplify. When adding and subtracting polynomials, only add and subtract the **coefficient**, or the number part; the variable and exponent stay the same.

THE FOIL METHOD

In general, multiplying polynomials is done by multiplying each term in one polynomial by each term in the other and adding the results. In the specific case for multiplying binomials, there is a useful acronym, FOIL, that can help you make sure to cover each combination of terms. The **FOIL method** for $(Ax + By)(Cx + Dy)$ would be:

F	Multiply the *first* terms of each binomial	$(\overset{first}{\overbrace{Ax}} + By)(\overset{first}{\overbrace{Cx}} + Dy)$	ACx^2
O	Multiply the *outer* terms	$(\overset{outer}{\overbrace{Ax}} + By)(Cx + \overset{outer}{\overbrace{Dy}})$	$ADxy$
I	Multiply the *inner* terms	$(Ax + \overset{inner}{\overbrace{By}})(\overset{inner}{\overbrace{Cx}} + Dy)$	$BCxy$
L	Multiply the *last* terms of each binomial	$(Ax + \overset{last}{\overbrace{By}})(Cx + \overset{last}{\overbrace{Dy}})$	BDy^2

Then, add up the result of each and combine like terms: $ACx^2 + (AD + BC)xy + BDy^2$.

For example, using the FOIL method on binomials $(x + 2)$ and $(x - 3)$:

$$\text{First:} \quad (\boxed{x} + 2)(\boxed{x} + (-3)) \quad \rightarrow \quad (x)(x) = x^2$$
$$\text{Outer:} \quad (\boxed{x} + 2)(x + \boxed{(-3)}) \quad \rightarrow \quad (x)(-3) = -3x$$
$$\text{Inner:} \quad (x + \boxed{2})(\boxed{x} + (-3)) \quad \rightarrow \quad (2)(x) = 2x$$
$$\text{Last:} \quad (x + \boxed{2})(x + \boxed{(-3)}) \quad \rightarrow \quad (2)(-3) = -6$$

This results in: $(x^2) + (-3x) + (2x) + (-6)$

Combine like terms: $x^2 + (-3 + 2)x + (-6) = x^2 - x - 6$

> **Review Video: Multiplying Terms Using the FOIL Method**
> Visit mometrix.com/academy and enter code: 854792

DIVIDING POLYNOMIALS

Use long division to divide a polynomial by either a monomial or another polynomial of equal or lesser degree.

When **dividing by a monomial**, divide each term of the polynomial by the monomial.

When **dividing by a polynomial**, begin by arranging the terms of each polynomial in order of one variable. You may arrange in ascending or descending order, but be consistent with both polynomials. To get the first term of the quotient, divide the first term of the dividend by the first term of the divisor. Multiply the first term of the quotient by the entire divisor and subtract that product from the dividend. Repeat for the second and successive terms until you either get a remainder of zero or a remainder whose degree is less than the degree of the divisor. If the quotient has a remainder, write the answer as a mixed expression in the form:

$$\text{quotient} + \frac{\text{remainder}}{\text{divisor}}$$

For example, we can evaluate the following expression in the same way as long division:

$$\frac{x^3 - 3x^2 - 2x + 5}{x - 5}$$

$$\begin{array}{r} x^2 + 2x + 8 \\ x-5{\overline{\smash{\big)}\,}} x^3 - 3x^2 - 2x + 5 \\ \underline{x^3 - 5x^2 } \\ 2x^2 - 2x \\ \underline{2x^2 -10x } \\ 8x + 5 \\ \underline{8x +40} \\ 45 \end{array}$$

$$\frac{x^3 - 3x^2 - 2x + 5}{x - 5} = x^2 + 2x + 8 + \frac{45}{x - 5}$$

When **factoring** a polynomial, first check for a common monomial factor, that is, look to see if each coefficient has a common factor or if each term has an x in it. If the factor is a trinomial but not a perfect trinomial square, look for a factorable form, such as one of these:

$$x^2 + (a + b)x + ab = (x + a)(x + b)$$
$$(ac)x^2 + (ad + bc)x + bd = (ax + b)(cx + d)$$

For factors with four terms, look for groups to factor. Once you have found the factors, write the original polynomial as the product of all the factors. Make sure all of the polynomial factors are prime. Monomial factors may be *prime* or *composite*. Check your work by multiplying the factors to make sure you get the original polynomial.

Below are patterns of some special products to remember to help make factoring easier:

- Perfect trinomial squares: $x^2 + 2xy + y^2 = (x + y)^2$ or $x^2 - 2xy + y^2 = (x - y)^2$
- Difference between two squares: $x^2 - y^2 = (x + y)(x - y)$
- Sum of two cubes: $x^3 + y^3 = (x + y)(x^2 - xy + y^2)$
  - Note: the second factor is *not* the same as a perfect trinomial square, so do not try to factor it further.
- Difference between two cubes: $x^3 - y^3 = (x - y)(x^2 + xy + y^2)$
  - Again, the second factor is *not* the same as a perfect trinomial square.
- Perfect cubes: $x^3 + 3x^2y + 3xy^2 + y^3 = (x + y)^3$ and $x^3 - 3x^2y + 3xy^2 - y^3 = (x - y)^3$

RATIONAL EXPRESSIONS

Rational expressions are fractions with polynomials in both the numerator and the denominator; the value of the polynomial in the denominator cannot be equal to zero. Be sure to keep track of values that make the denominator of the original expression zero as the final result inherits the same restrictions. For example, a denominator of $x - 3$ indicates that the expression is not defined when $x = 3$ and, as such, regardless of any operations done to the expression, it remains undefined there.

To **add or subtract** rational expressions, first find the common denominator, then rewrite each fraction as an equivalent fraction with the common denominator. Finally, add or subtract the numerators to get the numerator of the answer, and keep the common denominator as the denominator of the answer.

When **multiplying** rational expressions, factor each polynomial and cancel like factors (a factor which appears in both the numerator and the denominator). Then, multiply all remaining factors in the numerator to get the numerator of the product, and multiply the remaining factors in the denominator to get the denominator of the product. Remember: cancel entire factors, not individual terms.

To **divide** rational expressions, take the reciprocal of the divisor (the rational expression you are dividing by) and multiply by the dividend.

> **Review Video: Rational Expressions**
> Visit mometrix.com/academy and enter code: 415183

SIMPLIFYING RATIONAL EXPRESSIONS

To simplify a rational expression, factor the numerator and denominator completely. Factors that are the same and appear in the numerator and denominator have a ratio of 1. For example, look at the following expression:

$$\frac{x-1}{1-x^2}$$

The denominator, $(1 - x^2)$, is a difference of squares. It can be factored as $(1 - x)(1 + x)$. The factor $1 - x$ and the numerator $x - 1$ are opposites and have a ratio of -1. Rewrite the numerator as $-1(1 - x)$. So, the rational expression can be simplified as follows:

$$\frac{x-1}{1-x^2} = \frac{-1(1-x)}{(1-x)(1+x)} = \frac{-1}{1+x}$$

Note that since the original expression is only defined for $x \neq \{-1, 1\}$, the simplified expression has the same restrictions.

> **Review Video: Reducing Rational Expressions**
> Visit mometrix.com/academy and enter code: 788868

Quadratics

SOLVING QUADRATIC EQUATIONS

Quadratic equations are a special set of trinomials of the form $y = ax^2 + bx + c$ that occur commonly in math and real-world applications. The **roots** of a quadratic equation are the solutions that satisfy the equation when $y = 0$; in other words, where the graph touches the x-axis. There are several ways to determine these solutions including using the quadratic formula, factoring, completing the square, and graphing the function.

> **Review Video: Changing Constants in Graphs of Functions:**
> **Quadratic Equations**
> Visit mometrix.com/academy and enter code: 476276

QUADRATIC FORMULA

The **quadratic formula** is used to solve quadratic equations when other methods are more difficult. To use the quadratic formula to solve a quadratic equation, begin by rewriting the equation in standard form $ax^2 + bx + c = 0$, where a, b, and c are coefficients. Once you have identified the values of the coefficients, substitute those values into the quadratic formula

$$x = \frac{-b \pm \sqrt{b^2 - 4ac}}{2a}$$

Evaluate the equation and simplify the expression. Again, check each root by substituting into the original equation. In the quadratic formula, the portion of the formula under the radical $(b^2 - 4ac)$ is called the **discriminant**. If the discriminant is zero, there is only one root: $-\frac{b}{2a}$. If the discriminant is positive, there are two different real roots. If the discriminant is negative, there are no real roots; you will instead find complex roots. Often these solutions don't make sense in context and are ignored.

> **Review Video: Using the Quadratic Formula**
> Visit mometrix.com/academy and enter code: 163102

FACTORING

To solve a quadratic equation by factoring, begin by rewriting the equation in standard form, $x^2 + bx + c = 0$. Remember that the goal of factoring is to find numbers f and g such that $(x + f)(x + g) = x^2 + (f + g)x + fg$, in other words $(f + g) = b$ and $fg = c$. This can be a really useful method when b and c are integers. Determine the factors of c and look for pairs that could sum to b.

For example, consider finding the roots of $x^2 + 6x - 16 = 0$. The factors of -16 include, -4 and 4, -8 and 2, -2 and 8, -1 and 16, and 1 and -16. The factors that sum to 6 are -2 and 8. Write these factors as the product of two binomials, $0 = (x - 2)(x + 8)$. Finally, since these binomials multiply together to equal zero, set them each equal to zero and solve each for x. This results in $x - 2 = 0$, which simplifies to $x = 2$ and $x + 8 = 0$, which simplifies to $x = -8$. Therefore, the roots of the equation are 2 and -8.

> **Review Video: Factoring Quadratic Equations**
> Visit mometrix.com/academy and enter code: 336566

COMPLETING THE SQUARE

One way to find the roots of a quadratic equation is to find a way to manipulate it such that it follows the form of a perfect square $(x^2 + 2px + p^2)$ by adding and subtracting a constant. This process is called **completing the square**. In other words, if you are given a quadratic that is not a perfect square, $x^2 + bx + c = 0$, you can find a constant d that could be added in to make it a perfect square:

$$x^2 + bx + c + (d - d) = 0; \; \{\text{Let } b = 2p \text{ and } c + d = p^2\}$$
$$\text{then: } x^2 + 2px + p^2 - d = 0 \text{ and } d = \frac{b^2}{4} - c$$

Once you have completed the square you can find the roots of the resulting equation:

$$x^2 + 2px + p^2 - d = 0$$
$$(x + p)^2 = d$$
$$x + p = \pm\sqrt{d}$$
$$x = -p \pm \sqrt{d}$$

It is worth noting that substituting the original expressions into this solution gives the same result as the quadratic formula where $a = 1$:

$$x = -p \pm \sqrt{d} = -\frac{b}{2} \pm \sqrt{\frac{b^2}{4} - c} = -\frac{b}{2} \pm \frac{\sqrt{b^2 - 4c}}{2} = \frac{-b \pm \sqrt{b^2 - 4c}}{2}$$

Completing the square can be seen as arranging block representations of each of the terms to be as close to a square as possible and then filling in the gaps. For example, consider the quadratic expression $x^2 + 6x + 2$:

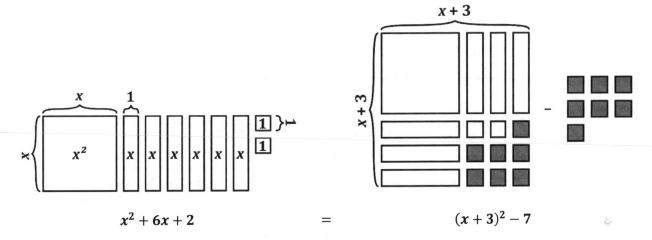

$$x^2 + 6x + 2 \qquad = \qquad (x + 3)^2 - 7$$

USING GIVEN ROOTS TO FIND QUADRATIC EQUATION

One way to find the roots of a quadratic equation is to factor the equation and use the **zero product property**, setting each factor of the equation equal to zero to find the corresponding root. We can use this technique in reverse to find an equation given its roots. Each root corresponds to a linear equation which in turn corresponds to a factor of the quadratic equation.

For example, we can find a quadratic equation whose roots are $x = 2$ and $x = -1$. The root $x = 2$ corresponds to the equation $x - 2 = 0$, and the root $x = -1$ corresponds to the equation $x + 1 = 0$.

These two equations correspond to the factors $(x - 2)$ and $(x + 1)$, from which we can derive the equation $(x - 2)(x + 1) = 0$, or $x^2 - x - 2 = 0$.

Any integer multiple of this entire equation will also yield the same roots, as the integer will simply cancel out when the equation is factored. For example, $2x^2 - 2x - 4 = 0$ factors as $2(x - 2)(x + 1) = 0$.

SOLVING A SYSTEM OF EQUATIONS CONSISTING OF A LINEAR EQUATION AND A QUADRATIC EQUATION

ALGEBRAICALLY

Generally, the simplest way to solve a system of equations consisting of a linear equation and a quadratic equation algebraically is through the method of substitution. One possible strategy is to solve the linear equation for y and then substitute that expression into the quadratic equation. After expansion and combining like terms, this will result in a new quadratic equation for x, which, like all quadratic equations, may have zero, one, or two solutions. Plugging each solution for x back into one of the original equations will then produce the corresponding value of y.

For example, consider the following system of equations:

$$x + y = 1$$
$$y = (x + 3)^2 - 2$$

We can solve the linear equation for y to yield $y = -x + 1$. Substituting this expression into the quadratic equation produces $-x + 1 = (x + 3)^2 - 2$. We can simplify this equation:

$$-x + 1 = (x + 3)^2 - 2$$
$$-x + 1 = x^2 + 6x + 9 - 2$$
$$-x + 1 = x^2 + 6x + 7$$
$$0 = x^2 + 7x + 6$$

This quadratic equation can be factored as $(x + 1)(x + 6) = 0$. It therefore has two solutions: $x_1 = -1$ and $x_2 = -6$. Plugging each of these back into the original linear equation yields $y_1 = -x_1 + 1 = -(-1) + 1 = 2$ and $y_2 = -x_2 + 1 = -(-6) + 1 = 7$. Thus, this system of equations has two solutions, $(-1,2)$ and $(-6,7)$.

It may help to check your work by putting each x and y value back into the original equations and verifying that they do provide a solution.

GRAPHICALLY

To solve a system of equations consisting of a linear equation and a quadratic equation graphically, plot both equations on the same graph. The linear equation will, of course, produce a straight line, while the quadratic equation will produce a parabola. These two graphs will intersect at zero, one, or two points; each point of intersection is a solution of the system.

For example, consider the following system of equations:

$$y = -2x + 2$$
$$y = -2x^2 + 4x + 2$$

The linear equation describes a line with a y-intercept of $(0,2)$ and a slope of -2.

To graph the quadratic equation, we can first find the vertex of the parabola: the x-coordinate of the vertex is $h = -\dfrac{b}{2a} = -\dfrac{4}{2(-2)} = 1$, and the y coordinate is $k = -2(1)^2 + 4(1) + 2 = 4$. Thus, the vertex lies at $(1,4)$. To get a feel for the rest of the parabola, we can plug in a few more values of x to find more points; by putting in $x = 2$ and $x = 3$ in the quadratic equation, we find that the points

(2,2) and (3, −4) lie on the parabola; by symmetry, so must (0, 2) and (−1, −4). We can now plot both equations:

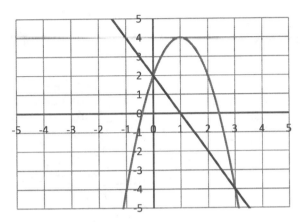

These two curves intersect at the points (0,2) and (3, −4), thus these are the solutions of the equation.

Linear Algebra

MATRIX BASICS

A **matrix** (plural: matrices) is a rectangular array of numbers or variables, often called **elements**, which are arranged in columns and rows. A matrix is generally represented by a capital letter, with its elements represented by the corresponding lowercase letter with two subscripts indicating the row and column of the element. For example, n_{ab} represents the element in row a column b of matrix N.

$$N = \begin{bmatrix} n_{11} & n_{12} & n_{13} \\ n_{21} & n_{22} & n_{23} \end{bmatrix}$$

A matrix can be described in terms of the number of rows and columns it contains in the format $a \times b$, where a is the number of rows and b is the number of columns. The matrix shown above is a 2×3 matrix. Any $a \times b$ matrix where $a = b$ is a square matrix. A **vector** is a matrix that has exactly one column (**column vector**) or exactly one row (**row vector**).

The **main diagonal** of a matrix is the set of elements on the diagonal from the top left to the bottom right of a matrix. Because of the way it is defined, only square matrices will have a main diagonal. For the matrix shown below, the main diagonal consists of the elements $n_{11}, n_{22}, n_{33}, n_{44}$.

$$\begin{bmatrix} n_{11} & n_{12} & n_{13} & n_{14} \\ n_{21} & n_{22} & n_{23} & n_{24} \\ n_{31} & n_{32} & n_{33} & n_{34} \\ n_{41} & n_{42} & n_{43} & n_{44} \end{bmatrix}$$

A 3×4 matrix such as the one shown below would not have a main diagonal because there is no straight line of elements between the top left corner and the bottom right corner that joins the elements.

$$\begin{bmatrix} n_{11} & n_{12} & n_{13} & n_{14} \\ n_{21} & n_{22} & n_{23} & n_{24} \\ n_{31} & n_{32} & n_{33} & n_{34} \end{bmatrix}$$

49

A **diagonal matrix** is a square matrix that has a zero for every element in the matrix except the elements on the main diagonal. All the elements on the main diagonal must be nonzero numbers.

$$\begin{bmatrix} n_{11} & 0 & 0 & 0 \\ 0 & n_{22} & 0 & 0 \\ 0 & 0 & n_{33} & 0 \\ 0 & 0 & 0 & n_{44} \end{bmatrix}$$

If every element on the main diagonal of a diagonal matrix is equal to one, the matrix is called an **identity matrix**. The identity matrix is often represented by the letter I.

$$I = \begin{bmatrix} 1 & 0 & 0 & 0 \\ 0 & 1 & 0 & 0 \\ 0 & 0 & 1 & 0 \\ 0 & 0 & 0 & 1 \end{bmatrix}$$

A **zero matrix** is a matrix that has zero as the value for every element in the matrix.

$$\begin{bmatrix} 0 & 0 & 0 & 0 \\ 0 & 0 & 0 & 0 \\ 0 & 0 & 0 & 0 \\ 0 & 0 & 0 & 0 \end{bmatrix}$$

The zero matrix is the *identity for matrix addition*. Do not confuse the zero matrix with the identity matrix.

The **negative of a matrix** is also known as the additive inverse of a matrix. If matrix N is the given matrix, then matrix $-N$ is its negative. This means that every element n_{ab} is equal to $-n_{ab}$ in the negative. To find the negative of a given matrix, change the sign of every element in the matrix and keep all elements in their original corresponding positions in the matrix.

If two matrices have the same order and all corresponding elements in the two matrices are the same, then the two matrices are **equal matrices**.

A matrix N may be **transposed** to matrix N^T by changing all rows into columns and changing all columns into rows. The easiest way to accomplish this is to swap the positions of the row and column notations for each element. For example, suppose the element in the second row of the third column of matrix N is $n_{23} = 6$. In the transposed matrix N^T, the transposed element would be $n_{32} = 6$, and it would be placed in the third row of the second column.

$$N = \begin{bmatrix} 1 & 2 & 3 \\ 4 & 5 & 6 \end{bmatrix}; \ N^T = \begin{bmatrix} 1 & 4 \\ 2 & 5 \\ 3 & 6 \end{bmatrix}$$

To quickly transpose a matrix by hand, begin with the first column and rewrite a new matrix with those same elements in the same order in the first row. Write the elements from the second column of the original matrix in the second row of the transposed matrix. Continue this process until all columns have been completed. If the original matrix is identical to the transposed matrix, the matrices are symmetric.

The **determinant** of a matrix is a scalar value that is calculated by taking into account all the elements of a square matrix. A determinant only exists for square matrices. Finding the determinant of a 2 × 2 matrix is as simple as remembering a simple equation. For a 2 × 2 matrix

$M = \begin{bmatrix} m_{11} & m_{12} \\ m_{21} & m_{22} \end{bmatrix}$, the determinant is obtained by the equation $|M| = m_{11}m_{22} - m_{12}m_{21}$. Anything larger than 2×2 requires multiple steps. Take matrix $N = \begin{bmatrix} a & b & c \\ d & e & f \\ g & h & j \end{bmatrix}$. The determinant of N is calculated as $|N| = a\begin{vmatrix} e & f \\ h & j \end{vmatrix} - b\begin{vmatrix} d & f \\ g & j \end{vmatrix} + c\begin{vmatrix} d & e \\ g & h \end{vmatrix}$ or $|N| = a(ej - fh) - b(dj - fg) + c(dh - eg)$.

There is a shortcut for 3×3 matrices: add the products of each unique set of elements diagonally left-to-right and subtract the products of each unique set of elements diagonally right-to-left. In matrix N, the left-to-right diagonal elements are (a, e, j), (b, f, g), and (c, d, h). The right-to-left diagonal elements are (a, f, h), (b, d, j), and (c, e, g). $\det(N) = aej + bfg + cdh - afh - bdj - ceg$.

Calculating the determinants of matrices larger than 3×3 is rarely, if ever, done by hand.

The **inverse** of a matrix M is the matrix that, when multiplied by matrix M, yields a product that is the identity matrix. Multiplication of matrices will be explained in greater detail shortly. Not all matrices have inverses. Only a square matrix whose determinant is not zero has an inverse. If a matrix has an inverse, that inverse is unique to that matrix. For any matrix M that has an inverse, the inverse is represented by the symbol M^{-1}. To calculate the inverse of a 2×2 square matrix, use the following pattern:

$$M = \begin{bmatrix} m_{11} & m_{12} \\ m_{21} & m_{22} \end{bmatrix}; \quad M^{-1} = \begin{bmatrix} \dfrac{m_{22}}{|M|} & \dfrac{-m_{12}}{|M|} \\ \dfrac{-m_{21}}{|M|} & \dfrac{m_{11}}{|M|} \end{bmatrix}$$

Another way to find the inverse of a matrix by hand is use an augmented matrix and elementary row operations. An **augmented matrix** is formed by appending the entries from one matrix onto the end of another. For example, given a 2×2 invertible matrix $N = \begin{bmatrix} a & b \\ c & d \end{bmatrix}$, you can find the inverse N^{-1} by creating an augmented matrix by appending a 2×2 identity matrix: $\begin{bmatrix} a & b & | & 1 & 0 \\ c & d & | & 0 & 1 \end{bmatrix}$. To find the inverse of the original 2×2 matrix, perform elementary row operations to convert the original matrix on the left to an identity matrix: $\begin{bmatrix} 1 & 0 & | & e & f \\ 0 & 1 & | & g & h \end{bmatrix}$. For instance, the first step might be to multiply the second row by $\dfrac{b}{d}$ and then subtract it from the first row to make its second column a zero. The end result is that the 2×2 section on the right will become the inverse of the original matrix: $N^{-1} = \begin{bmatrix} e & f \\ g & h \end{bmatrix}$.

ELEMENTARY ROW OPERATIONS

Elementary row operations include multiplying a row by a non-zero scalar, adding scalar multiples of two rows, and switching rows. These operations can be done using matrix multiplication with specialized transformation matrices. **Row switching** is achieved by swapping the corresponding rows in the identity matrix. For example, consider switching row 2 and row 3 in a 3×3 matrix:

$$M_{R_2 \leftrightarrow R_3} = \begin{bmatrix} 1 & 0 & 0 \\ 0 & 0 & 1 \\ 0 & 1 & 0 \end{bmatrix}$$

The transformation matrix for **row multiplication** is also based on the identity matrix with the scalar multiplication factor in place of the 1 in the corresponding row. Multiplying row 1 by -4 in a 3×3 matrix:

$$M_{-4R_1 \to R_1} = \begin{bmatrix} -4 & 0 & 0 \\ 0 & 1 & 0 \\ 0 & 0 & 1 \end{bmatrix}$$

The transformation matrix for **row addition** consists of the identity matrix with a 1 in the element corresponding to the two rows being added in the column where you want the result to go. Adding row 2 to row 1 in a 3×3 matrix:

$$M_{R_1 + R_2 \to R_1} = \begin{bmatrix} 1 & 0 & 0 \\ 1 & 1 & 0 \\ 0 & 0 & 1 \end{bmatrix}$$

BASIC OPERATIONS WITH MATRICES

There are two categories of basic operations with regard to matrices: operations between a matrix and a scalar, and operations between two matrices.

SCALAR OPERATIONS

A scalar being added to a matrix is treated as though it were being added to each element of the matrix:

$$M + \mathrm{k} = \begin{bmatrix} m_{11} + k & m_{12} + k \\ m_{21} + k & m_{22} + k \end{bmatrix}$$

The same is true for the other three operations.

Subtraction:

$$M - k = \begin{bmatrix} m_{11} - k & m_{12} - k \\ m_{21} - k & m_{22} - k \end{bmatrix}$$

Multiplication:

$$M \times k = \begin{bmatrix} m_{11} \times k & m_{12} \times k \\ m_{21} \times k & m_{22} \times k \end{bmatrix}$$

Division:

$$M \div k = \begin{bmatrix} m_{11} \div k & m_{12} \div k \\ m_{21} \div k & m_{22} \div k \end{bmatrix}$$

MATRIX ADDITION AND SUBTRACTION

All four of the basic operations can be used with operations between matrices (although division is usually discarded in favor of multiplication by the inverse), but there are restrictions on the situations in which they can be used. Matrices that meet all the qualifications for a given operation are called **conformable matrices**. However, conformability is specific to the operation; two matrices that are conformable for addition are not necessarily conformable for multiplication.

For two matrices to be conformable for addition or subtraction, they must be of the same dimension; otherwise the operation is not defined. If matrix M is a 3×2 matrix and matrix N is a 2×3 matrix, the operations $M + N$ and $M - N$ are meaningless. If matrices M and N are the same size, the operation is as simple as adding or subtracting all of the corresponding elements:

$$\begin{bmatrix} m_{11} & m_{12} \\ m_{21} & m_{22} \end{bmatrix} + \begin{bmatrix} n_{11} & n_{12} \\ n_{21} & n_{22} \end{bmatrix} = \begin{bmatrix} m_{11} + n_{11} & m_{12} + n_{12} \\ m_{21} + n_{21} & m_{22} + n_{22} \end{bmatrix}$$

$$\begin{bmatrix} m_{11} & m_{12} \\ m_{21} & m_{22} \end{bmatrix} - \begin{bmatrix} n_{11} & n_{12} \\ n_{21} & n_{22} \end{bmatrix} = \begin{bmatrix} m_{11} - n_{11} & m_{12} - n_{12} \\ m_{21} - n_{21} & m_{22} - n_{22} \end{bmatrix}$$

The result of addition or subtraction is a matrix of the same dimension as the two original matrices involved in the operation.

MATRIX MULTIPLICATION

The first thing it is necessary to understand about matrix multiplication is that it is not commutative. In scalar multiplication, the operation is commutative, meaning that $a \times b = b \times a$. For matrix multiplication, this is not the case: $A \times B \neq B \times A$. The terminology must be specific when describing matrix multiplication. The operation $A \times B$ can be described as A multiplied (or **post-multiplied**) by B, or B **pre-multiplied** by A.

For two matrices to be conformable for multiplication, they need not be of the same dimension, but specific dimensions must correspond. Taking the example of two matrices M and N to be multiplied $M \times N$, matrix M must have the same number of columns as matrix N has rows. Put another way, if matrix M has the dimensions $a \times b$ and matrix N has the dimensions $c \times d$, b must equal c if the two matrices are to be conformable for this multiplication. The matrix that results from the multiplication will have the dimensions $a \times d$. If a and d are both equal to 1, the product is simply a scalar. Square matrices of the same dimensions are always conformable for multiplication, and their product is always a matrix of the same size.

The simplest type of matrix multiplication is a 1×2 matrix (a row vector) times a 2×1 matrix (a column vector). These will multiply in the following way:

$$\begin{bmatrix} m_{11} & m_{12} \end{bmatrix} \times \begin{bmatrix} n_{11} \\ n_{21} \end{bmatrix} = m_{11}n_{11} + m_{12}n_{21}$$

The two matrices are conformable for multiplication because matrix M has the same number of columns as matrix N has rows. Because the other dimensions are both 1, the result is a scalar. Expanding our matrices to 1×3 and 3×1, the process is the same:

$$\begin{bmatrix} m_{11} & m_{12} & m_{13} \end{bmatrix} \times \begin{bmatrix} n_{11} \\ n_{21} \\ n_{31} \end{bmatrix} = m_{11}n_{11} + m_{12}n_{21} + m_{13}n_{31}$$

Once again, the result is a scalar. This type of basic matrix multiplication is the building block for the multiplication of larger matrices.

To multiply larger matrices, treat each **row from the first matrix** and each **column from the second matrix** as individual vectors and follow the pattern for multiplying vectors. The scalar value found from multiplying the first-row vector by the first column vector is placed in the first row, first column of the new matrix. The scalar value found from multiplying the second-row vector by the first column vector is placed in the second row, first column of the new matrix. Continue this pattern until each row of the first matrix has been multiplied by each column of the second vector.

Below is an example of the multiplication of a 3×2 matrix and a 2×3 matrix.

$$\begin{bmatrix} m_{11} & m_{12} \\ m_{21} & m_{22} \\ m_{31} & m_{32} \end{bmatrix} \times \begin{bmatrix} n_{11} & n_{12} & n_{13} \\ n_{21} & n_{22} & n_{23} \end{bmatrix} = \begin{bmatrix} m_{11}n_{11} + m_{12}n_{21} & m_{11}n_{12} + m_{12}n_{22} & m_{11}n_{13} + m_{12}n_{23} \\ m_{21}n_{11} + m_{22}n_{21} & m_{21}n_{12} + m_{22}n_{22} & m_{21}n_{13} + m_{22}n_{23} \\ m_{31}n_{11} + m_{32}n_{21} & m_{31}n_{12} + m_{32}n_{22} & m_{31}n_{13} + m_{32}n_{23} \end{bmatrix}$$

This process starts by taking the first column of the second matrix and running it through each row of the first matrix. Removing all but the first M row and first N column, we would see only the following:

$$[m_{11} \quad m_{12}] \times \begin{bmatrix} n_{11} \\ n_{21} \end{bmatrix} = m_{11}n_{11} + m_{12}n_{21}$$

The first product would then be $m_{11}n_{11} + m_{12}n_{21}$. This process will be continued for each column of the N matrix to find the first full row of the product matrix, as shown below.

$$[m_{11}n_{11} + m_{12}n_{21} \quad m_{11}n_{12} + m_{12}n_{22} \quad m_{11}n_{13} + m_{12}n_{23}]$$

After completing the first row, the next step would be to simply move to the second row of the M matrix and repeat the process until all of the rows have been finished. The result is a 3×3 matrix.

$$\begin{bmatrix} m_{11} & m_{12} \\ m_{21} & m_{22} \\ m_{31} & m_{32} \end{bmatrix} \times \begin{bmatrix} n_{11} & n_{12} & n_{13} \\ n_{21} & n_{22} & n_{23} \end{bmatrix} = \begin{bmatrix} m_{11}n_{11} + m_{12}n_{21} & m_{11}n_{12} + m_{12}n_{22} & m_{11}n_{13} + m_{12}n_{23} \\ m_{21}n_{11} + m_{22}n_{21} & m_{21}n_{12} + m_{22}n_{22} & m_{21}n_{13} + m_{22}n_{23} \\ m_{31}n_{11} + m_{32}n_{21} & m_{31}n_{12} + m_{32}n_{22} & m_{31}n_{13} + m_{32}n_{23} \end{bmatrix}$$

If the operation were done in reverse ($N \times M$), the result would be a 2×2 matrix.

$$\begin{bmatrix} n_{11} & n_{12} & n_{13} \\ n_{21} & n_{22} & n_{23} \end{bmatrix} \times \begin{bmatrix} m_{11} & m_{12} \\ m_{21} & m_{22} \\ m_{31} & m_{32} \end{bmatrix} = \begin{bmatrix} m_{11}n_{11} + m_{21}n_{12} + m_{31}n_{13} & m_{12}n_{11} + m_{22}n_{12} + m_{32}n_{13} \\ m_{11}n_{21} + m_{21}n_{22} + m_{31}n_{23} & m_{12}n_{21} + m_{22}n_{22} + m_{32}n_{23} \end{bmatrix}$$

SOLVING SYSTEMS OF EQUATIONS

Matrices can be used to represent the coefficients of a system of linear equations and can be very useful in solving those systems. Take for instance three equations with three variables where all a, b, c, and d are known constants:

$$a_1 x + b_1 y + c_1 z = d_1$$
$$a_2 x + b_2 y + c_2 z = d_2$$
$$a_3 x + b_3 y + c_3 z = d_3$$

To solve this system, define three matrices:

$$A = \begin{bmatrix} a_1 & b_1 & c_1 \\ a_2 & b_2 & c_2 \\ a_3 & b_3 & c_3 \end{bmatrix}; \quad D = \begin{bmatrix} d_1 \\ d_2 \\ d_3 \end{bmatrix}; \quad X = \begin{bmatrix} x \\ y \\ z \end{bmatrix}$$

The three equations in our system can be fully represented by a single matrix equation:

$$AX = D$$

We know that the identity matrix times X is equal to X, and we know that any matrix multiplied by its inverse is equal to the identity matrix.

$$A^{-1}AX = IX = X; \text{thus } X = A^{-1}D$$

Our goal then is to find the inverse of A, or A^{-1}. Once we have that, we can pre-multiply matrix D by A^{-1} (post-multiplying here is an undefined operation) to find matrix X.

> **Review Video: Comparison of Methods for Solving Systems**
> Visit mometrix.com/academy and enter code: 281590

Systems of equations can also be solved using the transformation of an augmented matrix in a process similar to that for finding a matrix inverse. Begin by arranging each equation of the system in the following format:

$$a_1x + b_1y + c_1z = d_1$$
$$a_2x + b_2y + c_2z = d_2$$
$$a_3x + b_3y + c_3z = d_3$$

Define matrices A and D and combine them into augmented matrix A_a:

$$A = \begin{bmatrix} a_1 & b_1 & c_1 \\ a_2 & b_2 & c_2 \\ a_3 & b_3 & c_3 \end{bmatrix}; \quad D = \begin{bmatrix} d_1 \\ d_2 \\ d_3 \end{bmatrix}; \quad A_a = \begin{bmatrix} a_1 & b_1 & c_1 & d_1 \\ a_2 & b_2 & c_2 & d_2 \\ a_3 & b_3 & c_3 & d_3 \end{bmatrix}$$

To solve the augmented matrix and the system of equations, use elementary row operations to form an identity matrix in the first 3×3 section. When this is complete, the values in the last column are the solutions to the system of equations:

$$\begin{bmatrix} 1 & 0 & 0 & x \\ 0 & 1 & 0 & y \\ 0 & 0 & 1 & z \end{bmatrix}$$

If an identity matrix is not possible, the system of equations has no unique solution. Sometimes only a partial solution will be possible. The following are partial solutions you may find:

$$\begin{bmatrix} 1 & 0 & k_1 & x_0 \\ 0 & 1 & k_2 & y_0 \\ 0 & 0 & 0 & 0 \end{bmatrix}$$ gives the non-unique solution $x = x_0 - k_1z$; $y = y_0 - k_2z$

$$\begin{bmatrix} 1 & j_1 & k_1 & x_0 \\ 0 & 0 & 0 & 0 \\ 0 & 0 & 0 & 0 \end{bmatrix}$$ gives the non-unique solution $x = x_0 - j_1y - k_1z$

This process can be used to solve systems of equations with any number of variables, but three is the upper limit for practical purposes. Anything more ought to be done with a graphing calculator.

REDUCED ROW-ECHELON FORMS

When a system of equations has a solution, finding the transformation of the augmented matrix will result in one of three reduced row-echelon forms. Only one of these forms will give a unique solution to the system of equations, however. The following examples show the solutions indicated by particular results:

$$\begin{bmatrix} 1 & 0 & 0 & x_0 \\ 0 & 1 & 0 & y_0 \\ 0 & 0 & 1 & z_0 \end{bmatrix}$$ gives the unique solution $x = x_0$; $y = y_0$; $z = z_0$

$$\begin{bmatrix} 1 & 0 & k_1 & x_0 \\ 0 & 1 & k_2 & y_0 \\ 0 & 0 & 0 & 0 \end{bmatrix}$$ gives a non-unique solution $x = x_0 - k_1z$; $y = y_0 - k_2z$

$$\begin{bmatrix} 1 & j_1 & k_1 & x_0 \\ 0 & 0 & 0 & 0 \\ 0 & 0 & 0 & 0 \end{bmatrix}$$ gives a non-unique solution $x = x_0 - j_1y - k_1z$

GEOMETRIC TRANSFORMATIONS

The four *geometric transformations* are **translations**, **reflections**, **rotations**, and **dilations**. When geometric transformations are expressed as matrices, the process of performing the transformations is simplified. For calculations of the geometric transformations of a planar figure, make a $2 \times n$ matrix, where n is the number of vertices in the planar figure. Each column represents the rectangular coordinates of one vertex of the figure, with the top row containing the values of the x-coordinates and the bottom row containing the values of the y-coordinates. For example, given a planar triangular figure with coordinates (x_1, y_1), (x_2, y_2), and (x_3, y_3), the corresponding matrix is $\begin{bmatrix} x_1 & x_2 & x_3 \\ y_1 & y_2 & y_3 \end{bmatrix}$. You can then perform the necessary transformations on this matrix to determine the coordinates of the resulting figure.

TRANSLATION

A **translation** moves a figure along the x-axis, the y-axis, or both axes without changing the size or shape of the figure. To calculate the new coordinates of a planar figure following a translation, set up a matrix of the coordinates and a matrix of the translation values and add the two matrices.

$$\begin{bmatrix} h & h & h \\ v & v & v \end{bmatrix} + \begin{bmatrix} x_1 & x_2 & x_3 \\ y_1 & y_2 & y_3 \end{bmatrix} = \begin{bmatrix} h + x_1 & h + x_2 & h + x_3 \\ v + y_1 & v + y_2 & v + y_3 \end{bmatrix}$$

where h is the number of units the figure is moved along the x-axis (horizontally) and v is the number of units the figure is moved along the y-axis (vertically).

REFLECTION

To find the **reflection** of a planar figure over the x-axis, set up a matrix of the coordinates of the vertices and pre-multiply the matrix by the 2×2 matrix $\begin{bmatrix} 1 & 0 \\ 0 & -1 \end{bmatrix}$ so that $\begin{bmatrix} 1 & 0 \\ 0 & -1 \end{bmatrix}\begin{bmatrix} x_1 & x_2 & x_3 \\ y_1 & y_2 & y_3 \end{bmatrix} = \begin{bmatrix} x_1 & x_2 & x_3 \\ -y_1 & -y_2 & -y_3 \end{bmatrix}$. To find the reflection of a planar figure over the y-axis, set up a matrix of the coordinates of the vertices and pre-multiply the matrix by the 2×2 matrix $\begin{bmatrix} -1 & 0 \\ 0 & 1 \end{bmatrix}$ so that $\begin{bmatrix} -1 & 0 \\ 0 & 1 \end{bmatrix}\begin{bmatrix} x_1 & x_2 & x_3 \\ y_1 & y_2 & y_3 \end{bmatrix} = \begin{bmatrix} -x_1 & -x_2 & -x_3 \\ y_1 & y_2 & y_3 \end{bmatrix}$. To find the reflection of a planar figure over the line $y = x$, set up a matrix of the coordinates of the vertices and pre-multiply the matrix by the 2×2 matrix $\begin{bmatrix} 0 & 1 \\ 1 & 0 \end{bmatrix}$ so that $\begin{bmatrix} 0 & 1 \\ 1 & 0 \end{bmatrix}\begin{bmatrix} x_1 & x_2 & x_3 \\ y_1 & y_2 & y_3 \end{bmatrix} = \begin{bmatrix} y_1 & y_2 & y_3 \\ x_1 & x_2 & x_3 \end{bmatrix}$. Remember that the order of multiplication is important when multiplying matrices. The commutative property does not apply.

ROTATION

To find the coordinates of the figure formed by rotating a planar figure about the origin θ degrees in a counterclockwise direction, set up a matrix of the coordinates of the vertices and pre-multiply the matrix by the 2×2 matrix $\begin{bmatrix} \cos\theta & \sin\theta \\ -\sin\theta & \cos\theta \end{bmatrix}$. For example, if you want to rotate a figure 90° clockwise around the origin, you would have to convert the degree measure to 270° counterclockwise and solve the 2×2 matrix you have set as the pre-multiplier: $\begin{bmatrix} \cos 270° & \sin 270° \\ -\sin 270° & \cos 270° \end{bmatrix} = \begin{bmatrix} 0 & -1 \\ 1 & 0 \end{bmatrix}$. Use this as the pre-multiplier for the matrix $\begin{bmatrix} x_1 & x_2 & x_3 \\ y_1 & y_2 & y_3 \end{bmatrix}$ and solve to find the new coordinates.

DILATION

To find the **dilation** of a planar figure by a scale factor of k, set up a matrix of the coordinates of the vertices of the planar figure and pre-multiply the matrix by the 2×2 matrix $\begin{bmatrix} k & 0 \\ 0 & k \end{bmatrix}$ so that $\begin{bmatrix} k & 0 \\ 0 & k \end{bmatrix} \begin{bmatrix} x_1 & x_2 & x_3 \\ y_1 & y_2 & y_3 \end{bmatrix} = \begin{bmatrix} kx_1 & kx_2 & kx_3 \\ ky_1 & ky_2 & ky_3 \end{bmatrix}$. This is effectively the same as multiplying the matrix by the scalar k, but the matrix equation would still be necessary if the figure were being dilated by different factors in vertical and horizontal directions. The scale factor k will be greater than 1 if the figure is being enlarged, and between 0 and 1 if the figure is being shrunk. Again, remember that when multiplying matrices, the order of the matrices is important. The commutative property does not apply, and the matrix with the coordinates of the figure must be the second matrix.

Functions

Basic Functions

FUNCTION AND RELATION

When expressing functional relationships, the **variables** x and y are typically used. These values are often written as the **coordinates** (x, y). The x-value is the independent variable and the y-value is the dependent variable. A **relation** is a set of data in which there is not a unique y-value for each x-value in the dataset. This means that there can be two of the same x-values assigned to different y-values. A relation is simply a relationship between the x- and y-values in each coordinate but does not apply to the relationship between the values of x and y in the data set. A **function** is a relation where one quantity depends on the other. For example, the amount of money that you make depends on the number of hours that you work. In a function, each x-value in the data set has one unique y-value because the y-value depends on the x-value.

> **Review Video: Definition of a Function**
> Visit mometrix.com/academy and enter code: 784611

FUNCTIONS

A function has exactly one value of **output variable** (dependent variable) for each value of the **input variable** (independent variable). The set of all values for the input variable (here assumed to be x) is the domain of the function, and the set of all corresponding values of the output variable (here assumed to be y) is the range of the function. When looking at a graph of an equation, the easiest way to determine if the equation is a function or not is to conduct the vertical line test. If a vertical line drawn through any value of x crosses the graph in more than one place, the equation is not a function.

FINDING THE DOMAIN AND RANGE OF A FUNCTION

The **domain** of a function $f(x)$ is the set of all input values for which the function is defined. The **range** of a function $f(x)$ is the set of all possible output values of the function—that is, of every possible value of $f(x)$, for any value of x in the function's domain. For a function expressed in a table, every input-output pair is given explicitly. To find the domain, we just list all the x values and to find the range, we just list all the values of $f(x)$. Consider the following example:

x	-1	4	2	1	0	3	8	6
$f(x)$	3	0	3	−1	−1	2	4	6

In this case, the domain would be {-1, 4, 2, 1, 0, 3, 8, 6}, or, putting them in ascending order, {-1, 0, 1, 2, 3, 4, 6, 8}. (Putting the values in ascending order isn't strictly necessary, but generally makes the set easier to read.) The range would be {3, 0, 3, −1, −1, 2, 4, 6}. Note that some of these values appear more than once. This is entirely permissible for a function; while each value of x must be matched to a unique value of $f(x)$, the converse is not true. We don't need to list each value more than once, so eliminating duplicates, the range is {3, 0, −1, 2, 4, 6}, or, putting them in ascending order, {−1, 0, 2, 3, 4, 6}.

58

Note that by definition of a function, no input value can be matched to more than one output value. It is good to double-check to make sure that the data given follows this and is therefore actually a function.

DETERMINING A FUNCTION

You can determine whether an equation is a **function** by substituting different values into the equation for x. You can display and organize these numbers in a data table. A **data table** contains the values for x and y, which you can also list as coordinates. In order for a function to exist, the table cannot contain any repeating x-values that correspond with different y-values. If each x-coordinate has a unique y-coordinate, the table contains a function. However, there can be repeating y-values that correspond with different x-values. An example of this is when the function contains an exponent. For example, if $x^2 = y$, $2^2 = 4$, and $(-2)^2 = 4$.

WRITING A FUNCTION RULE USING A TABLE

If given a set of data, place the corresponding x- and y-values into a table and analyze the relationship between them. Consider what you can do to each x-value to obtain the corresponding y-value. Try adding or subtracting different numbers to and from x and then try multiplying or dividing different numbers to and from x. If none of these **operations** give you the y-value, try combining the operations. Once you find a rule that works for one pair, make sure to try it with each additional set of ordered pairs in the table. If the same operation or combination of operations satisfies each set of coordinates, then the table contains a function. The rule is then used to write the equation of the function in "$y =$" form.

DIRECT AND INVERSE VARIATIONS OF VARIABLES

Variables that vary directly are those that either both increase at the same rate or both decrease at the same rate. For example, in the functions $y = kx$ or $y = kx^n$, where k and n are positive, the value of y increases as the value of x increases and decreases as the value of x decreases.

Variables that vary inversely are those where one increases while the other decreases. For example, in the functions $y = \frac{k}{x}$ or $y = \frac{k}{x^n}$ where k and n are positive, the value of y increases as the value of x decreases and decreases as the value of x increases.

In both cases, k is the constant of variation.

PROPERTIES OF FUNCTIONS

There are many different ways to classify functions based on their structure or behavior. Important features of functions include:

- **End behavior**: the behavior of the function at extreme values ($f(x)$ as $x \to \pm\infty$)
- **y-intercept**: the value of the function at $f(0)$
- **Roots**: the values of x where the function equals zero ($f(x) = 0$)
- **Extrema**: minimum or maximum values of the function or where the function changes direction ($f(x) \geq k$ or $f(x) \leq k$)

CLASSIFICATION OF FUNCTIONS

An **invertible function** is defined as a function, $f(x)$, for which there is another function, $f^{-1}(x)$, such that $f^{-1}(f(x)) = x$. For example, if $f(x) = 3x - 2$ the inverse function, $f^{-1}(x)$, can be found:

$$x = 3(f^{-1}(x)) - 2$$
$$\frac{x + 2}{3} = f^{-1}(x)$$

$$f^{-1}(f(x)) = \frac{3x - 2 + 2}{3}$$
$$= \frac{3x}{3}$$
$$= x$$

Note that $f^{-1}(x)$ is a valid function over all values of x.

In a **one-to-one function**, each value of x has exactly one value for y on the coordinate plane (this is the definition of a function) and each value of y has exactly one value for x. While the vertical line test will determine if a graph is that of a function, the horizontal line test will determine if a function is a one-to-one function. If a horizontal line drawn at any value of y intersects the graph in more than one place, the graph is not that of a one-to-one function. Do not make the mistake of using the horizontal line test exclusively in determining if a graph is that of a one-to-one function. A one-to-one function must pass both the vertical line test and the horizontal line test. As such, one-to-one functions are invertible functions.

A **many-to-one function** is a function whereby the relation is a function, but the inverse of the function is not a function. In other words, each element in the domain is mapped to one and only one element in the range. However, one or more elements in the range may be mapped to the same element in the domain. A graph of a many-to-one function would pass the vertical line test, but not the horizontal line test. This is why many-to-one functions are not invertible.

A **monotone function** is a function whose graph either constantly increases or constantly decreases. Examples include the functions $f(x) = x$, $f(x) = -x$, or $f(x) = x^3$.

An **even function** has a graph that is symmetric with respect to the y-axis and satisfies the equation $f(x) = f(-x)$. Examples include the functions $f(x) = x^2$ and $f(x) = ax^n$, where a is any real number and n is a positive even integer.

An **odd function** has a graph that is symmetric with respect to the origin and satisfies the equation $f(x) = -f(-x)$. Examples include the functions $f(x) = x^3$ and $f(x) = ax^n$, where a is any real number and n is a positive odd integer.

Constant functions are given by the equation $f(x) = b$, where b is a real number. There is no independent variable present in the equation, so the function has a constant value for all x. The graph of a constant function is a horizontal line of slope 0 that is positioned b units from the x-axis. If b is positive, the line is above the x-axis; if b is negative, the line is below the x-axis.

Identity functions are identified by the equation $f(x) = x$, where every value of the function is equal to its corresponding value of x. The only zero is the point $(0, 0)$. The graph is a line with a slope of 1.

In **linear functions**, the value of the function changes in direct proportion to x. The rate of change, represented by the slope on its graph, is constant throughout. The standard form of a linear equation is $ax + cy = d$, where a, c, and d are real numbers. As a function, this equation is commonly in the form $y = mx + b$ or $f(x) = mx + b$ where $m = -\frac{a}{c}$ and $b = \frac{d}{c}$. This is known as

60

the slope-intercept form, because the coefficients give the slope of the graphed function (m) and its y-intercept (b). Solve the equation $mx + b = 0$ for x to get $x = -\dfrac{b}{m}$, which is the only zero of the function. The domain and range are both the set of all real numbers.

Algebraic functions are those that exclusively use polynomials and roots. These would include polynomial functions, rational functions, square root functions, and all combinations of these functions, such as polynomials as the radicand. These combinations may be joined by addition, subtraction, multiplication, or division, but may not include variables as exponents.

ABSOLUTE VALUE FUNCTIONS

An **absolute value function** is in the format $f(x) = |ax + b|$. Like other functions, the domain is the set of all real numbers. However, because absolute value indicates positive numbers, the range is limited to positive real numbers. To find the zero of an absolute value function, set the portion inside the absolute value sign equal to zero and solve for x. An absolute value function is also known as a piecewise function because it must be solved in pieces—one for if the value inside the absolute value sign is positive, and one for if the value is negative. The function can be expressed as

$$f(x) = \begin{cases} ax + b & \text{if } ax + b \geq 0 \\ -(ax + b) & \text{if } ax + b < 0 \end{cases}$$

This will allow for an accurate statement of the range. The graph of an example absolute value function, $f(x) = |2x - 1|$, is below:

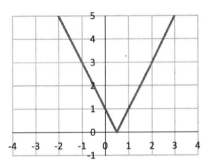

PIECEWISE FUNCTIONS

A **piecewise function** is a function that has different definitions on two or more different intervals. The following, for instance, is one example of a piecewise-defined function:

$$f(x) = \begin{cases} x^2, & x < 0 \\ x, & 0 \leq x \leq 2 \\ (x - 2)^2, & x > 2 \end{cases}$$

To graph this function, you would simply graph each part separately in the appropriate domain. The final graph would look like this:

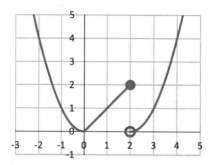

Note the filled and hollow dots at the discontinuity at $x = 2$. This is important to show which side of the graph that point corresponds to. Because $f(x) = x$ on the closed interval $0 \leq x \leq 2$, $f(2) = 2$. The point $(2, 2)$ is therefore marked with a filled circle, and the point $(2,0)$, which is the endpoint of the rightmost $(x - 2)^2$ part of the graph but *not actually part of the function*, is marked with a hollow dot to indicate this.

QUADRATIC FUNCTIONS

A **quadratic function** is a function in the form $y = ax^2 + bx + c$, where a does not equal 0. While a linear function forms a line, a quadratic function forms a **parabola**, which is a u-shaped figure that either opens upward or downward. A parabola that opens upward is said to be a **positive quadratic function,** and a parabola that opens downward is said to be a **negative quadratic function**. The shape of a parabola can differ, depending on the values of a, b, and c. All parabolas contain a **vertex**, which is the highest possible point, the **maximum**, or the lowest possible point, the **minimum**. This is the point where the graph begins moving in the opposite direction. A quadratic function can have zero, one, or two solutions, and therefore zero, one, or two x-intercepts. Recall that the x-intercepts are referred to as the zeros, or roots, of a function. A quadratic function will have only one y-intercept. Understanding the basic components of a quadratic function can give you an idea of the shape of its graph.

Example graph of a positive quadratic function, $x^2 + 2x - 3$:

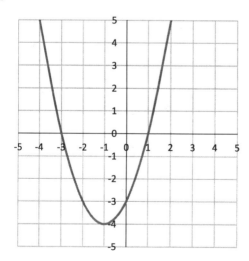

62

POLYNOMIAL FUNCTIONS

A **polynomial function** is a function with multiple terms and multiple powers of x, such as:

$$f(x) = a_n x^n + a_{n-1} x^{n-1} + a_{n-2} x^{n-2} + \cdots + a_1 x + a_0$$

where n is a non-negative integer that is the highest exponent in the polynomial and $a_n \neq 0$. The domain of a polynomial function is the set of all real numbers. If the greatest exponent in the polynomial is even, the polynomial is said to be of even degree and the range is the set of real numbers that satisfy the function. If the greatest exponent in the polynomial is odd, the polynomial is said to be odd and the range, like the domain, is the set of all real numbers.

> **Review Video: Simplifying Rational Polynomial Functions**
> Visit mometrix.com/academy and enter code: 351038

RATIONAL FUNCTIONS

A **rational function** is a function that can be constructed as a ratio of two polynomial expressions: $f(x) = \frac{p(x)}{q(x)}$, where $p(x)$ and $q(x)$ are both polynomial expressions and $q(x) \neq 0$. The domain is the set of all real numbers, except any values for which $q(x) = 0$. The range is the set of real numbers that satisfies the function when the domain is applied. When you graph a rational function, you will have vertical asymptotes wherever $q(x) = 0$. If the polynomial in the numerator is of lesser degree than the polynomial in the denominator, the x-axis will also be a horizontal asymptote. If the numerator and denominator have equal degrees, there will be a horizontal asymptote not on the x-axis. If the degree of the numerator is exactly one greater than the degree of the denominator, the graph will have an oblique, or diagonal, asymptote. The asymptote will be along the line $y = \frac{p_n}{q_{n-1}} x + \frac{p_{n-1}}{q_{n-1}}$, where p_n and q_{n-1} are the coefficients of the highest degree terms in their respective polynomials.

SQUARE ROOT FUNCTIONS

A **square root function** is a function that contains a radical and is in the format $f(x) = \sqrt{ax + b}$. The domain is the set of all real numbers that yields a positive radicand or a radicand equal to zero. Because square root values are assumed to be positive unless otherwise identified, the range is all real numbers from zero to infinity. To find the zero of a square root function, set the radicand equal to zero and solve for x. The graph of a square root function is always to the right of the zero and always above the x-axis.

Example graph of a square root function, $f(x) = \sqrt{2x + 1}$:

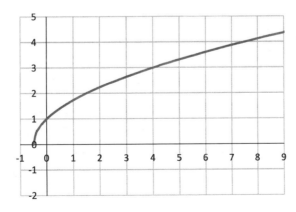

Advanced Functions

STEP FUNCTIONS

The double brackets indicate a step function. For a step function, the value inside the double brackets is rounded down to the nearest integer. The graph of the function $f_0(x) = [\![x]\!]$ appears on the left graph. In comparison $f(x) = 2\left[\!\left[\frac{1}{3}(x-1)\right]\!\right]$ is on the right graph. The coefficient of 2 shows that it's stretched vertically by a factor of 2 (so there's a vertical distance of 2 units between successive "steps"). The coefficient of $\frac{1}{3}$ in front of the x shows that it's stretched horizontally by a factor of 3 (so each "step" is three units long), and the $x - 1$ shows that it's displaced one unit to the right.

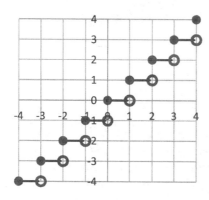 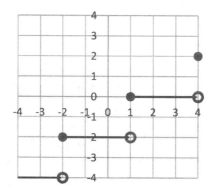

TRANSCENDENTAL FUNCTIONS

Transcendental functions are all functions that are non-algebraic. Any function that includes logarithms, trigonometric functions, variables as exponents, or any combination that includes any of these is not algebraic in nature, even if the function includes polynomials or roots.

EXPONENTIAL FUNCTIONS

Exponential functions are equations that have the format $y = b^x$, where base $b > 0$ and $b \neq 1$. The exponential function can also be written $f(x) = b^x$. Recall the properties of exponents, like the product of terms with the same base is equal to the base raised to the sum of the exponents $(a^x \times a^y = a^{x+y})$ and a term with an exponent that is raised to an exponent is equal to the base of the original term raised to the product of the exponents: $((a^x)^y = a^{xy})$. The graph of an example exponential function, $f(x) = 2^x$, is below:

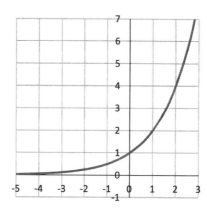

64

Note in the graph that the y-value approaches zero to the left and infinity to the right. One of the key features of an exponential function is that there will be one end that goes off to infinity and another that asymptotically approaches a lower bound. Common forms of exponential functions include:

Geometric sequences: $a_n = a_1 \times r^{n-1}$, where u_n is the value of the nth term, a_1 is the initial value, r is the common ratio, and n is the number of terms. Note that $a_1 \times r^{1-1} = a_1 \times r^0 = a_1 \times 1 = a_1$.

Population growth: $f(t) = ae^{rt}$, where $f(t)$ is the population at time $t \geq 0$, a is the initial population, e is the mathematical constant known as Euler's number, and r is the growth rate.

Compound interest: $f(t) = P\left(1 + \frac{r}{n}\right)^{nt}$, where $f(t)$ is the account value at a certain number of time periods $t \geq 0$, P is the initial principle balance, r is the interest rate, and n is the number of times the interest is applied per time period.

General exponential growth or decay: $f(t) = a(1 + r)^t$, where $f(t)$ is the future count, a is the current or initial count, r is the growth or decay rate, and t is the time.

For example, suppose the initial population of a town was 1,200 people. The population growth is 5%. The current population is 2,400. To find out how much time has passed since the town was founded, we can use the following function:

$$2400 = 1200e^{0.05t}.$$

The general form for population growth may be represented as $f(t) = ae^{rt}$, where $f(t)$ represents the current population, a represents the initial population, r represents the growth rate, and t represents the time. Thus, substituting the initial population, current population, and rate into this form gives the equation above.

The number of years that have passed were found by first dividing both sides of the equation by 1,200. Doing so gives $2 = e^{0.05t}$. Taking the natural logarithm of both sides gives $\ln(2) = ln(e^{0.05t})$. Applying the power property of logarithms, the equation may be rewritten as $\ln(2) = 0.05t \times \ln(e)$, which simplifies as $\ln(2) = 0.05t$. Dividing both sides of this equation by 0.05 gives $t \approx 13.86$. Thus, approximately 13.86 years passed.

> **Review Video: Biology Application - Exponential Growth Function**
> Visit mometrix.com/academy and enter code: 336069

LOGARITHMIC FUNCTIONS

Logarithmic functions are equations that have the format $y = \log_b x$ or $f(x) = \log_b x$. The base b may be any number except one; however, the most common bases for logarithms are base 10 and base e. The log base e is the natural logarithm, or ln, expressed by the function $f(x) = \ln x$.

Any logarithm that does not have an assigned value of b is assumed to be base 10: $\log x = \log_{10} x$. Exponential functions and logarithmic functions are related in that one is the inverse of the other. If $f(x) = b^x$, then $f^{-1}(x) = \log_b x$. This can perhaps be expressed more clearly by the two equations: $y = b^x$ and $x = \log_b y$.

The following properties apply to logarithmic expressions:

Property	Description
$\log_b 1 = 0$	The log of 1 is equal to 0 for any base
$\log_b b = 1$	The log of the base is equal to 1
$\log_b b^p = p$	The log of the base raised to a power is equal to that power
$\log_b MN = \log_b M + \log_b N$	The log of a product is the sum of the log of each factor
$\log_b \dfrac{M}{N} = \log_b M - \log_b N$	The log of a quotient is equal to the log of the dividend minus the log of the divisor
$\log_b M^p = p \log_b M$	The log of a value raised to a power is equal to the power times the log of the value

The graph of an example logarithmic function, $f(x) = \log_2(x + 2)$, is below:

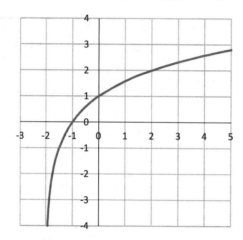

TRIGONOMETRIC FUNCTIONS

Trigonometric functions are periodic, meaning that they repeat the same form over and over. The basic trigonometric functions are sine (abbreviated 'sin'), cosine (abbreviated 'cos'), and tangent (abbreviated 'tan'). The simplest way to think of them is as describing the ratio of the side lengths of a right triangle in relation to the angles of the triangle.

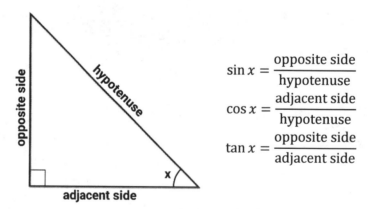

$$\sin x = \frac{\text{opposite side}}{\text{hypotenuse}}$$

$$\cos x = \frac{\text{adjacent side}}{\text{hypotenuse}}$$

$$\tan x = \frac{\text{opposite side}}{\text{adjacent side}}$$

Using sine as an example, trigonometric functions take the form $f(x) = A\sin(Bx + C) + D$, where the **amplitude** is simply equal to A. The **period** is the distance between successive peaks or troughs, essentially the length of the repeated pattern. In this form, the period is equal to $2\pi/B$. As for C, this is the **phase shift** or the horizontal shift of the function. The last term, D, is the vertical shift and determines the **midline** as $y = D$.

For instance, consider the function $f(x) = 2 + \frac{3}{2}\sin\left(\pi x + \frac{\pi}{2}\right)$. Here $A = \frac{3}{2}$, $B = \pi$, $C = \frac{\pi}{2}$, and $D = 2$, so the midline is at $y = 2$, the amplitude is $\frac{3}{2}$, and the period is $2\pi/\pi = 2$. To graph this function, we center the sine wave on the midline and extend it to a height above and below the midline equal to the amplitude—so this graph would have a minimum value of $2 - \frac{3}{2} = \frac{1}{2}$ and a maximum of $2 + \frac{3}{2} = \frac{7}{2}$. So, the function would be graphed as follows:

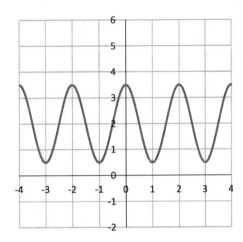

MANIPULATION OF FUNCTIONS

Translation occurs when values are added to or subtracted from the x or y values. If a constant is added to the y portion of each point, the graph shifts up. If a constant is subtracted from the y portion of each point, the graph shifts down. This is represented by the expression $f(x) \pm k$, where k is a constant. If a constant is added to the x portion of each point, the graph shifts left. If a constant is subtracted from the x portion of each point, the graph shifts right. This is represented by the expression $f(x \pm k)$, where k is a constant.

Stretching, compression, and reflection occur when different parts of a function are multiplied by different groups of constants. If the function as a whole is multiplied by a real number constant greater than 1, $(k \times f(x))$, the graph is stretched vertically. If k in the previous equation is greater than zero but less than 1, the graph is compressed vertically. If k is less than zero, the graph is reflected about the x-axis, in addition to being either stretched or compressed vertically if k is less than or greater than -1, respectively. If instead, just the x-term is multiplied by a constant greater than 1 $(f(k \times x))$, the graph is compressed horizontally. If k in the previous equation is greater than zero but less than 1, the graph is stretched horizontally. If k is less than zero, the graph is reflected about the y-axis, in addition to being either stretched or compressed horizontally if k is greater than or less than -1, respectively.

ALGEBRAIC THEOREMS

According to the **fundamental theorem of algebra**, every non-constant, single-variable polynomial has exactly as many roots as the polynomial's highest exponent. For example, if x^4 is the largest exponent of a term, the polynomial will have exactly 4 roots. However, some of these roots may have multiplicity or be non-real numbers. For instance, in the polynomial function $f(x) = x^4 - 4x + 3$, the only real roots are 1 and -1. The root 1 has multiplicity of 2 and there is one non-real root $(-1 - \sqrt{2}i)$.

67

The **remainder theorem** is useful for determining the remainder when a polynomial is divided by a binomial. The remainder theorem states that if a polynomial function $f(x)$ is divided by a binomial $x - a$, where a is a real number, the remainder of the division will be the value of $f(a)$. If $f(a) = 0$, then a is a root of the polynomial.

The **factor theorem** is related to the remainder theorem and states that if $f(a) = 0$ then $(x-a)$ is a factor of the function.

According to the **rational root theorem,** any rational root of a polynomial function $f(x) = a_n x^n + a_{n-1} x^{n-1} + \cdots + a_1 x + a_0$ with integer coefficients will, when reduced to its lowest terms, be a positive or negative fraction such that the numerator is a factor of a_0 and the denominator is a factor of a_n. For instance, if the polynomial function $f(x) = x^3 + 3x^2 - 4$ has any rational roots, the numerators of those roots can only be factors of 4 (1, 2, 4), and the denominators can only be factors of 1 (1). The function in this example has roots of 1 $\left(\text{or } \frac{1}{1}\right)$ and -2 $\left(\text{or } -\frac{2}{1}\right)$.

APPLYING THE BASIC OPERATIONS TO FUNCTIONS

For each of the basic operations, we will use these functions as examples: $f(x) = x^2$ and $g(x) = x$.

To find the sum of two functions f and g, assuming the domains are compatible, simply add the two functions together: $(f + g)(x) = f(x) + g(x) = x^2 + x$

To find the difference of two functions f and g, assuming the domains are compatible, simply subtract the second function from the first: $(f - g)(x) = f(x) - g(x) = x^2 - x$.

To find the product of two functions f and g, assuming the domains are compatible, multiply the two functions together: $(f \times g)(x) = f(x) \times g(x) = x^2 \times x = x^3$.

To find the quotient of two functions f and g, assuming the domains are compatible, divide the first function by the second: $\frac{f}{g}(x) = \frac{f(x)}{g(x)} = \frac{x^2}{x} = x \; ; x \neq 0$.

The example given in each case is fairly simple, but on a given problem, if you are looking only for the value of the sum, difference, product, or quotient of two functions at a particular x-value, it may be simpler to solve the functions individually and then perform the given operation using those values.

The composite of two functions f and g, written as $(f \circ g)(x)$ simply means that the output of the second function is used as the input of the first. This can also be written as $f(g(x))$. In general, this can be solved by substituting $g(x)$ for all instances of x in $f(x)$ and simplifying. Using the example functions $f(x) = x^2 - x + 2$ and $g(x) = x + 1$, we can find that $(f \circ g)(x)$ or $f(g(x))$ is equal to $f(x + 1) = (x + 1)^2 - (x + 1) + 2$, which simplifies to $x^2 + x + 2$.

It is important to note that $(f \circ g)(x)$ is not necessarily the same as $(g \circ f)(x)$. The process is not always commutative like addition or multiplication expressions. It *can* be commutative, but most often this is not the case.

Sequences

SEQUENCES

A **sequence** is a set of numbers that continues on in a defined pattern. The function that defines a sequence has a domain composed of the set of positive integers. Each member of the sequence is an element, or individual term. Each element is identified by the notation a_n, where a is the term of the sequence, and n is the integer identifying which term in the sequence a is. There are two different ways to represent a sequence that contains the element a_n. The first is the simple notation $\{a_n\}$. The expanded notation of a sequence is $a_1, a_2, a_3, \ldots a_n, \ldots$. Notice that the expanded form does not end with the nth term. There is no indication that the nth term is the last term in the sequence, only that the nth term is an element of the sequence.

ARITHMETIC SEQUENCES

An **arithmetic sequence**, or arithmetic progression, is a special kind of sequence in which each term has a specific quantity, called the common difference, that is added to the previous term. The common difference may be positive or negative. The general form of an arithmetic sequence containing n terms is $a_1, a_1 + d, a_1 + 2d, \ldots, a_1 + (n-1)d$, where d is the common difference. The formula for the general term of an arithmetic sequence is $a_n = a_1 + (n-1)d$, where a_n is the term you are looking for and d is the common difference. To find the sum of the first n terms of an arithmetic sequence, use the formula $s_n = \frac{n}{2}(a_1 + a_n)$.

> **Review Video: Arithmetic Sequence**
> Visit mometrix.com/academy and enter code: 676885

MONOTONIC SEQUENCES

A **monotonic sequence** is a sequence that is either nonincreasing or nondecreasing. A **nonincreasing** sequence is one whose terms either get progressively smaller in value or remain the same—a sequence that is bounded above. This means that all elements of the sequence must be less than a given real number. A **nondecreasing** sequence is one whose terms either get progressively larger in value or remain the same—a sequence that is bounded below. This means that all elements of the sequence must be greater than a given real number.

RECURSIVE SEQUENCES

When one element of a sequence is defined in terms of a previous element or elements of the sequence, the sequence is a **recursive sequence**. For example, given the recursive definition $a_1 = 1; a_2 = 1; a_n = a_{n-1} + a_{n-2}$ for all $n > 2$, you get the sequence $1, 1, 2, 3, 5, 8, \ldots$. This particular sequence is known as the Fibonacci sequence, and is defined as the numbers zero and one, and a continuing sequence of numbers, with each number in the sequence equal to the sum of the two previous numbers. It is important to note that the Fibonacci sequence can also be defined as the first two terms being equal to one, with the remaining terms equal to the sum of the previous two terms. Both definitions are considered correct in mathematics. Make sure you know which definition you are working with when dealing with Fibonacci numbers.

Sometimes one term of a sequence with a recursive definition can be found without knowing the previous terms of the sequence. This case is known as a **closed-form** expression for a recursive definition. In this case, an alternate formula will apply to the sequence to generate the same sequence of numbers. However, not all sequences based on recursive definitions will have a closed-form expression. Some sequences will require the use of the recursive definition.

GOLDEN RATIO AND FIBONACCI SEQUENCE

The golden ratio is approximately 1.6180339887498948482... and is often represented by the Greek letter phi, Φ. The exact value of Φ is $(1 + \sqrt{5})/2$ and it is one of the solutions to $x - \frac{1}{x} = 1$.

The golden ratio is represented within the Fibonacci sequence, since the ratio of a term to the previous term approaches Φ as the sequence approaches infinity:

n	a_n	a_{n-1}	$\dfrac{a_n}{a_{n-1}}$
3	2	1	2
4	3	2	1.5
5	5	3	$1.\overline{6}$
6	8	5	1.6
7	13	8	1.625
8	21	13	$1.\overline{615384}$
9	34	21	$1.\overline{619047}$
⋮	⋮	⋮	⋮
20	6765	4181	1.618033963

GEOMETRIC SEQUENCES

Any function with the set of all natural numbers as the domain is also called a sequence. An element of a sequence is denoted by the symbol a_n, which represents the nth element of sequence a. Sequences may be arithmetic or geometric and may be defined by a recursive definition, closed-form expression or both. Arithmetic and geometric sequences both have recursive definitions based on the first term of the sequence, as well as both having formulas to find the sum of the first n terms in the sequence, assuming you know what the first term is. The sum of all the terms in a sequence is called a **series**. Consider the following example of a geometric sequence: Andy opens a savings account with $10. During each subsequent week, he plans to double the amount deposited during the previous week.

Sequence: 10, 20, 40, 80, 160, ...

Function: $a_n = 10 \times 2^{n-1}$

The sequence is a geometric sequence, with a common ratio of 2. All geometric sequences represent exponential functions. The nth term in any geometric sequence is represented by the general form, $a_n = a_1 \times r^{n-1}$, where a_n represents the value of the nth term, a_1 represents the value of the initial term, r represents the common ratio, and n represents the number of terms. Thus, substituting the initial value of 10 and common ratio of 2 gives the function, $a_n = 10 \times 2^{n-1}$.

LIMIT OF A SEQUENCE

Some sequences will have a **limit**, or a value the sequence approaches or sometimes even reaches but never passes. A sequence that has a limit is known as a convergent sequence because all the values of the sequence seemingly converge at that point. Sequences that do not converge at a particular limit are divergent sequences. The easiest way to determine whether a sequence converges or diverges is to find the limit of the sequence. If the limit is a real number, the sequence is a convergent sequence. If the limit is infinity, the sequence is a divergent sequence.

Remember the following rules for finding limits:

- $\lim\limits_{n\to\infty} k = k$, for all real numbers k
- $\lim\limits_{n\to\infty} \dfrac{1}{n} = 0$
- $\lim\limits_{n\to\infty} n = \infty$

- $\lim\limits_{n\to\infty}\dfrac{k}{n^p}=0$, for all real numbers k and positive rational numbers p
- The limit of the sums of two sequences is equal to the sum of the limits of the two sequences: $\lim\limits_{n\to\infty}(a_n+b_n)=\lim\limits_{n\to\infty}a_n+\lim\limits_{n\to\infty}b_n$.
- The limit of the difference between two sequences is equal to the difference between the limits of the two sequences: $\lim\limits_{n\to\infty}(a_n-b_n)=\lim\limits_{n\to\infty}a_n-\lim\limits_{n\to\infty}b_n$
- The limit of the product of two sequences is equal to the product of the limits of the two sequences: $\lim\limits_{n\to\infty}(a_n\times b_n)=\lim\limits_{n\to\infty}a_n\times\lim\limits_{n\to\infty}b_n$
- The limit of the quotient of two sequences is equal to the quotient of the limits of the two sequences, with some exceptions: $\lim\limits_{n\to\infty}\left(\dfrac{a_n}{b_n}\right)=\dfrac{\lim\limits_{n\to\infty}a_n}{\lim\limits_{n\to\infty}b_n}$. In the quotient formula, it is important to consider that $b_n\neq 0$ and $\lim\limits_{n\to\infty}b_n\neq 0$.
- The limit of a sequence multiplied by a scalar is equal to the scalar multiplied by the limit of the sequence: $\lim\limits_{n\to\infty}ka_n=k\lim\limits_{n\to\infty}a_n$, where k is any real number.

INFINITE SERIES

An **infinite series**, also referred to as just a series, is a series of partial sums of a defined sequence. Each infinite sequence represents an infinite series according to the equation $\sum_{n=1}^{\infty}a_n=a_1+a_2+a_3+\cdots+a_n+\cdots$. This notation can be shortened to $\sum_{n=1}^{\infty}a_n$ or $\sum a_n$. Every series is a sequence of partial sums, where the first partial sum is equal to the first element of the series, the second partial sum is equal to the sum of the first two elements of the series, and the nth partial sum is equal to the sum of the first n elements of the series.

Every infinite sequence of partial sums (infinite series) either converges or diverges. Like the test for convergence in a sequence, finding the limit of the sequence of partial sums will indicate whether it is a converging series or a diverging series. If there exists a real number S such that $\lim\limits_{n\to\infty}S_n=S$, where S_n is the sequence of partial sums, then the series converges. If the limit equals infinity, then the series diverges. If $\lim\limits_{n\to\infty}S_n=S$ and S is a real number, then S is also the convergence value of the series.

To find the sum as n approaches infinity for the sum of two convergent series, find the sum as n approaches infinity for each individual series and add the results.

$$\sum_{n=1}^{\infty}(a_n+b_n)=\sum_{n=1}^{\infty}a_n+\sum_{n=1}^{\infty}b_n$$

To find the sum as n approaches infinity for the difference between two convergent series, find the sum as n approaches infinity for each individual series and subtract the results.

$$\sum_{n=1}^{\infty}(a_n-b_n)=\sum_{n=1}^{\infty}a_n-\sum_{n=1}^{\infty}b_n$$

To find the sum as n approaches infinity for the product of a constant, also called a scalar, and a convergent series, find the sum as n approaches infinity for the series and multiply the result by the scalar.

$$\sum_{n=1}^{\infty} ka_n = k \sum_{n=1}^{\infty} a_n$$

The **nth term test for divergence** involves taking the limit of the nth term of a sequence and determining whether or not the limit is equal to zero. If the limit of the nth term is not equal to zero, then the series is a diverging series. This test only works to prove divergence, however. If the nth term is equal to zero, the test is inconclusive.

Trigonometry

DEGREES, RADIANS, AND THE UNIT CIRCLE

It is important to understand the deep connection between trigonometry and circles. Specifically, the two main units, **degrees** (°) and **radians** (rad), that are used to measure angles are related this way: 360° in one full circle and 2π radians in one full circle: (360° = 2π rad). The conversion factor relating the two is often stated as $\frac{180°}{\pi}$. For example, to convert $\frac{3\pi}{2}$ radians to degrees, multiply by the conversion factor: $\frac{3\pi}{2} \times \frac{180°}{\pi} = 270°$. As another example, to convert 60° to radians, divide by the conversion factor or multiply by the reciprocal: $60° \times \frac{\pi}{180°} = \frac{\pi}{3}$ radians.

Recall that the standard equation for a circle is $(x - h)^2 + (y - k)^2 = r^2$. A **unit circle** is a circle with a radius of 1 ($r = 1$) that has its center at the origin ($h = 0, k = 0$). Thus, the equation for the unit circle simplifies from the standard equation down to $x^2 + y^2 = 1$.

Standard position is the position of an angle of measure θ whose vertex is at the origin, the initial side crosses the unit circle at the point (1, 0), and the terminal side crosses the unit circle at some other point (a, b). In the standard position, $\sin \theta = b$, $\cos \theta = a$, and $\tan \theta = \frac{b}{a}$.

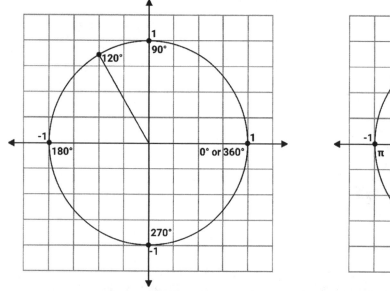
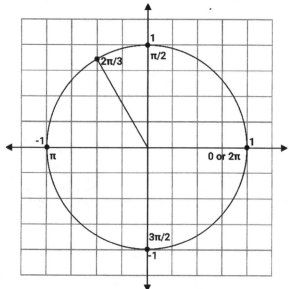

Review Video: Unit Circles and Standard Position
Visit mometrix.com/academy and enter code: 333922

72

BASIC TRIGONOMETRIC FUNCTIONS

SINE

The **sine** (sin) function has a period of 360° or 2π radians. This means that its graph makes one complete cycle every 360° or 2π. Because $\sin 0 = 0$, the graph of $y = \sin x$ begins at the origin, with the x-axis representing the angle measure, and the y-axis representing the sine of the angle. The graph of the sine function is a smooth curve that begins at the origin, peaks at the point $\left(\frac{\pi}{2}, 1\right)$, crosses the x-axis at $(\pi, 0)$, has its lowest point at $\left(\frac{3\pi}{2}, -1\right)$, and returns to the x-axis to complete one cycle at $(2\pi, 0)$.

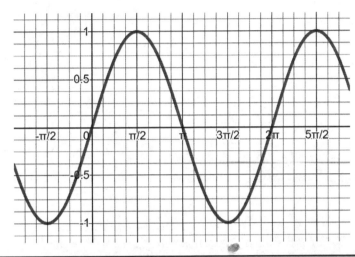

Review Video: Upper Level Trig: Sine
Visit mometrix.com/academy and enter code: 193339

COSINE

The **cosine** (cos) function also has a period of 360° or 2π radians, which means that its graph also makes one complete cycle every 360° or 2π. Because $\cos 0° = 1$, the graph of $y = \cos x$ begins at the point $(0, 1)$, with the x-axis representing the angle measure, and the y-axis representing the cosine of the angle. The graph of the cosine function is a smooth curve that begins at the point $(0,1)$, crosses the x-axis at the point $\left(\frac{\pi}{2}, 0\right)$, has its lowest point at $(\pi, -1)$, crosses the x-axis again at the point $\left(\frac{3\pi}{2}, 0\right)$, and returns to a peak at the point $(2\pi, 1)$ to complete one cycle.

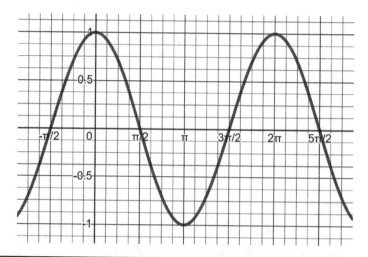

TANGENT

The **tangent** (tan) function has a period of 180° or π radians, which means that its graph makes one complete cycle every 180° or π radians. The x-axis represents the angle measure, and the y-axis represents the tangent of the angle. The graph of the tangent function is a series of smooth curves that cross the x-axis at every 180° or π radians and have an asymptote every $k \times 90°$ or $\frac{k\pi}{2}$ radians, where k is an odd integer. This can be explained by the fact that the tangent is calculated by dividing the sine by the cosine, since the cosine equals zero at those asymptote points.

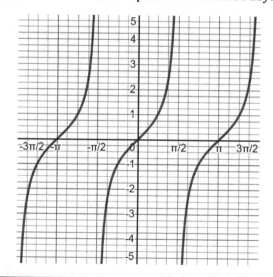

DEFINED AND RECIPROCAL FUNCTIONS

The tangent function is defined as the ratio of the sine to the cosine: $\tan x = \frac{\sin x}{\cos x}$

To take the reciprocal of a number means to place that number as the denominator of a fraction with a numerator of 1. The reciprocal functions are thus defined quite simply.

Cosecant	$\csc x$	$\frac{1}{\sin x}$
Secant	$\sec x$	$\frac{1}{\cos x}$
Cotangent	$\cot x$	$\frac{1}{\tan x}$

It is important to know these reciprocal functions, but they are not as commonly used as the three basic functions.

INVERSE FUNCTIONS

Each of the trigonometric functions accepts an angular measure, either degrees or radians, and gives a numerical value as the output. The inverse functions do the opposite; they accept a numerical value and give an angular measure as the output. The inverse of sine, or arcsine, commonly written as either $\sin^{-1} x$ or $\arcsin x$, gives the angle whose sine is x. Similarly:

The inverse of $\cos x$ is written as $\cos^{-1} x$ or $\arccos x$ and means the angle whose cosine is x.
The inverse of $\tan x$ is written as $\tan^{-1} x$ or $\arctan x$ and means the angle whose tangent is x.
The inverse of $\csc x$ is written as $\csc^{-1} x$ or $\text{arccsc}\, x$ and means the angle whose cosecant is x.
The inverse of $\sec x$ is written as $\sec^{-1} x$ or $\text{arcsec}\, x$ and means the angle whose secant is x.
The inverse of $\cot x$ is written as $\cot^{-1} x$ or $\text{arccot}\, x$ and means the angle whose cotangent is x.

IMPORTANT NOTE ABOUT SOLVING TRIGONOMETRIC EQUATIONS

Trigonometric and algebraic equations are solved following the same rules, but while algebraic expressions have one unique solution, trigonometric equations could have multiple solutions, and you must find them all. When solving for an angle with a known trigonometric value, you must consider the sign and include all angles with that value. Your calculator will probably only give one value as an answer, typically in the following ranges:

- For $\sin^{-1} x$, $\left[-\frac{\pi}{2}, \frac{\pi}{2}\right]$ or $[-90°, 90°]$
- For $\cos^{-1} x$, $[0, \pi]$ or $[0°, 180°]$
- For $\tan^{-1} x$, $\left[-\frac{\pi}{2}, \frac{\pi}{2}\right]$ or $[-90°, 90°]$

It is important to determine if there is another angle in a different quadrant that also satisfies the problem. To do this, find the other quadrant(s) with the same sign for that trigonometric function and find the angle that has the same reference angle. Then check whether this angle is also a solution.

- In the first quadrant, all six trigonometric functions are positive.
- In the second quadrant, sin and csc are positive.
- In the third quadrant, tan and cot are positive.
- In the fourth quadrant, cos and sec are positive.

If you remember the phrase, "ALL Students Take Classes," you will be able to remember the sign of each trigonometric function in each quadrant. ALL represents all the signs in the first quadrant. The "S" in "Students" represents the sine function and its reciprocal in the second quadrant. The "T" in "Take" represents the tangent function and its reciprocal in the third quadrant. The "C" in "Classes" represents the cosine function and its reciprocal.

DOMAIN, RANGE, AND ASYMPTOTES IN TRIGONOMETRY

The domain is the set of all possible real number values of x on the graph of a trigonometric function. Some graphs will impose limits on the values of x.

The range is the set of all possible real number values of y on the graph of a trigonometric function. Some graphs will impose limits on the values of y.

Asymptotes are lines that the graph of a trigonometric function approaches but never reaches. Asymptotes exist for values of x in the graphs of the tangent, cotangent, secant, and cosecant. The sine and cosine graphs do not have any asymptotes.

DOMAIN, RANGE, AND ASYMPTOTES OF THE SIX TRIGONOMETRIC FUNCTIONS

The domain, range, and asymptotes for each of the trigonometric functions are as follows:

- In the **sine** function, the domain is all real numbers, the range is $-1 \leq y \leq 1$, and there are no asymptotes.
- In the **cosine** function, the domain is all real numbers, the range is $-1 \leq y \leq 1$, and there are no asymptotes.
- In the **tangent** function, the domain is $x \in$ all real numbers; $x \neq \frac{\pi}{2} + k\pi$, the range is all real numbers, and the asymptotes are the lines $x = \frac{\pi}{2} + k\pi$.
- In the **cosecant** function, the domain is $x \in$ all real numbers; $x \neq k\pi$, the range is $(-\infty, -1]$ and $[1, \infty)$, and the asymptotes are the lines $x = k\pi$.

- In the **secant** function, the domain is $x \in$ all real numbers; $x \neq \frac{\pi}{2} + k\pi$, the range is $(-\infty, 1]$ and $[1, \infty)$, and the asymptotes are the lines $x = \frac{\pi}{2} + k\pi$.
- In the **cotangent** function, the domain is $x \in$ all real numbers; $x \neq k\pi$, the range is all real numbers, and the asymptotes are the lines $x = k\pi$.

In each of the above cases, k represents any integer.

TRIGONOMETRIC IDENTITIES
SUM AND DIFFERENCE

To find the sine, cosine, or tangent of the sum or difference of two angles, use one of the following formulas where α and β are two angles with known sine, cosine, or tangent values as needed:

$$\sin(\alpha \pm \beta) = \sin\alpha\cos\beta \pm \cos\alpha\sin\beta$$
$$\cos(\alpha \pm \beta) = \cos\alpha\cos\beta \mp \sin\alpha\sin\beta$$
$$\tan(\alpha \pm \beta) = \frac{\tan\alpha \pm \tan\beta}{1 \mp \tan\alpha\tan\beta}$$

HALF ANGLE

To find the sine or cosine of half of a known angle, use the following formulas where θ is an angle with a known exact cosine value:

$$\sin(\theta/2) = \pm\sqrt{(1 - \cos\theta)/2}$$
$$\cos(\theta/2) = \pm\sqrt{(1 + \cos\theta)/2}$$

To determine the sign of the answer, you must recognize which quadrant the given angle is in and apply the correct sign for the trigonometric function you are using. If you need to find an expression for the exact sine or cosine of an angle that you do not know, such as sine 22.5°, you can rewrite the given angle as a half angle, such as $\sin\left(\frac{45°}{2}\right)$, and use the formula above:

$$\sin\left(\frac{45°}{2}\right) = \pm\sqrt{(1 - \cos(45°))/2} = \pm\sqrt{\left(1 - \frac{\sqrt{2}}{2}\right)/2} = \pm\sqrt{(2 - \sqrt{2})/4} = \pm\frac{1}{2}\sqrt{(2 - \sqrt{2})}$$

To find the tangent or cotangent of half of a known angle, use the following formulas where θ is an angle with known exact sine and cosine values:

$$\tan\frac{\theta}{2} = \frac{\sin\theta}{1 + \cos\theta}$$
$$\cot\frac{\theta}{2} = \frac{\sin\theta}{1 - \cos\theta}$$

These formulas will work for finding the tangent or cotangent of half of any angle unless the cosine of θ happens to make the denominator of the identity equal to 0.

The Pythagorean theorem states that $a^2 + b^2 = c^2$ for all right triangles. The trigonometric identity that derives from this principle is stated in this way: $\sin^2\theta + \cos^2\theta = 1$

Dividing each term by either $\sin^2\theta$ or $\cos^2\theta$ yields two other identities, respectively:

$$1 + \cot^2\theta = \csc^2\theta$$
$$\tan^2\theta + 1 = \sec^2\theta$$

DOUBLE ANGLES

In each case, use one of the double angle formulas. To find the sine or cosine of twice a known angle, use one of the following formulas:

$$\sin(2\theta) = 2\sin\theta\cos\theta$$

$$\cos(2\theta) = \cos^2\theta - \sin^2\theta$$
$$= 2\cos^2\theta - 1$$
$$= 1 - 2\sin^2\theta$$

To find the tangent or cotangent of twice a known angle, use the formulas where θ is an angle with known exact sine, cosine, tangent, and cotangent values:

$$\tan(2\theta) = \frac{2\tan\theta}{1 - \tan^2\theta}$$
$$\cot(2\theta) = \frac{\cot\theta - \tan\theta}{2}$$

PRODUCTS

To find the product of the sines and cosines of two different angles, use one of the following formulas where α and β are two unique angles:

$$\sin\alpha\sin\beta = \frac{1}{2}[\cos(\alpha - \beta) - \cos(\alpha + \beta)]$$
$$\cos\alpha\cos\beta = \frac{1}{2}[\cos(\alpha + \beta) + \cos(\alpha - \beta)]$$
$$\sin\alpha\cos\beta = \frac{1}{2}[\sin(\alpha + \beta) + \sin(\alpha - \beta)]$$
$$\cos\alpha\sin\beta = \frac{1}{2}[\sin(\alpha + \beta) - \sin(\alpha - \beta)]$$

COMPLEMENTARY

The trigonometric cofunction identities use the trigonometric relationships of complementary angles (angles whose sum is 90°). These are:

$$\cos x = \sin(90° - x)$$
$$\csc x = \sec(90° - x)$$
$$\cot x = \tan(90° - x)$$

Review Video: Complementary Angles
Visit mometrix.com/academy and enter code: 919405

78

TABLE OF COMMONLY ENCOUNTERED ANGLES

$0° = 0$ radians, $30° = \frac{\pi}{6}$ radians, $45° = \frac{\pi}{4}$ radians, $60° = \frac{\pi}{3}$ radians, and $90° = \frac{\pi}{2}$ radians

$\sin 0° = 0$	$\cos 0° - 1$	$\tan 0° = 0$
$\sin 30° = \frac{1}{2}$	$\cos 30° = \frac{\sqrt{3}}{2}$	$\tan 30° = \frac{\sqrt{3}}{3}$
$\sin 45° = \frac{\sqrt{2}}{2}$	$\cos 45° = \frac{\sqrt{2}}{2}$	$\tan 45° = 1$
$\sin 60° = \frac{\sqrt{3}}{2}$	$\cos 60° = \frac{1}{2}$	$\tan 60° = \sqrt{3}$
$\sin 90° = 1$	$\cos 90° = 0$	$\tan 90° =$ undefined
$\csc 0° =$ undefined	$\sec 0° = 1$	$\cot 0° =$ undefined
$\csc 30° = 2$	$\sec 30° = \frac{2\sqrt{3}}{3}$	$\cot 30° = \sqrt{3}$
$\csc 45° = \sqrt{2}$	$\sec 45° = \sqrt{2}$	$\cot 45° = 1$
$\csc 60° = \frac{2\sqrt{3}}{3}$	$\sec 60° = 2$	$\cot 60° = \frac{\sqrt{3}}{3}$
$\csc 90° = 1$	$\sec 90° =$ undefined	$\cot 90° = 0$

The values in the upper half of this table are values you should have memorized or be able to find quickly and those in the lower half can easily be determined as the reciprocal of the corresponding function.

Review Video: Commonly Encountered Angles
Visit mometrix.com/academy and enter code: 204098

RECTANGULAR AND POLAR COORDINATES

Rectangular coordinates are those that lie on the square grids of the Cartesian plane. They should be quite familiar to you. The polar coordinate system is based on a circular graph, rather than the square grid of the Cartesian system. Points in the polar coordinate system are in the format (r, θ), where r is the distance from the origin (think radius of the circle) and θ is the smallest positive angle (moving counterclockwise around the circle) made with the positive horizontal axis.

To convert a point from rectangular (x, y) format to polar (r, θ) format, use the formula (x, y) to $(r, \theta) \Rightarrow r = \sqrt{x^2 + y^2}; \theta = \arctan\frac{y}{x}$ when $x \neq 0$

Review Video: Converting Between Polar and Rectangular Formats
Visit mometrix.com/academy and enter code: 281325

If x is positive, use the positive square root value for r. If x is negative, use the negative square root value for r. If $x = 0$, use the following rules:

- If $y = 0$, then $\theta = 0$
- If $y > 0$, then $\theta = \frac{\pi}{2}$
- If $y < 0$, then $\theta = \frac{3\pi}{2}$

To convert a point from polar (r, θ) format to rectangular (x, y) format, use the formula (r, θ) to $(x, y) \Rightarrow x = r \cos \theta \, ; y = r \sin \theta$

DE MOIVRE'S THEOREM

De Moivre's theorem is used to find the powers of complex numbers (numbers that contain the imaginary number i) written in polar form. Given a trigonometric expression that contains i, such as $z = r \cos x + ir \sin x$, where r is a real number and x is an angle measurement in polar form, use the formula $z^n = r^n(\cos nx + i \sin nx)$, where r and n are real numbers, x is the angle measure in polar form, and i is the imaginary number $i = \sqrt{-1}$. The expression $\cos x + i \sin x$ can be written cis x, making the formula appear in the format $z^n = r^n$ cis nx.

Note that De Moivre's theorem is only for angles in polar form. If you are given an angle in degrees, you must convert to polar form before using the formula.

Geometry

Lines and Planes

POINTS AND LINES

A **point** is a fixed location in space, has no size or dimensions, and is commonly represented by a dot. A **line** is a set of points that extends infinitely in two opposite directions. It has length, but no width or depth. A line can be defined by any two distinct points that it contains. A **line segment** is a portion of a line that has definite endpoints. A **ray** is a portion of a line that extends from a single point on that line in one direction along the line. It has a definite beginning, but no ending.

INTERACTIONS BETWEEN LINES

Intersecting lines are lines that have exactly one point in common. **Concurrent lines** are multiple lines that intersect at a single point. **Perpendicular lines** are lines that intersect at right angles. They are represented by the symbol ⊥. The shortest distance from a line to a point not on the line is a perpendicular segment from the point to the line. **Parallel lines** are lines in the same plane that have no points in common and never meet. It is possible for lines to be in different planes, have no points in common, and never meet, but they are not parallel because they are in different planes.

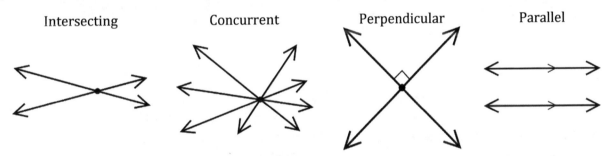

A **transversal** is a line that intersects at least two other lines, which may or may not be parallel to one another. A transversal that intersects parallel lines is a common occurrence in geometry. A **bisector** is a line or line segment that divides another line segment into two equal lengths. A **perpendicular bisector** of a line segment is composed of points that are equidistant from the endpoints of the segment it is dividing.

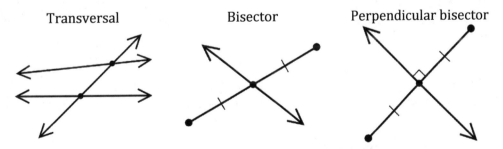

The **projection of a point on a line** is the point at which a perpendicular line drawn from the given point to the given line intersects the line. This is also the shortest distance from the given point to

81

the line. The **projection of a segment on a line** is a segment whose endpoints are the points formed when perpendicular lines are drawn from the endpoints of the given segment to the given line. This is similar to the length a diagonal line appears to be when viewed from above.

Projection of a point on a line   Projection of a segment on a line

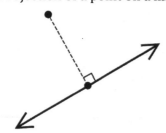
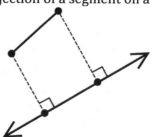

PLANES

A **plane** is a two-dimensional flat surface defined by three non-collinear points. A plane extends an infinite distance in all directions in those two dimensions. It contains an infinite number of points, parallel lines and segments, intersecting lines and segments, as well as parallel or intersecting rays. A plane will never contain a three-dimensional figure or skew lines, which are lines that don't intersect and are not parallel. Two given planes are either parallel or they intersect at a line. A plane may intersect a circular conic surface to form **conic sections**, such as a parabola, hyperbola, circle or ellipse.

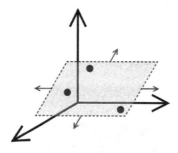

> **Review Video: Lines and Planes**
> Visit mometrix.com/academy and enter code: 554267

Angles

ANGLES AND VERTICES

An **angle** is formed when two lines or line segments meet at a common point. It may be a common starting point for a pair of segments or rays, or it may be the intersection of lines. Angles are represented by the symbol ∠.

The **vertex** is the point at which two segments or rays meet to form an angle. If the angle is formed by intersecting rays, lines, and/or line segments, the vertex is the point at which four angles are formed. The pairs of angles opposite one another are called vertical angles, and their measures are equal.

- An **acute** angle is an angle with a degree measure less than 90°.
- A **right** angle is an angle with a degree measure of exactly 90°.
- An **obtuse** angle is an angle with a degree measure greater than 90° but less than 180°.

82

- A **straight angle** is an angle with a degree measure of exactly 180°. This is also a semicircle.
- A **reflex angle** is an angle with a degree measure greater than 180° but less than 360°.
- A **full angle** is an angle with a degree measure of exactly 360°.

RELATIONSHIPS BETWEEN ANGLES

Two angles whose sum is exactly 90° are said to be **complementary**. The two angles may or may not be adjacent. In a right triangle, the two acute angles are complementary.

Two angles whose sum is exactly 180° are said to be **supplementary**. The two angles may or may not be adjacent. Two intersecting lines always form two pairs of supplementary angles. Adjacent supplementary angles will always form a straight line.

Two angles that have the same vertex and share a side are said to be **adjacent**. Vertical angles are not adjacent because they share a vertex but no common side.

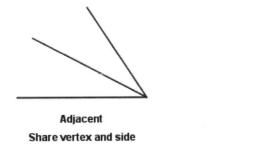

Adjacent

Share vertex and side

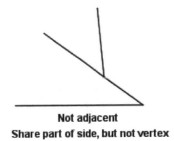

Not adjacent

Share part of side, but not vertex

When two parallel lines are cut by a transversal, the angles that are between the two parallel lines are **interior angles**. In the diagram below, angles 3, 4, 5, and 6 are interior angles.

When two parallel lines are cut by a transversal, the angles that are outside the parallel lines are **exterior angles**. In the diagram below, angles 1, 2, 7, and 8 are exterior angles.

When two parallel lines are cut by a transversal, the angles that are in the same position relative to the transversal and a parallel line are **corresponding angles**. The diagram below has four pairs of corresponding angles: angles 1 and 5, angles 2 and 6, angles 3 and 7, and angles 4 and 8. Corresponding angles formed by parallel lines are congruent.

When two parallel lines are cut by a transversal, the two interior angles that are on opposite sides of the transversal are called **alternate interior angles**. In the diagram below, there are two pairs of alternate interior angles: angles 3 and 6, and angles 4 and 5. Alternate interior angles formed by parallel lines are congruent.

When two parallel lines are cut by a transversal, the two exterior angles that are on opposite sides of the transversal are called **alternate exterior angles**.

> **Review Video: Angles**
> Visit mometrix.com/academy and enter code: 264624

In the diagram below, there are two pairs of alternate exterior angles: angles 1 and 8, and angles 2 and 7. Alternate exterior angles formed by parallel lines are congruent.

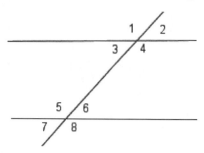

When two lines intersect, four angles are formed. The non-adjacent angles at this vertex are called vertical angles. Vertical angles are congruent. In the diagram, $\angle ABD \cong \angle CBE$ and $\angle ABC \cong \angle DBE$.

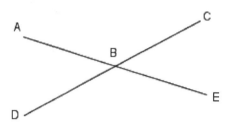

Transformations

ROTATION

A **rotation** is a transformation that turns a figure around a point called the **center of rotation**, which can lie anywhere in the plane. If a line is drawn from a point on a figure to the center of rotation, and another line is drawn from the center to the rotated image of that point, the angle between the two lines is the **angle of rotation**. The vertex of the angle of rotation is the center of rotation.

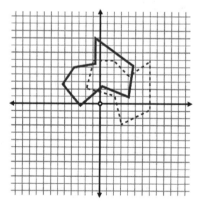

TRANSLATION AND DILATION

A **translation** is a transformation which slides a figure from one position in the plane to another position in the plane. The original figure and the translated figure have the same size, shape, and orientation. A **dilation** is a transformation which proportionally stretches or shrinks a figure by a

scale factor. The dilated image is the same shape and orientation as the original image but a different size. A polygon and its dilated image are similar.

Translation

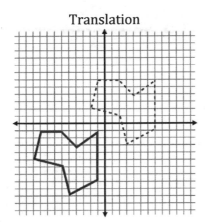

Dilation

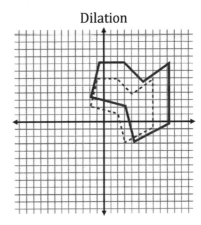

REFLECTION

A **reflection of a figure over a line** (a "flip") creates a congruent image that is the same distance from the line as the original figure but on the opposite side. The **line of reflection** is the perpendicular bisector of any line segment drawn from a point on the original figure to its reflected image (unless the point and its reflected image happen to be the same point, which happens when a figure is reflected over one of its own sides). A **reflection of a figure over a point** (an inversion) in two dimensions is the same as the rotation of the figure 180° about that point. The image of the figure is congruent to the original figure. The **point of reflection** is the midpoint of a line segment which connects a point in the figure to its image (unless the point and its reflected image happen to be the same point, which happens when a figure is reflected in one of its own points).

Reflection of a figure over a line

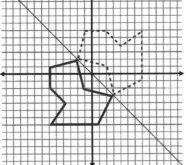

Reflection of a figure over a point

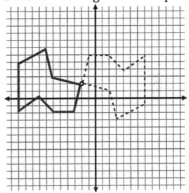

Review Video: <u>Rotation</u>
Visit mometrix.com/academy and enter code: 602600
Review Video: <u>Translation</u>
Visit mometrix.com/academy and enter code: 718628
Review Video: <u>Dilation</u>
Visit mometrix.com/academy and enter code: 471630
Review Video: <u>Reflection</u>
Visit mometrix.com/academy and enter code: 955068

Two-Dimensional Shapes

POLYGONS

A **polygon** is a closed, two-dimensional figure with three or more straight line segments called **sides**. The point at which two sides of a polygon intersect is called the **vertex**. In a polygon, the number of sides is always equal to the number of vertices. A polygon with all sides congruent and all angles equal is called a **regular polygon**. Common polygons are:

$$\begin{aligned}
\text{Triangle} &= 3 \text{ sides} \\
\text{Quadrilateral} &= 4 \text{ sides} \\
\text{Pentagon} &= 5 \text{ sides} \\
\text{Hexagon} &= 6 \text{ sides} \\
\text{Heptagon} &= 7 \text{ sides} \\
\text{Octagon} &= 8 \text{ sides} \\
\text{Nonagon} &= 9 \text{ sides} \\
\text{Decagon} &= 10 \text{ sides} \\
\text{Dodecagon} &= 12 \text{ sides}
\end{aligned}$$

More generally, an n-gon is a polygon that has n angles and n sides.

The sum of the interior angles of an n-sided polygon is $(n - 2) \times 180°$. For example, in a triangle $n = 3$. So the sum of the interior angles is $(3 - 2) \times 180° = 180°$. In a quadrilateral, $n = 4$, and the sum of the angles is $(4 - 2) \times 180° = 360°$.

APOTHEM AND RADIUS

A line segment from the center of a polygon that is perpendicular to a side of the polygon is called the **apothem**. A line segment from the center of a polygon to a vertex of the polygon is called a **radius**. In a regular polygon, the apothem can be used to find the area of the polygon using the formula $A = \frac{1}{2}ap$, where a is the apothem, and p is the perimeter.

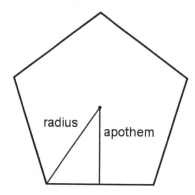

A **diagonal** is a line segment that joins two non-adjacent vertices of a polygon. The number of diagonals a polygon has can be found by using the formula:

$$\text{number of diagonals} = \frac{n(n - 3)}{2}$$

Note that *n* is the number of sides in the polygon. This formula works for all polygons, not just regular polygons.

> **Review Video: Diagonals of Parallelograms, Rectangles, and Rhombi**
> Visit mometrix.com/academy and enter code: 320040

CONVEX AND CONCAVE POLYGONS

A **convex polygon** is a polygon whose diagonals all lie within the interior of the polygon. A **concave polygon** is a polygon with a least one diagonal that is outside the polygon. In the diagram below, quadrilateral *ABCD* is concave because diagonal $\overline{AC}$ lies outside the polygon and quadrilateral *EFGH* is convex because both diagonals lie inside the polygon

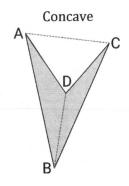
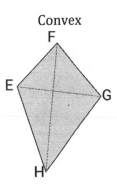

CONGRUENCE AND SIMILARITY

Congruent figures are geometric figures that have the same size and shape. All corresponding angles are equal, and all corresponding sides are equal. Congruence is indicated by the symbol ≅.

Congruent polygons

Similar figures are geometric figures that have the same shape, but do not necessarily have the same size. All corresponding angles are equal, and all corresponding sides are proportional, but they do not have to be equal. It is indicated by the symbol ~.

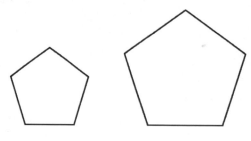

Similar polygons

Note that all congruent figures are also similar, but not all similar figures are congruent.

Review Video: Polygons, Similarity, and Congruence
Visit mometrix.com/academy and enter code: 686174

Review Video: Polygons
Visit mometrix.com/academy and enter code: 271869

LINE OF SYMMETRY

A line that divides a figure or object into congruent parts is called a **line of symmetry**. An object may have no lines of symmetry, one line of symmetry, or multiple (i.e., more than one) lines of symmetry.

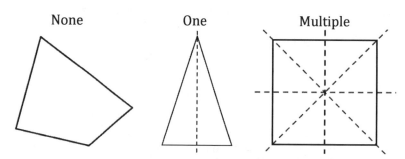

Review Video: Symmetry
Visit mometrix.com/academy and enter code: 528106

88

TRIANGLES

A triangle is a three-sided figure with the sum of its interior angles being 180°. The **perimeter of any triangle** is found by summing the three side lengths; $P = a + b + c$. For an equilateral triangle, this is the same as $P = 3a$, where a is any side length, since all three sides are the same length.

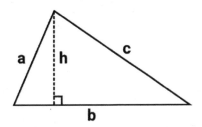

The **area of any triangle** can be found by taking half the product of one side length referred to as the base, often given the variable b and the perpendicular distance from that side to the opposite vertex called the altitude or height and given the variable h. In equation form that is $A = \frac{1}{2}bh$. Another formula that works for any triangle is $A = \sqrt{s(s-a)(s-b)(s-c)}$, where s is the semiperimeter: $\frac{a+b+c}{2}$, and a, b, and c are the lengths of the three sides. Special cases include isosceles triangles, $A = \frac{1}{2}b\sqrt{a^2 - \frac{b^2}{4}}$, where b is the unique side and a is the length of one of the two congruent sides, and equilateral triangles, $A = \frac{\sqrt{3}}{4}a^2$, where a is the length of a side.

> **Review Video: Area and Perimeter of a Triangle**
> Visit mometrix.com/academy and enter code: 853779

PARTS OF A TRIANGLE

An **altitude** of a triangle is a line segment drawn from one vertex perpendicular to the opposite side. In the diagram that follows, $\overline{BE}$, $\overline{AD}$, and $\overline{CF}$ are altitudes. The length of an altitude is also called the height of the triangle. The three altitudes in a triangle are always concurrent. The point of concurrency of the altitudes of a triangle, O, is called the **orthocenter**. Note that in an obtuse triangle, the orthocenter will be outside the triangle, and in a right triangle, the orthocenter is the vertex of the right angle.

A **median** of a triangle is a line segment drawn from one vertex to the midpoint of the opposite side. In the diagram that follows, $\overline{BH}$, $\overline{AG}$, and $\overline{CI}$ are medians. This is not the same as the altitude, except the altitude to the base of an isosceles triangle and all three altitudes of an equilateral triangle. The point of concurrency of the medians of a triangle, T, is called the **centroid**. This is the same point as the orthocenter only in an equilateral triangle. Unlike the orthocenter, the centroid is always inside the triangle. The centroid can also be considered the exact center of the triangle. Any shape triangle can be perfectly balanced on a tip placed at the centroid. The centroid is also the point that is two-thirds the distance from the vertex to the opposite side.

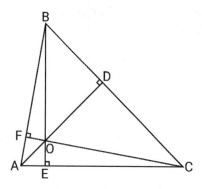 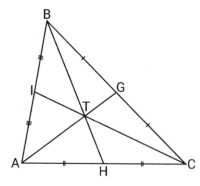

QUADRILATERALS

A **quadrilateral** is a closed two-dimensional geometric figure that has four straight sides. The sum of the interior angles of any quadrilateral is 360°.

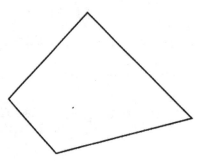

KITE

A **kite** is a quadrilateral with two pairs of adjacent sides that are congruent. A result of this is perpendicular diagonals. A kite can be concave or convex and has one line of symmetry.

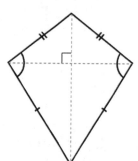 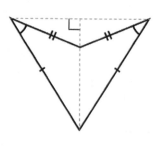

TRAPEZOID

Trapezoid: A trapezoid is defined as a quadrilateral that has at least one pair of parallel sides. There are no rules for the second pair of sides. So there are no rules for the diagonals and no lines of symmetry for a trapezoid.

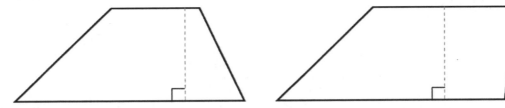

The **area of a trapezoid** is found by the formula $A = \frac{1}{2}h(b_1 + b_2)$, where h is the height (segment joining and perpendicular to the parallel bases), and b_1 and b_2 are the two parallel sides (bases). Do not use one of the other two sides as the height unless that side is also perpendicular to the parallel bases.

The **perimeter of a trapezoid** is found by the formula $P = a + b_1 + c + b_2$, where a, b_1, c, and b_2 are the four sides of the trapezoid.

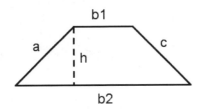

Review Video: Area and Perimeter of a Trapezoid
Visit mometrix.com/academy and enter code: 587523

Isosceles trapezoid: A trapezoid with equal base angles. This gives rise to other properties including: the two nonparallel sides have the same length, the two non-base angles are also equal, and there is one line of symmetry through the midpoints of the parallel sides.

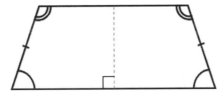

PARALLELOGRAM

A **parallelogram** is a quadrilateral that has two pairs of opposite parallel sides. As such it is a special type of trapezoid. The sides that are parallel are also congruent. The opposite interior angles are always congruent, and the consecutive interior angles are supplementary. The diagonals of a parallelogram divide each other. Each diagonal divides the parallelogram into two congruent triangles. A parallelogram has no line of symmetry, but does have 180-degree rotational symmetry about the midpoint.

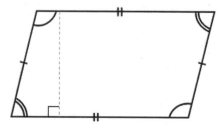

The **area of a parallelogram** is found by the formula $A = bh$, where b is the length of the base, and h is the height. Note that the base and height correspond to the length and width in a rectangle, so this formula would apply to rectangles as well. Do not confuse the height of a parallelogram with the length of the second side. The two are only the same measure in the case of a rectangle.

The **perimeter of a parallelogram** is found by the formula $P = 2a + 2b$ or $P = 2(a + b)$, where a and b are the lengths of the two sides.

> **Review Video: Parallelogram**
> Visit mometrix.com/academy and enter code: 129981
>
> **Review Video: Area and Perimeter of a Parallelogram**
> Visit mometrix.com/academy and enter code: 718313

RECTANGLE

A **rectangle** is a quadrilateral with four right angles. All rectangles are parallelograms and trapezoids, but not all parallelograms or trapezoids are rectangles. The diagonals of a rectangle are congruent. Rectangles have two lines of symmetry (through each pair of opposing midpoints) and 180-degree rotational symmetry about the midpoint.

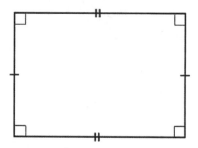

The **area of a rectangle** is found by the formula $A = lw$, where A is the area of the rectangle, l is the length (usually considered to be the longer side) and w is the width (usually considered to be the shorter side). The numbers for l and w are interchangeable.

The **perimeter of a rectangle** is found by the formula $P = 2l + 2w$ or $P = 2(l + w)$, where l is the length, and w is the width. It may be easier to add the length and width first and then double the result, as in the second formula.

> **Review Video: Area and Perimeter of a Rectangle**
> Visit mometrix.com/academy and enter code: 933707

RHOMBUS

A **rhombus** is a quadrilateral with four congruent sides. All rhombuses are parallelograms and kites; thus, they inherit all the properties of both types of quadrilaterals. The diagonals of a rhombus are perpendicular to each other. Rhombi have two lines of symmetry (along each of the diagonals) and 180° rotational symmetry. The **area of a rhombus** is half the product of the diagonals: $A = \frac{d_1 d_2}{2}$ and the perimeter of a rhombus is: $P = 2\sqrt{(d_1)^2 + (d_2)^2}$

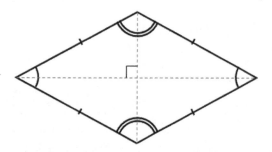

SQUARE

A **square** is a quadrilateral with four right angles and four congruent sides. Squares satisfy the criteria of all other types of quadrilaterals. The diagonals of a square are congruent and perpendicular to each other. Squares have four lines of symmetry (through each pair of opposing midpoints and along each of the diagonals) as well as 90° rotational symmetry about the midpoint.

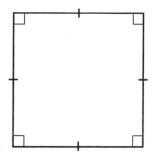

The **area of a square** is found by using the formula $A = s^2$, where s is the length of one side. The **perimeter of a square** is found by using the formula $P = 4s$, where s is the length of one side. Because all four sides are equal in a square, it is faster to multiply the length of one side by 4 than to add the same number four times. You could use the formulas for rectangles and get the same answer.

HIERARCHY OF QUADRILATERALS

The hierarchy of quadrilaterals is as follows:

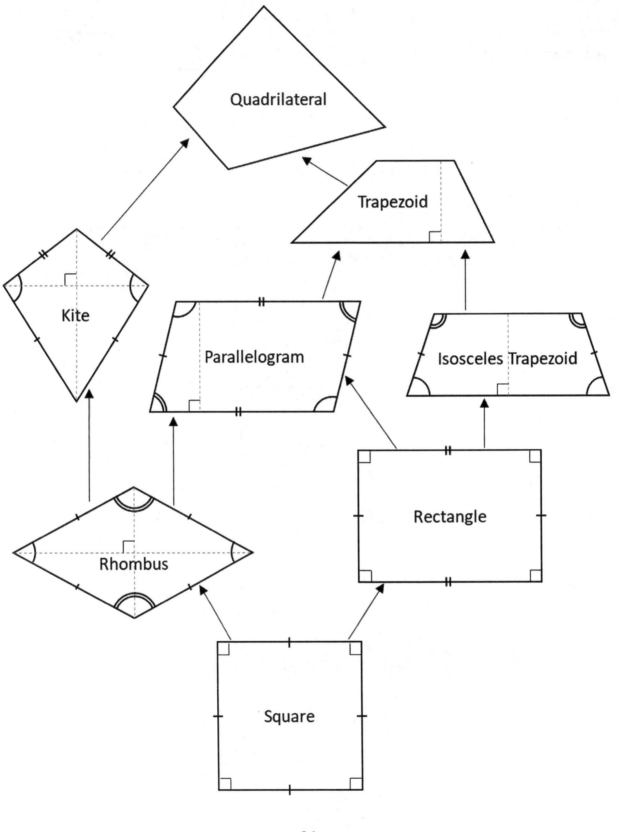

CIRCLES

The **center** of a circle is the single point from which every point on the circle is **equidistant**. The **radius** is a line segment that joins the center of the circle and any one point on the circle. All radii of a circle are equal. Circles that have the same center but not the same length of radii are **concentric**. The **diameter** is a line segment that passes through the center of the circle and has both endpoints on the circle. The length of the diameter is exactly twice the length of the radius. Point O in the diagram below is the center of the circle, segments $\overline{OX}$, $\overline{OY}$, and $\overline{OZ}$ are radii; and segment $\overline{XZ}$ is a diameter.

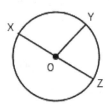

Review Video: Points of a Circle
Visit mometrix.com/academy and enter code: 420746

Review Video: The Diameter, Radius, and Circumference of Circles
Visit mometrix.com/academy and enter code: 448988

The **area of a circle** is found by the formula $A = \pi r^2$, where r is the length of the radius. If the diameter of the circle is given, remember to divide it in half to get the length of the radius before proceeding.

The **circumference** of a circle is found by the formula $C = 2\pi r$, where r is the radius. Again, remember to convert the diameter if you are given that measure rather than the radius.

Review Video: Area and Circumference of a Circle
Visit mometrix.com/academy and enter code: 243015

INSCRIBED AND CIRCUMSCRIBED FIGURES

These terms can both be used to describe a given arrangement of figures, depending on perspective. If each of the vertices of figure A lie on figure B, then it can be said that figure A is **inscribed** in figure B, but it can also be said that figure B is **circumscribed** about figure A. The following table and examples help to illustrate the concept. Note that the figures cannot both be circles, as they would be completely overlapping and neither would be inscribed or circumscribed.

Given	Description	Equivalent Description	Figures
Each of the sides of a pentagon is tangent to a circle	The circle is inscribed in the pentagon	The pentagon is circumscribed about the circle	
Each of the vertices of a pentagon lie on a circle	The pentagon is inscribed in the circle	The circle is circumscribed about the pentagon	

95

Mometrix

Three-Dimensional Shapes

SOLIDS

The **surface area of a solid object** is the area of all sides or exterior surfaces. For objects such as prisms and pyramids, a further distinction is made between base surface area (B) and lateral surface area (LA). For a prism, the total surface area (SA) is $SA = LA + 2B$. For a pyramid or cone, the total surface area is $SA = LA + B$.

> **Review Video: How to Calculate the Volume of 3D Objects**
> Visit mometrix.com/academy and enter code: 163343

The **surface area of a sphere** can be found by the formula $A = 4\pi r^2$, where r is the radius. The volume is given by the formula $V = \frac{4}{3}\pi r^3$, where r is the radius. Both quantities are generally given in terms of π.

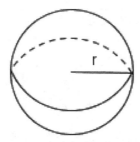

> **Review Video: Volume and Surface Area of a Sphere**
> Visit mometrix.com/academy and enter code: 786928

The **volume of any prism** is found by the formula $V = Bh$, where B is the area of the base, and h is the height (perpendicular distance between the bases). The surface area of any prism is the sum of the areas of both bases and all sides. It can be calculated as $SA = 2B + Ph$, where P is the perimeter of the base.

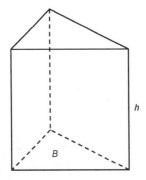

For a **rectangular prism**, the volume can be found by the formula $V = lwh$, where V is the volume, l is the length, w is the width, and h is the height. The surface area can be calculated as $SA = 2lw + 2hl + 2wh$ or $SA = 2(lw + hl + wh)$.

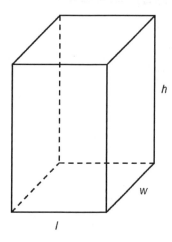

The **volume of a cube** can be found by the formula $V = s^3$, where s is the length of a side. The surface area of a cube is calculated as $SA = 6s^2$, where SA is the total surface area and s is the length of a side. These formulas are the same as the ones used for the volume and surface area of a rectangular prism, but simplified since all three quantities (length, width, and height) are the same.

> **Review Video: <u>Volume and Surface Area of a Cube</u>**
> Visit mometrix.com/academy and enter code: 664455

The **volume of a cylinder** can be calculated by the formula $V = \pi r^2 h$, where r is the radius, and h is the height. The surface area of a cylinder can be found by the formula $SA = 2\pi r^2 + 2\pi rh$. The first term is the base area multiplied by two, and the second term is the perimeter of the base multiplied by the height.

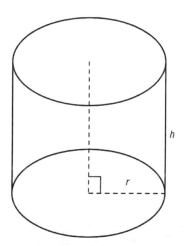

> **Review Video: <u>Volume and Surface Area of a Right Circular Cylinder</u>**
> Visit mometrix.com/academy and enter code: 226463

The **volume of a pyramid** is found by the formula $V = \frac{1}{3}Bh$, where B is the area of the base, and h is the height (perpendicular distance from the vertex to the base). Notice this formula is the same as $\frac{1}{3}$ times the volume of a prism. Like a prism, the base of a pyramid can be any shape.

Finding the **surface area of a pyramid** is not as simple as the other shapes we've looked at thus far. If the pyramid is a right pyramid, meaning the base is a regular polygon and the vertex is directly over the center of that polygon, the surface area can be calculated as $SA = B + \frac{1}{2}Ph_s$, where P is the perimeter of the base, and h_s is the slant height (distance from the vertex to the midpoint of one side of the base). If the pyramid is irregular, the area of each triangle side must be calculated individually and then summed, along with the base.

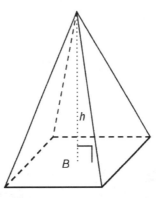

Review Video: Volume and Surface Area of a Pyramid
Visit mometrix.com/academy and enter code: 621932

The **volume of a cone** is found by the formula $V = \frac{1}{3}\pi r^2 h$, where r is the radius, and h is the height. Notice this is the same as $\frac{1}{3}$ times the volume of a cylinder. The surface area can be calculated as $SA = \pi r^2 + \pi r s$, where s is the slant height. The slant height can be calculated using the Pythagorean theorem to be $\sqrt{r^2 + h^2}$, so the surface area formula can also be written as $SA = \pi r^2 + \pi r\sqrt{r^2 + h^2}$.

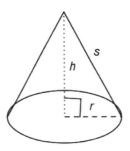

Review Video: Volume and Surface Area of a Right Circular Cone
Visit mometrix.com/academy and enter code: 573574

Triangle Classification and Properties

CLASSIFICATIONS OF TRIANGLES

A **scalene triangle** is a triangle with no congruent sides. A scalene triangle will also have three angles of different measures. The angle with the largest measure is opposite the longest side, and the angle with the smallest measure is opposite the shortest side. An **acute triangle** is a triangle whose three angles are all less than 90°. If two of the angles are equal, the acute triangle is also an **isosceles triangle**. An isosceles triangle will also have two congruent angles opposite the two congruent sides. If the three angles are all equal, the acute triangle is also an **equilateral triangle**. An equilateral triangle will also have three congruent angles, each 60°. All equilateral triangles are also acute triangles. An **obtuse triangle** is a triangle with exactly one angle greater than 90°. The other two angles may or may not be equal. If the two remaining angles are equal, the obtuse triangle is also an isosceles triangle. A **right triangle** is a triangle with exactly one angle equal to 90°. All right triangles follow the Pythagorean theorem. A right triangle can never be acute or obtuse.

The table below illustrates how each descriptor places a different restriction on the triangle:

Angles / Sides	Acute: All angles < 90°	Obtuse: One angle > 90°	Right: One angle = 90°
Scalene: No equal side lengths	$90° > \angle a > \angle b > \angle c$ $x > y > z$	$\angle a > 90° > \angle b > \angle c$ $x > y > z$	$90° = \angle a > \angle b > \angle c$ $x > y > z$
Isosceles: Two equal side lengths	$90° > \angle a, \angle b,$ or $\angle c$ $\angle b = \angle c, \qquad y = z$	$\angle a > 90° > \angle b = \angle c$ $x > y = z$	$\angle a = 90°, \angle b = \angle c$ $= 45°$ $x > y = z$
Equilateral: Three equal side lengths	$60° = \angle a = \angle b = \angle c$ $x = y = z$		

> **Review Video: Introduction to Types of Triangles**
> Visit mometrix.com/academy and enter code: 511711

SIMILARITY AND CONGRUENCE RULES

Similar triangles are triangles whose corresponding angles are equal and whose corresponding sides are proportional. Represented by AAA. Similar triangles whose corresponding sides are congruent are also congruent triangles.

Triangles can be shown to be **congruent** in 5 ways:

- **SSS**: Three sides of one triangle are congruent to the three corresponding sides of the second triangle.
- **SAS**: Two sides and the included angle (the angle formed by those two sides) of one triangle are congruent to the corresponding two sides and included angle of the second triangle.
- **ASA**: Two angles and the included side (the side that joins the two angles) of one triangle are congruent to the corresponding two angles and included side of the second triangle.

100

- **AAS**: Two angles and a non-included side of one triangle are congruent to the corresponding two angles and non-included side of the second triangle.
- **HL**: The hypotenuse and leg of one right triangle are congruent to the corresponding hypotenuse and leg of the second right triangle.

> **Review Video: <u>Similar Triangles</u>**
> Visit mometrix.com/academy and enter code: 398538

GENERAL RULES FOR TRIANGLES

The **triangle inequality theorem** states that the sum of the measures of any two sides of a triangle is always greater than the measure of the third side. If the sum of the measures of two sides were equal to the third side, a triangle would be impossible because the two sides would lie flat across the third side and there would be no vertex. If the sum of the measures of two of the sides was less than the third side, a closed figure would be impossible because the two shortest sides would never meet. In other words, for a triangle with sides lengths A, B, and C: $A + B > C$, $B + C > A$, and $A + C > B$.

The sum of the measures of the interior angles of a triangle is always $180°$. Therefore, a triangle can never have more than one angle greater than or equal to $90°$.

In any triangle, the angles opposite congruent sides are congruent, and the sides opposite congruent angles are congruent. The largest angle is always opposite the longest side, and the smallest angle is always opposite the shortest side.

The line segment that joins the midpoints of any two sides of a triangle is always parallel to the third side and exactly half the length of the third side.

> **Review Video: <u>General Rules (Triangle Inequality Theorem)</u>**
> Visit mometrix.com/academy and enter code: 166488

Introductory Trigonometry

PYTHAGOREAN THEOREM

The side of a triangle opposite the right angle is called the **hypotenuse**. The other two sides are called the legs. The Pythagorean theorem states a relationship among the legs and hypotenuse of a right triangle: $(a^2 + b^2 = c^2)$, where a and b are the lengths of the legs of a right triangle, and c is the length of the hypotenuse. Note that this formula will only work with right triangles.

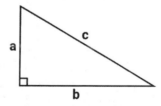

> **Review Video: <u>Pythagorean Theorem</u>**
> Visit mometrix.com/academy and enter code: 906576

TRIGONOMETRIC FORMULAS

In the diagram below, angle C is the right angle, and side c is the hypotenuse. Side a is the side opposite to angle A and side b is the side opposite to angle B. Using ratios of side lengths as a means to calculate the sine, cosine, and tangent of an acute angle only works for right triangles.

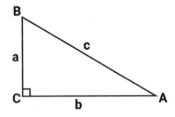

$$\sin A = \frac{\text{opposite side}}{\text{hypotenuse}} = \frac{a}{c} \qquad \csc A = \frac{1}{\sin A} = \frac{\text{hypotenuse}}{\text{opposite side}} = \frac{c}{a}$$

$$\cos A = \frac{\text{adjacent side}}{\text{hypotenuse}} = \frac{b}{c} \qquad \sec A = \frac{1}{\cos A} = \frac{\text{hypotenuse}}{\text{adjacent side}} = \frac{c}{b}$$

$$\tan A = \frac{\text{opposite side}}{\text{adjacent side}} = \frac{a}{b} \qquad \cot A = \frac{1}{\tan A} = \frac{\text{adjacent side}}{\text{opposite side}} = \frac{b}{a}$$

LAWS OF SINES AND COSINES

The **law of sines** states that $\frac{\sin A}{a} = \frac{\sin B}{b} = \frac{\sin C}{c}$, where A, B, and C are the angles of a triangle, and a, b, and c are the sides opposite their respective angles. This formula will work with all triangles, not just right triangles.

The **law of cosines** is given by the formula $c^2 = a^2 + b^2 - 2ab(\cos C)$, where a, b, and c are the sides of a triangle, and C is the angle opposite side c. This is a generalized form of the Pythagorean theorem that can be used on any triangle.

> **Review Video: Upper Level Trig (Law of Sines)**
> Visit mometrix.com/academy and enter code: 206844
>
> **Review Video: Law of Cosines**
> Visit mometrix.com/academy and enter code: 158911

Circle Properties

ARCS

An **arc** is a portion of a circle. Specifically, an arc is the set of points between and including two points on a circle. An arc does not contain any points inside the circle. When a segment is drawn from the endpoints of an arc to the center of the circle, a sector is formed. A **minor arc** is an arc that has a measure less than 180°. A **major arc** is an arc that has a measure of at least 180°. Every minor arc has a corresponding major arc that can be found by subtracting the measure of the minor arc from 360°. A **semicircle** is an arc whose endpoints are the endpoints of the diameter of a circle. A semicircle is exactly half of a circle.

Arc length is the length of that portion of the circumference between two points on the circle. The formula for arc length is $s = \frac{\pi r \theta}{180°}$, where s is the arc length, r is the length of the radius, and θ is the angular measure of the arc in degrees, or $s = r\theta$, where θ is the angular measure of the arc in radians (2π radians = 360 degrees).

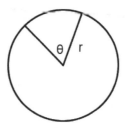

ANGLES OF CIRCLES

A **central angle** is an angle whose vertex is the center of a circle and whose legs intercept an arc of the circle. The measure of a central angle is equal to the measure of the minor arc it intercepts.

An **inscribed angle** is an angle whose vertex lies on a circle and whose legs contain chords of that circle. The portion of the circle intercepted by the legs of the angle is called the intercepted arc. The measure of the intercepted arc is exactly twice the measure of the inscribed angle. In the following diagram, angle ABC is an inscribed angle. $\widehat{AC} = 2(\text{m}\angle ABC)$.

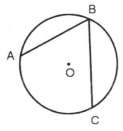

Any angle inscribed in a semicircle is a right angle. The intercepted arc is 180°, making the inscribed angle half that, or 90°. In the diagram below, angle ABC is inscribed in semicircle ABC, making angle ABC equal to 90°.

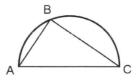

SECANTS, CHORDS, AND TANGENTS

A **secant** is a line that intersects a circle in two points. The segment of a secant line that is contained within the circle is called a **chord**. Two secants may intersect inside the circle, on the circle, or outside the circle. When the two secants intersect on the circle, an inscribed angle is formed. When two secants intersect inside a circle, the measure of each of two vertical angles is equal to half the sum of the two intercepted arcs. Consider the following diagram where $m\angle AEB = \frac{1}{2}(\widehat{AB} + \widehat{CD})$ and $m\angle BEC = \frac{1}{2}(\widehat{BC} + \widehat{AD})$.

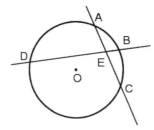

When two secants intersect outside a circle, the measure of the angle formed is equal to half the difference of the two arcs that lie between the two secants. In the diagram below, $m\angle AEB = \frac{1}{2}(\widehat{AB} - \widehat{CD})$.

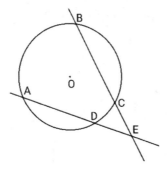

A **tangent** is a line in the same plane as a circle that touches the circle in exactly one point. The point at which a tangent touches a circle is called the **point of tangency**. While a line segment can be tangent to a circle as part of a line that is tangent, it is improper to say a tangent can be simply a line segment that touches the circle in exactly one point.

In the diagram below, $\overleftrightarrow{EB}$ is a secant and contains chord $\overline{EB}$, and $\overleftrightarrow{CD}$ is tangent to circle A. Notice that $\overline{FB}$ is not tangent to the circle. $\overline{FB}$ is a line segment that touches the circle in exactly one point, but if the segment were extended, it would touch the circle in a second point. In the diagram below, point B is the point of tangency.

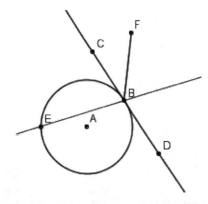

Review Video: <u>Tangent Lines of a Circle</u>
Visit mometrix.com/academy and enter code: 780167

SECTORS

A **sector** is the portion of a circle formed by two radii and their intercepted arc. While the arc length is exclusively the points that are also on the circumference of the circle, the sector is the entire area bounded by the arc and the two radii.

The **area of a sector** of a circle is found by the formula, $A = \frac{\theta r^2}{2}$, where A is the area, θ is the measure of the central angle in radians, and r is the radius. To find the area with the central angle in degrees, use the formula, $A = \frac{\theta \pi r^2}{360}$, where θ is the measure of the central angle and r is the radius.

Conic Sections

CONIC SECTIONS

Conic sections are a family of shapes that can be thought of as cross sections of a pair of infinite right cones stacked vertex to vertex. This is easiest to see with a visual representation:

A three-dimensional look at representative conic sections. (Note that a hyperbola intersects both cones.)

A side-on look at representative conic sections. (Note that the parabola is parallel to the slant of the cones.)

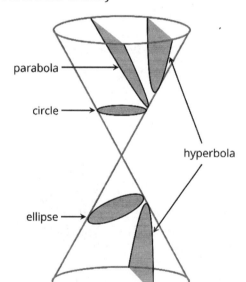

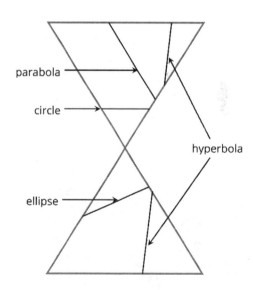

In short, a circle is a horizontal cross section, a parabola is a cross section parallel to the slant of the cone, an ellipse is a cross section at an angle *less than* the slant of the cone, and a hyperbola is a cross section at an angle *greater than* the slant of the cone.

ELLIPSE

An **ellipse** is the set of all points in a plane whose total distance from two fixed points called the **foci** (singular: focus) is constant, and whose center is the midpoint between the foci.

The standard equation of an ellipse that is taller than it is wide is $\frac{(x-h)^2}{a^2} + \frac{(y-k)^2}{b^2} = 1$, where a and b are coefficients. The center is the point (h, k) and the foci are the points $(h, k + c)$ and $(h, k - c)$, where $c^2 = a^2 - b^2$ and $a^2 > b^2$.

The major axis has length $2a$, and the minor axis has length $2b$.

Eccentricity (e) is a measure of how elongated an ellipse is, and is the ratio of the distance between the foci to the length of the major axis. Eccentricity will have a value between 0 and 1. The closer to 1 the eccentricity is, the closer the ellipse is to being a circle. The formula for eccentricity is $= \frac{c}{a}$.

PARABOLA

A **parabola** is the set of all points in a plane that are equidistant from a fixed line, called the **directrix**, and a fixed point not on the line, called the **focus**. The **axis** is the line perpendicular to the directrix that passes through the focus.

For parabolas that open up or down, the standard equation is $(x - h)^2 = 4c(y - k)$, where h, c, and k are coefficients. If c is positive, the parabola opens up. If c is negative, the parabola opens down. The vertex is the point (h, k). The directrix is the line having the equation $y = -c + k$, and the focus is the point $(h, c + k)$.

For parabolas that open left or right, the standard equation is $(y - k)^2 = 4c(x - h)$, where k, c, and h are coefficients. If c is positive, the parabola opens to the right. If c is negative, the parabola opens to the left. The vertex is the point (h, k). The directrix is the line having the equation $x = -c + h$, and the focus is the point $(c + h, k)$.

> **Review Video: Parabolas**
> Visit mometrix.com/academy and enter code: 129187

HYPERBOLA

A **hyperbola** is the set of all points in a plane, whose distance from two fixed points, called foci, has a constant difference.

The standard equation of a horizontal hyperbola is $\frac{(x-h)^2}{a^2} - \frac{(y-k)^2}{b^2} = 1$, where a, b, h, and k are real numbers. The center is the point (h, k), the vertices are the points $(h + a, k)$ and $(h - a, k)$, and the foci are the points that every point on one of the parabolic curves is equidistant from. The foci are found using the formulas $(h + c, k)$ and $(h - c, k)$, where $c^2 = a^2 + b^2$. The asymptotes are two lines the graph of the hyperbola approaches but never reaches, and are given by the equations $y = \left(\frac{b}{a}\right)(x - h) + k$ and $y = -\left(\frac{b}{a}\right)(x - h) + k$.

The standard equation of a vertical hyperbola is $\frac{(y-k)^2}{a^2} - \frac{(x-h)^2}{b^2} = 1$, where a, b, k, and h are real numbers. The center is the point (h, k), the vertices are the points $(h, k + a)$ and $(h, k - a)$, and the foci are the points that every point on one of the hyperbolic curves is equidistant from and are found using the formulas $(h, k + c)$ and $(h, k - c)$, where $c^2 = a^2 + b^2$. The asymptotes are two lines the graph of the hyperbola approaches but never reaches, and are given by the equations $y = \left(\frac{a}{b}\right)(x - h) + k$ and $y = -\left(\frac{a}{b}\right)(x - h) + k$.

Statistics and Probability

Statistics

STATISTICS

Statistics is the branch of mathematics that deals with collecting, recording, interpreting, illustrating, and analyzing large amounts of **data**. The following terms are often used in the discussion of data and **statistics**:

- **Data** – the collective name for pieces of information (singular is datum)
- **Quantitative data** – measurements (such as length, mass, and speed) that provide information about quantities in numbers
- **Qualitative data** – information (such as colors, scents, tastes, and shapes) that cannot be measured using numbers
- **Discrete data** – information that can be expressed only by a specific value, such as whole or half numbers. (e.g., since people can be counted only in whole numbers, a population count would be discrete data.)
- **Continuous data** – information (such as time and temperature) that can be expressed by any value within a given range
- **Primary data** – information that has been collected directly from a survey, investigation, or experiment, such as a questionnaire or the recording of daily temperatures. (Primary data that has not yet been organized or analyzed is called **raw data**.)
- **Secondary data** – information that has been collected, sorted, and processed by the researcher
- **Ordinal data** – information that can be placed in numerical order, such as age or weight
- **Nominal data** – information that *cannot* be placed in numerical order, such as names or places

DATA COLLECTION

POPULATION

In statistics, the **population** is the entire collection of people, plants, etc., that data can be collected from. For example, a study to determine how well students in local schools perform on a standardized test would have a population of all the students enrolled in those schools, although a study may include just a small sample of students from each school. A **parameter** is a numerical value that gives information about the population, such as the mean, median, mode, or standard deviation. Remember that the symbol for the mean of a population is μ and the symbol for the standard deviation of a population is σ.

SAMPLE

A **sample** is a portion of the entire population. Whereas a parameter helped describe the population, a **statistic** is a numerical value that gives information about the sample, such as mean, median, mode, or standard deviation. Keep in mind that the symbols for mean and standard deviation are different when they are referring to a sample rather than the entire population. For a sample, the symbol for mean is $\bar{x}$ and the symbol for standard deviation is s. The mean and standard deviation of a sample may or may not be identical to that of the entire population due to a sample only being a subset of the population. However, if the sample is random and large enough, statistically significant values can be attained. Samples are generally used when the population is

108

too large to justify including every element or when acquiring data for the entire population is impossible.

INFERENTIAL STATISTICS

Inferential statistics is the branch of statistics that uses samples to make predictions about an entire population. This type of statistic is often seen in political polls, where a sample of the population is questioned about a particular topic or politician to gain an understanding of the attitudes of the entire population of the country. Often, exit polls are conducted on election days using this method. Inferential statistics can have a large margin of error if you do not have a valid sample.

SAMPLING DISTRIBUTION

Statistical values calculated from various samples of the same size make up the **sampling distribution**. For example, if several samples of identical size are randomly selected from a large population and then the mean of each sample is calculated, the distribution of values of the means would be a sampling distribution.

The **sampling distribution of the mean** is the distribution of the sample mean, $\bar{x}$, derived from random samples of a given size. It has three important characteristics. First, the mean of the sampling distribution of the mean is equal to the mean of the population that was sampled. Second, assuming the standard deviation is non-zero, the standard deviation of the sampling distribution of the mean equals the standard deviation of the sampled population divided by the square root of the sample size. This is sometimes called the standard error. Finally, as the sample size gets larger, the sampling distribution of the mean gets closer to a normal distribution via the central limit theorem.

SURVEY STUDY

A **survey study** is a method of gathering information from a small group in an attempt to gain enough information to make accurate general assumptions about the population. Once a survey study is completed, the results are then put into a summary report.

Survey studies are generally in the format of surveys, interviews, or questionnaires as part of an effort to find opinions of a particular group or to find facts about a group.

It is important to note that the findings from a survey study are only as accurate as the sample chosen from the population.

CORRELATIONAL STUDIES

Correlational studies seek to determine how much one variable is affected by changes in a second variable. For example, correlational studies may look for a relationship between the amount of time a student spends studying for a test and the grade that student earned on the test or between student scores on college admissions tests and student grades in college.

It is important to note that correlational studies cannot show a cause and effect, but rather can show only that two variables are or are not potentially correlated.

EXPERIMENTAL STUDIES

Experimental studies take correlational studies one step farther, in that they attempt to prove or disprove a cause-and-effect relationship. These studies are performed by conducting a series of experiments to test the hypothesis. For a study to be scientifically accurate, it must have both an experimental group that receives the specified treatment and a control group that does not get the treatment. This is the type of study pharmaceutical companies do as part of drug trials for new medications. Experimental studies are only valid when the proper scientific method has been followed. In other words, the experiment must be well-planned and executed without bias in the testing process, all subjects must be selected at random, and the process of determining which subject is in which of the two groups must also be completely random.

OBSERVATIONAL STUDIES

Observational studies are the opposite of experimental studies. In observational studies, the tester cannot change or in any way control all of the variables in the test. For example, a study to determine which gender does better in math classes in school is strictly observational. You cannot change a person's gender, and you cannot change the subject being studied. The big downfall of observational studies is that you have no way of proving a cause-and-effect relationship because you cannot control outside influences. Events outside of school can influence a student's performance in school, and observational studies cannot take that into consideration.

RANDOM SAMPLES

For most studies, a **random sample** is necessary to produce valid results. Random samples should not have any particular influence to cause sampled subjects to behave one way or another. The goal is for the random sample to be a **representative sample**, or a sample whose characteristics give an accurate picture of the characteristics of the entire population. To accomplish this, you must make sure you have a proper **sample size**, or an appropriate number of elements in the sample.

BIASES

In statistical studies, biases must be avoided. **Bias** is an error that causes the study to favor one set of results over another. For example, if a survey to determine how the country views the president's job performance only speaks to registered voters in the president's party, the results will be skewed because a disproportionately large number of responders would tend to show approval, while a disproportionately large number of people in the opposite party would tend to express disapproval. **Extraneous variables** are, as the name implies, outside influences that can affect the outcome of a study. They are not always avoidable but could trigger bias in the result.

Statistical Analysis

MEASURES OF CENTRAL TENDENCY

A **measure of central tendency** is a statistical value that gives a reasonable estimate for the center of a group of data. There are several different ways of describing the measure of central tendency. Each one has a unique way it is calculated, and each one gives a slightly different perspective on the data set. Whenever you give a measure of central tendency, always make sure the units are the same. If the data has different units, such as hours, minutes, and seconds, convert all the data to the same unit, and use the same unit in the measure of central tendency. If no units are given in the data, do not give units for the measure of central tendency.

MEAN

The **statistical mean** of a group of data is the same as the arithmetic average of that group. To find the mean of a set of data, first convert each value to the same units, if necessary. Then find the sum of all the values, and count the total number of data values, making sure you take into consideration each individual value. If a value appears more than once, count it more than once. Divide the sum of the values by the total number of values and apply the units, if any. Note that the mean does not have to be one of the data values in the set, and may not divide evenly.

$$\text{mean} = \frac{\text{sum of the data values}}{\text{quantity of data values}}$$

For instance, the mean of the data set {88, 72, 61, 90, 97, 68, 88, 79, 86, 93, 97, 71, 80, 84, 89} would be the sum of the fifteen numbers divided by 15:

$$\frac{88 + 72 + 61 + 90 + 97 + 68 + 88 + 79 + 86 + 93 + 97 + 71 + 80 + 84 + 88}{15} = \frac{1242}{15}$$
$$= 82.8$$

While the mean is relatively easy to calculate and averages are understood by most people, the mean can be very misleading if used as the sole measure of central tendency. If the data set has outliers (data values that are unusually high or unusually low compared to the rest of the data values), the mean can be very distorted, especially if the data set has a small number of values. If unusually high values are countered with unusually low values, the mean is not affected as much. For example, if five of twenty students in a class get a 100 on a test, but the other 15 students have an average of 60 on the same test, the class average would appear as 70. Whenever the mean is skewed by outliers, it is always a good idea to include the median as an alternate measure of central tendency.

A **weighted mean**, or weighted average, is a mean that uses "weighted" values. The formula is weighted mean $= \frac{w_1 x_1 + w_2 x_2 + w_3 x_3 \dots + w_n x_n}{w_1 + w_2 + w_3 + \dots + w_n}$. Weighted values, such as $w_1, w_2, w_3, \dots w_n$ are assigned to each member of the set $x_1, x_2, x_3, \dots x_n$. If calculating weighted mean, make sure a weight value for each member of the set is used.

MEDIAN

The **statistical median** is the value in the middle of the set of data. To find the median, list all data values in order from smallest to largest or from largest to smallest. Any value that is repeated in the set must be listed the number of times it appears. If there are an odd number of data values, the median is the value in the middle of the list. If there is an even number of data values, the median is the arithmetic mean of the two middle values.

For example, the median of the data set {88, 72, 61, 90, 97, 68, 88, 79, 86, 93, 97, 71, 80, 84, 88} is 86 since the ordered set is {61, 68, 71, 72, 79, 80, 84, **86**, 88, 88, 88, 90, 93, 97, 97}.

The big disadvantage of using the median as a measure of central tendency is that is relies solely on a value's relative size as compared to the other values in the set. When the individual values in a set of data are evenly dispersed, the median can be an accurate tool. However, if there is a group of rather large values or a group of rather small values that are not offset by a different group of values, the information that can be inferred from the median may not be accurate because the distribution of values is skewed.

MODE

The **statistical mode** is the data value that occurs the greatest number of times in the data set. It is possible to have exactly one mode, more than one mode, or no mode. To find the mode of a set of data, arrange the data like you do to find the median (all values in order, listing all multiples of data values). Count the number of times each value appears in the data set. If all values appear an equal number of times, there is no mode. If one value appears more than any other value, that value is the mode. If two or more values appear the same number of times, but there are other values that appear fewer times and no values that appear more times, all of those values are the modes.

For example, the mode of the data set {**88**, 72, 61, 90, 97, 68, **88**, 79, 86, 93, 97, 71, 80, 84, **88**} is 88.

The main disadvantage of the mode is that the values of the other data in the set have no bearing on the mode. The mode may be the largest value, the smallest value, or a value anywhere in between in the set. The mode only tells which value or values, if any, occurred the greatest number of times. It does not give any suggestions about the remaining values in the set.

> **Review Video: Mean, Median, and Mode**
> Visit mometrix.com/academy and enter code: 286207

DISPERSION

A **measure of dispersion** is a single value that helps to "interpret" the measure of central tendency by providing more information about how the data values in the set are distributed about the measure of central tendency. The measure of dispersion helps to eliminate or reduce the disadvantages of using the mean, median, or mode as a single measure of central tendency, and give a more accurate picture of the dataset as a whole. To have a measure of dispersion, you must know or calculate the range, standard deviation, or variance of the data set.

RANGE

The **range** of a set of data is the difference between the greatest and lowest values of the data in the set. To calculate the range, you must first make sure the units for all data values are the same, and then identify the greatest and lowest values. If there are multiple data values that are equal for the highest or lowest, just use one of the values in the formula. Write the answer with the same units as the data values you used to do the calculations.

STANDARD DEVIATION

Standard deviation is a measure of dispersion that compares all the data values in the set to the mean of the set to give a more accurate picture. To find the standard deviation of a sample, use the formula

$$s = \sqrt{\frac{\sum_{i=1}^{n}(x_i - \bar{x})^2}{n-1}}$$

Note that s is the standard deviation of a sample, x represents the individual values in the data set, $\bar{x}$ is the mean of the data values in the set, and n is the number of data values in the set. The higher the value of the standard deviation is, the greater the variance of the data values from the mean. The units associated with the standard deviation are the same as the units of the data values.

> **Review Video: Standard Deviation**
> Visit mometrix.com/academy and enter code: 419469

VARIANCE

The **variance** of a sample, or just variance, is the square of the standard deviation of that sample. While the mean of a set of data gives the average of the set and gives information about where a specific data value lies in relation to the average, the variance of the sample gives information about the degree to which the data values are spread out and tells you how close an individual value is to the average compared to the other values. The units associated with variance are the same as the units of the data values squared.

PERCENTILE

Percentiles and quartiles are other methods of describing data within a set. **Percentiles** tell what percentage of the data in the set fall below a specific point. For example, achievement test scores are often given in percentiles. A score at the 80th percentile is one which is equal to or higher than 80 percent of the scores in the set. In other words, 80 percent of the scores were lower than that score.

Quartiles are percentile groups that make up quarter sections of the data set. The first quartile is the 25th percentile. The second quartile is the 50th percentile; this is also the median of the dataset. The third quartile is the 75th percentile.

SKEWNESS

Skewness is a way to describe the symmetry or asymmetry of the distribution of values in a dataset. If the distribution of values is symmetrical, there is no skew. In general the closer the mean of a data set is to the median of the data set, the less skew there is. Generally, if the mean is to the right of the median, the data set is *positively skewed*, or right-skewed, and if the mean is to the left of the median, the data set is *negatively skewed*, or left-skewed. However, this rule of thumb is not infallible. When the data values are graphed on a curve, a set with no skew will be a perfect bell curve.

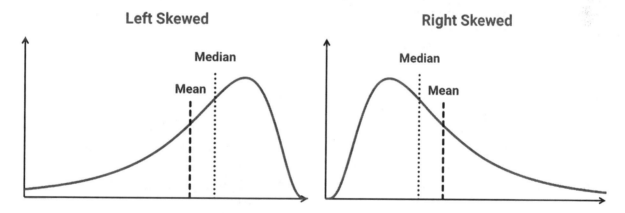

To estimate skew, use the formula:

$$\text{skew} = \frac{\sqrt{n(n-1)}}{n-2}\left(\frac{\frac{1}{n}\sum_{i=1}^{n}(x_i - \bar{x})^3}{\left(\frac{1}{n}\sum_{i=1}^{n}(x_i - \bar{x})^2\right)^{\frac{3}{2}}}\right)$$

Note that n is the datapoints in the set, x_i is the ith value in the set, and $\bar{x}$ is the mean of the set.

Review Video: Skew
Visit mometrix.com/academy and enter code: 661486

UNIMODAL VS. BIMODAL

If a distribution has a single peak, it would be considered **unimodal**. If it has two discernible peaks it would be considered **bimodal**. Bimodal distributions may be an indication that the set of data being considered is actually the combination of two sets of data with significant differences. A **uniform distribution** is a distribution in which there is *no distinct peak or variation* in the data. No values or ranges are particularly more common than any other values or ranges.

OUTLIER

An outlier is an extremely high or extremely low value in the data set. It may be the result of measurement error, in which case, the outlier is not a valid member of the data set. However, it may also be a valid member of the distribution. Unless a measurement error is identified, the experimenter cannot know for certain if an outlier is or is not a member of the distribution. There are arbitrary methods that can be employed to designate an extreme value as an outlier. One method designates an outlier (or possible outlier) to be any value less than $Q_1 - 1.5(IQR)$ or any value greater than $Q_3 + 1.5(IQR)$.

DATA ANALYSIS

SIMPLE REGRESSION

In statistics, **simple regression** is using an equation to represent a relation between independent and dependent variables. The independent variable is also referred to as the explanatory variable or the predictor and is generally represented by the variable x in the equation. The dependent variable, usually represented by the variable y, is also referred to as the response variable. The equation may be any type of function – linear, quadratic, exponential, etc. The best way to handle this task is to use the regression feature of your graphing calculator. This will easily give you the curve of best fit and provide you with the coefficients and other information you need to derive an equation.

LINE OF BEST FIT

In a scatter plot, the **line of best fit** is the line that best shows the trends of the data. The line of best fit is given by the equation $\hat{y} = ax + b$, where a and b are the regression coefficients. The regression coefficient a is also the slope of the line of best fit, and b is also the y-coordinate of the point at which the line of best fit crosses the y-axis. Not every point on the scatter plot will be on the line of best fit. The differences between the y-values of the points in the scatter plot and the corresponding y-values according to the equation of the line of best fit are the residuals. The line of best fit is also called the least-squares regression line because it is also the line that has the lowest sum of the squares of the residuals.

CORRELATION COEFFICIENT

The **correlation coefficient** is the numerical value that indicates how strong the relationship is between the two variables of a linear regression equation. A correlation coefficient of –1 is a perfect negative correlation. A correlation coefficient of +1 is a perfect positive correlation. Correlation coefficients close to –1 or +1 are very strong correlations. A correlation coefficient equal to zero indicates there is no correlation between the two variables. This test is a good indicator of whether or not the equation for the line of best fit is accurate. The formula for the correlation coefficient is

$$r = \frac{\sum_{i=1}^{n}(x_i - \bar{x})(y_i - \bar{y})}{\sqrt{\sum_{i=1}^{n}(x_i - \bar{x})^2}\sqrt{\sum_{i=1}^{n}(y_i - \bar{y})^2}}$$

where r is the correlation coefficient, n is the number of data values in the set, (x_i, y_i) is a point in the set, and $\bar{x}$ and $\bar{y}$ are the means.

Z-SCORE

A **z-score** is an indication of how many standard deviations a given value falls from the mean. To calculate a z-score, use the formula $\frac{x-\mu}{\sigma}$, where x is the data value, μ is the mean of the data set, and σ is the standard deviation of the population. If the z-score is positive, the data value lies above the mean. If the z-score is negative, the data value falls below the mean. These scores are useful in interpreting data such as standardized test scores, where every piece of data in the set has been counted, rather than just a small random sample. In cases where standard deviations are calculated from a random sample of the set, the z-scores will not be as accurate.

CENTRAL LIMIT THEOREM

According to the **central limit theorem**, regardless of what the original distribution of a sample is, the distribution of the means tends to get closer and closer to a normal distribution as the sample size gets larger and larger (this is necessary because the sample is becoming more all-encompassing of the elements of the population). As the sample size gets larger, the distribution of the sample mean will approach a normal distribution with a mean of the population mean and a variance of the population variance divided by the sample size.

Displaying Information

FREQUENCY TABLES

Frequency tables show how frequently each unique value appears in a set. A **relative frequency table** is one that shows the proportions of each unique value compared to the entire set. Relative frequencies are given as percentages; however, the total percent for a relative frequency table will not necessarily equal 100 percent due to rounding. An example of a frequency table with relative frequencies is below.

Favorite Color	Frequency	Relative Frequency
Blue	4	13%
Red	7	22%
Green	3	9%
Purple	6	19%
Cyan	12	38%

Review Video: Data Interpretation of Graphs
Visit mometrix.com/academy and enter code: 200439

CIRCLE GRAPHS

Circle graphs, also known as *pie charts*, provide a visual depiction of the relationship of each type of data compared to the whole set of data. The circle graph is divided into sections by drawing radii to create central angles whose percentage of the circle is equal to the individual data's percentage of the whole set. Each 1% of data is equal to 3.6° in the circle graph. Therefore, data represented by a 90° section of the circle graph makes up 25% of the whole. When complete, a circle graph often looks like a pie cut into uneven wedges. The pie chart below shows the data from the frequency table referenced earlier where people were asked their favorite color.

Favorite Color

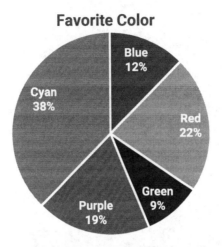

PICTOGRAPHS

A **pictograph** is a graph, generally in the horizontal orientation, that uses pictures or symbols to represent the data. Each pictograph must have a key that defines the picture or symbol and gives the quantity each picture or symbol represents. Pictures or symbols on a pictograph are not always shown as whole elements. In this case, the fraction of the picture or symbol shown represents the same fraction of the quantity a whole picture or symbol stands for. For example, a row with $3\frac{1}{2}$ ears of corn, where each ear of corn represents 100 stalks of corn in a field, would equal $3\frac{1}{2} \times 100 = 350$ stalks of corn in the field.

LINE GRAPHS

Line graphs have one or more lines of varying styles (solid or broken) to show the different values for a set of data. The individual data are represented as ordered pairs, much like on a Cartesian plane. In this case, the x- and y-axes are defined in terms of their units, such as dollars or time. The individual plotted points are joined by line segments to show whether the value of the data is increasing (line sloping upward), decreasing (line sloping downward), or staying the same (horizontal line). Multiple sets of data can be graphed on the same line graph to give an easy visual comparison. An example of this would be graphing achievement test scores for different groups of students over the same time period to see which group had the greatest increase or decrease in performance from year to year (as shown below).

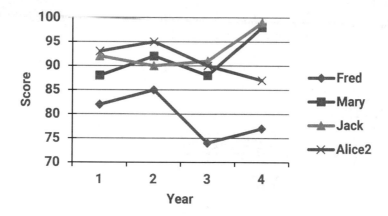

LINE PLOTS

A **line plot**, also known as a *dot plot*, has plotted points that are not connected by line segments. In this graph, the horizontal axis lists the different possible values for the data, and the vertical axis lists the number of times the individual value occurs. A single dot is graphed for each value to show the number of times it occurs. This graph is more closely related to a bar graph than a line graph. Do not connect the dots in a line plot or it will misrepresent the data.

STEM AND LEAF PLOTS

A **stem and leaf plot** is useful for depicting groups of data that fall into a range of values. Each piece of data is separated into two parts: the first, or left, part is called the stem; the second, or right, part is called the leaf. Each stem is listed in a column from smallest to largest. Each leaf that has the common stem is listed in that stem's row from smallest to largest. For example, in a set of two-digit numbers, the digit in the tens place is the stem, and the digit in the ones place is the leaf. With a stem and leaf plot, you can easily see which subset of numbers (10s, 20s, 30s, etc.) is the largest. This information is also readily available by looking at a histogram, but a stem and leaf plot also allows you to look closer and see exactly which values fall in that range. Using all of the test scores from above, we can assemble a stem and leaf plot like the one below.

Test Scores							
7	4	8					
8	2	5	7	8	8		
9	0	0	1	2	2	3	5	8	9

BAR GRAPHS

A **bar graph** is one of the few graphs that can be drawn correctly in two different configurations – both horizontally and vertically. A bar graph is similar to a line plot in the way the data is organized on the graph. Both axes must have their categories defined for the graph to be useful. Rather than placing a single dot to mark the point of the data's value, a bar, or thick line, is drawn from zero to the exact value of the data, whether it is a number, percentage, or other numerical value. Longer bar lengths correspond to greater data values. To read a bar graph, read the labels for the axes to find the units being reported. Then, look where the bars end in relation to the scale given on the corresponding axis and determine the associated value.

The bar chart below represents the responses from our favorite-color survey.

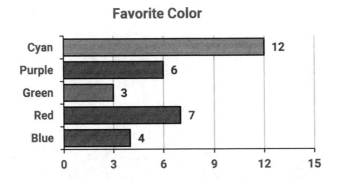

HISTOGRAMS

At first glance, a **histogram** looks like a vertical bar graph. The difference is that a bar graph has a separate bar for each piece of data and a histogram has one continuous bar for each *range* of data. For example, a histogram may have one bar for the range 0–9, one bar for 10–19, etc. While a bar graph has numerical values on one axis, a histogram has numerical values on both axes. Each range is of equal size, and they are ordered left to right from lowest to highest. The height of each column on a histogram represents the number of data values within that range. Like a stem and leaf plot, a histogram makes it easy to glance at the graph and quickly determine which range has the greatest quantity of values. A simple example of a histogram is below.

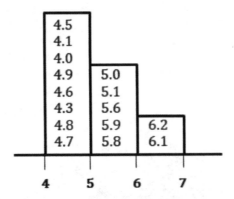

BIVARIATE DATA

Bivariate data is simply data from two different variables. (The prefix *bi-* means *two*.) In a *scatter plot*, each value in the set of data is plotted on a grid similar to a Cartesian plane, where each axis represents one of the two variables. By looking at the pattern formed by the points on the grid, you can often determine whether or not there is a relationship between the two variables, and what that relationship is, if it exists. The variables may be directly proportionate, inversely proportionate, or show no proportion at all. It may also be possible to determine if the data is linear, and if so, to find an equation to relate the two variables. The following scatter plot shows the relationship between preference for brand "A" and the age of the consumers surveyed.

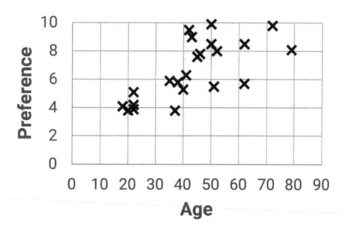

SCATTER PLOTS

Scatter plots are also useful in determining the type of function represented by the data and finding the simple regression. Linear scatter plots may be positive or negative. Nonlinear scatter plots are generally exponential or quadratic. Below are some common types of scatter plots:

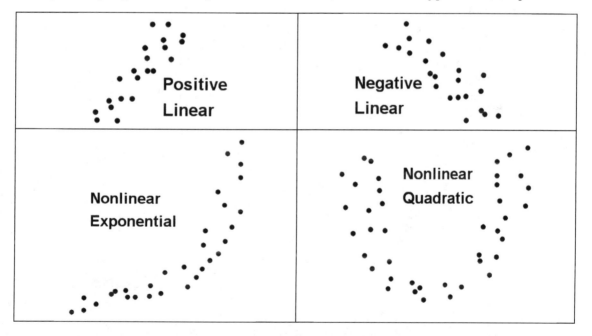

Review Video: Scatter Plot
Visit mometrix.com/academy and enter code: 596526

5-NUMBER SUMMARY

The **5-number summary** of a set of data gives a very informative picture of the set. The five numbers in the summary include the minimum value, maximum value, and the three quartiles. This information gives the reader the range and median of the set, as well as an indication of how the data is spread about the median.

BOX AND WHISKER PLOTS

A **box-and-whisker plot** is a graphical representation of the 5-number summary. To draw a box-and-whisker plot, plot the points of the 5-number summary on a number line. Draw a box whose ends are through the points for the first and third quartiles. Draw a vertical line in the box through the median to divide the box in half. Draw a line segment from the first quartile point to the minimum value and from the third quartile point to the maximum value.

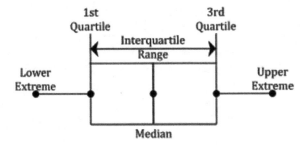

68-95-99.7 RULE

The **68–95–99.7 rule** describes how a normal distribution of data should appear when compared to the mean. This is also a description of a normal bell curve. According to this rule, 68 percent of the data values in a normally distributed set should fall within one standard deviation of the mean (34 percent above and 34 percent below the mean), 95 percent of the data values should fall within two standard deviations of the mean (47.5 percent above and 47.5 percent below the mean), and 99.7 percent of the data values should fall within three standard deviations of the mean, again, equally distributed on either side of the mean. This means that only 0.3 percent of all data values should fall more than three standard deviations from the mean. On the graph below, the normal curve is centered on the *y*-axis. The *x*-axis labels are how many standard deviations away from the center you are. Therefore, it is easy to see how the 68-95-99.7 rule can apply.

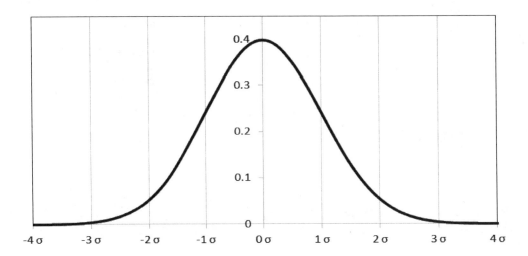

Probability

PROBABILITY

Probability is the likelihood of a certain outcome occurring for a given event. An **event** is any situation that produces a result. It could be something as simple as flipping a coin or as complex as launching a rocket. Determining the probability of an outcome for an event can be equally simple or complex. As such, there are specific terms used in the study of probability that need to be understood:

- **Compound event** – event that involves two or more independent events (rolling a pair of dice and taking the sum)
- **Desired outcome** (or success) – an outcome that meets a particular set of criteria (a roll of 1 or 2 if we are looking for numbers less than 3)
- **Independent events** – two or more events whose outcomes do not affect one another (two coins tossed at the same time)
- **Dependent events** – two or more events whose outcomes affect one another (two cards drawn consecutively from the same deck)
- **Certain outcome** – probability of outcome is 100% or 1
- **Impossible outcome** – probability of outcome is 0% or 0
- **Mutually exclusive outcomes** – two or more outcomes whose criteria cannot all be satisfied in a single event (a coin coming up heads and tails on the same toss)
- **Random variable** – refers to all possible outcomes of a single event which may be discrete or continuous.

> **Review Video: Intro to Probability**
> Visit mometrix.com/academy and enter code: 212374

THEORETICAL AND EXPERIMENTAL PROBABILITY

Theoretical probability can usually be determined without actually performing the event. The likelihood of an outcome occurring, or the probability of an outcome occurring, is given by the formula:

$$P(A) = \frac{\text{Number of acceptable outcomes}}{\text{Number of possible outcomes}}$$

Note that $P(A)$ is the probability of an outcome A occurring, and each outcome is just as likely to occur as any other outcome. If each outcome has the same probability of occurring as every other possible outcome, the outcomes are said to be equally likely to occur. The total number of acceptable outcomes must be less than or equal to the total number of possible outcomes. If the two are equal, then the outcome is certain to occur and the probability is 1. If the number of acceptable outcomes is zero, then the outcome is impossible and the probability is 0. For example, if there are 20 marbles in a bag and 5 are red, then the theoretical probability of randomly selecting a red marble is 5 out of 20, ($\frac{5}{20} = \frac{1}{4}$, 0.25, or 25%).

If the theoretical probability is unknown or too complicated to calculate, it can be estimated by an experimental probability. **Experimental probability**, also called empirical probability, is an estimate of the likelihood of a certain outcome based on repeated experiments or collected data. In other words, while theoretical probability is based on what *should* happen, experimental probability is based on what *has* happened. Experimental probability is calculated in the same way as theoretical, except that actual outcomes are used instead of possible outcomes. The more experiments performed or datapoints gathered, the better the estimate should be.

Theoretical and experimental probability do not always line up with one another. Theoretical probability says that out of 20 coin-tosses, 10 should be heads. However, if we were actually to toss 20 coins, we might record just 5 heads. This doesn't mean that our theoretical probability is incorrect; it just means that this particular experiment had results that were different from what was predicted. A practical application of empirical probability is the insurance industry. There are no set functions that define lifespan, health, or safety. Insurance companies look at factors from hundreds of thousands of individuals to find patterns that they then use to set the formulas for insurance premiums.

> **Review Video: Empirical Probability**
> Visit mometrix.com/academy and enter code: 513468

OBJECTIVE AND SUBJECTIVE PROBABILITY

Objective probability is based on mathematical formulas and documented evidence. Examples of objective probability include raffles or lottery drawings where there is a pre-determined number of possible outcomes and a predetermined number of outcomes that correspond to an event. Other cases of objective probability include probabilities of rolling dice, flipping coins, or drawing cards. Most gambling games are based on objective probability.

In contrast, **subjective probability** is based on personal or professional feelings and judgments. Often, there is a lot of guesswork following extensive research. Areas where subjective probability is applicable include sales trends and business expenses. Attractions set admission prices based on subjective probabilities of attendance based on varying admission rates in an effort to maximize their profit.

SAMPLE SPACE

The total set of all possible results of a test or experiment is called a **sample space**, or sometimes a universal sample space. The sample space, represented by one of the variables S, Ω, or U (for universal sample space) has individual elements called outcomes. Other terms for outcome that may be used interchangeably include elementary outcome, simple event, or sample point. The number of outcomes in a given sample space could be infinite or finite, and some tests may yield multiple unique sample sets. For example, tests conducted by drawing playing cards from a standard deck would have one sample space of the card values, another sample space of the card suits, and a third sample space of suit-denomination combinations. For most tests, the sample spaces considered will be finite.

An **event**, represented by the variable E, is a portion of a sample space. It may be one outcome or a group of outcomes from the same sample space. If an event occurs, then the test or experiment will generate an outcome that satisfies the requirement of that event. For example, given a standard deck of 52 playing cards as the sample space, and defining the event as the collection of face cards, then the event will occur if the card drawn is a J, Q, or K. If any other card is drawn, the event is said to have not occurred.

For every sample space, each possible outcome has a specific likelihood, or probability, that it will occur. The probability measure, also called the **distribution**, is a function that assigns a real number probability, from zero to one, to each outcome. For a probability measure to be accurate, every outcome must have a real number probability measure that is greater than or equal to zero and less than or equal to one. Also, the probability measure of the sample space must equal one, and the probability measure of the union of multiple outcomes must equal the sum of the individual probability measures.

Probabilities of events are expressed as real numbers from zero to one. They give a numerical value to the chance that a particular event will occur. The probability of an event occurring is the sum of the probabilities of the individual elements of that event. For example, in a standard deck of 52 playing cards as the sample space and the collection of face cards as the event, the probability of drawing a specific face card is $\frac{1}{52} = 0.019$, but the probability of drawing any one of the twelve face cards is $12(0.019) = 0.228$. Note that rounding of numbers can generate different results. If you multiplied 12 by the fraction $\frac{1}{52}$ before converting to a decimal, you would get the answer $\frac{12}{52} = 0.231$.

TREE DIAGRAM

For a simple sample space, possible outcomes may be determined by using a **tree diagram** or an organized chart. In either case, you can easily draw or list out the possible outcomes. For example, to determine all the possible ways three objects can be ordered, you can draw a tree diagram:

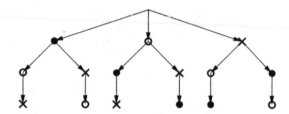

You can also make a chart to list all the possibilities:

First object	Second object	Third object
●	X	O
●	O	X
O	●	X
O	X	●
X	●	O
X	O	●

Either way, you can easily see there are six possible ways the three objects can be ordered.

If two events have no outcomes in common, they are said to be **mutually exclusive**. For example, in a standard deck of 52 playing cards, the event of all card suits is mutually exclusive to the event of all card values. If two events have no bearing on each other so that one event occurring has no influence on the probability of another event occurring, the two events are said to be independent. For example, rolling a standard six-sided die multiple times does not change that probability that a particular number will be rolled from one roll to the next. If the outcome of one event does affect the probability of the second event, the two events are said to be dependent. For example, if cards are drawn from a deck, the probability of drawing an ace after an ace has been drawn is different than the probability of drawing an ace if no ace (or no other card, for that matter) has been drawn.

In probability, the **odds in favor of an event** are the number of times the event will occur compared to the number of times the event will not occur. To calculate the odds in favor of an event, use the formula $\frac{P(A)}{1-P(A)}$, where $P(A)$ is the probability that the event will occur. Many times, odds in favor is given as a ratio in the form $\frac{a}{b}$ or $a{:}b$, where a is the probability of the event occurring and b is the complement of the event, the probability of the event not occurring. If the odds in favor are given as 2:5, that means that you can expect the event to occur two times for every 5 times that it does not occur. In other words, the probability that the event will occur is $\frac{2}{2+5} = \frac{2}{7}$.

In probability, the **odds against an event** are the number of times the event will not occur compared to the number of times the event will occur. To calculate the odds against an event, use the formula $\frac{1-P(A)}{P(A)}$, where $P(A)$ is the probability that the event will occur. Many times, odds against is given as a ratio in the form $\frac{b}{a}$ or $b{:}a$, where b is the probability the event will not occur (the complement of the event) and a is the probability the event will occur. If the odds against an event are given as 3:1, that means that you can expect the event to not occur 3 times for every one time it does occur. In other words, 3 out of every 4 trials will fail.

PERMUTATIONS AND COMBINATIONS

When trying to calculate the probability of an event using the $\frac{\text{desired outcomes}}{\text{total outcomes}}$ formula, you may frequently find that there are too many outcomes to individually count them. **Permutation** and **combination formulas** offer a shortcut to counting outcomes. A permutation is an arrangement of a specific number of a set of objects in a specific order. The number of **permutations** of r items given a set of n items can be calculated as $_nP_r = \frac{n!}{(n-r)!}$. Combinations are similar to permutations, except there are no restrictions regarding the order of the elements. While ABC is considered a different permutation than BCA, ABC and BCA are considered the same combination. The number of **combinations** of r items given a set of n items can be calculated as $_nC_r = \frac{n!}{r!(n-r)!}$ or $_nC_r = \frac{_nP_r}{r!}$.

Suppose you want to calculate how many different 5-card hands can be drawn from a deck of 52 cards. This is a combination since the order of the cards in a hand does not matter. There are 52 cards available, and 5 to be selected. Thus, the number of different hands is $_{52}C_5 = \frac{52!}{5! \times 47!} = 2{,}598{,}960$.

> **Review Video: Probability - Permutation and Combination**
> Visit mometrix.com/academy and enter code: 907664

UNION AND INTERSECTION OF TWO SETS OF OUTCOMES

If A and B are each a set of elements or outcomes from an experiment, then the **union** (symbol $\cup$) of the two sets is the set of elements found in set A or set B. For example, if $A = \{2, 3, 4\}$ and $B = \{3, 4, 5\}$, $A \cup B = \{2, 3, 4, 5\}$. Note that the outcomes 3 and 4 appear only once in the union. For statistical events, the union is equivalent to "or"; $P(A \cup B)$ is the same thing as $P(A \text{ or } B)$. The **intersection** (symbol $\cap$) of two sets is the set of outcomes common to both sets. For the above sets A and B, $A \cap B = \{3, 4\}$. For statistical events, the intersection is equivalent to "and"; $P(A \cap B)$ is the same thing as $P(A \text{ and } B)$. It is important to note that union and intersection operations commute. That is:

$$A \cup B = B \cup A \text{ and } A \cap B = B \cap A$$

COMPLEMENT OF AN EVENT

Sometimes it may be easier to calculate the possibility of something not happening, or the **complement of an event**. Represented by the symbol $\bar{A}$, the complement of A is the probability that event A does not happen. When you know the probability of event A occurring, you can use the formula $P(\bar{A}) = 1 - P(A)$, where $P(\bar{A})$ is the probability of event A not occurring, and $P(A)$ is the probability of event A occurring.

ADDITION RULE

The **addition rule** for probability is used for finding the probability of a compound event. Use the formula $P(A \text{ or } B) = P(A) + P(B) - P(A \text{ and } B)$, where $P(A \text{ and } B)$ is the probability of both events occurring to find the probability of a compound event. The probability of both events occurring at the same time must be subtracted to eliminate any overlap in the first two probabilities.

CONDITIONAL PROBABILITY

Given two events A and B, the **conditional probability** $P(A|B)$ is the probability that event B will occur, given that event A has occurred. The conditional probability cannot be calculated simply from $P(A)$ and $P(B)$; these probabilities alone do not give sufficient information to determine the conditional probability. It can, however, be determined if you are also given the probability of the intersection of events A and B, $P(A \cap B)$, the probability that events A and B both occur. Specifically, $P(A|B) = \frac{P(A \cap B)}{P(B)}$. For instance, suppose you have a jar containing two red marbles and two blue marbles, and you draw two marbles at random. Consider event A being the event that the first marble drawn is red, and event B being the event that the second marble drawn is blue. $P(A)$ is $\frac{1}{2}$, and $P(A \cap B)$ is $\frac{1}{3}$. (The latter may not be obvious, but may be determined by finding the product of $\frac{1}{2}$ and $\frac{2}{3}$). Therefore $P(A|B) = \frac{1/3}{1/2} = \frac{2}{3}$.

CONDITIONAL PROBABILITY IN EVERYDAY SITUATIONS

Conditional probability often arises in everyday situations in, for example, estimating the risk or benefit of certain activities. The conditional probability of having a heart attack given that you exercise daily may be smaller than the overall probability of having a heart attack. The conditional probability of having lung cancer given that you are a smoker is larger than the overall probability of having lung cancer. Note that changing the order of the conditional probability changes the meaning: the conditional probability of having lung cancer given that you are a smoker is a very different thing from the probability of being a smoker given that you have lung cancer. In an extreme case, suppose that a certain rare disease is caused only by eating a certain food, but even then, it is unlikely. Then the conditional probability of having that disease given that you eat the dangerous food is nonzero but low, but the conditional probability of having eaten that food given that you have the disease is 100%!

> **Review Video: Conditional Probability**
> Visit mometrix.com/academy and enter code: 397924

INDEPENDENCE

The conditional probability $P(A|B)$ is the probability that event B will occur given that event A occurs. If the two events are independent, we do not expect that whether or not event A occurs should have any effect on whether or not event B occurs. In other words, we expect $P(A|B) = P(A)$.

This can be proven using the usual equations for conditional probability and the joint probability of independent events. The conditional probability $P(A|B) = \frac{P(A \cap B)}{P(B)}$. If A and B are independent, then

$P(A \cap B) = P(A)P(B)$. So $P(A|B) = \frac{P(A)P(B)}{P(B)} = P(A)$. By similar reasoning, if A and B are independent then $P(B|A) = P(B)$.

TWO-WAY FREQUENCY TABLES

If we have a two-way frequency table, it is generally a straightforward matter to read off the probabilities of any two events A and B, as well as the joint probability of both events occurring, $P(A \cap B)$. We can then find the conditional probability $P(A|B)$ by calculating $P(A|B) = \frac{P(A \cap B)}{P(B)}$. We could also check whether or not events are independent by verifying whether $P(A)P(B) = P(A \cap B)$.

For example, a certain store's recent T-shirt sales:

Size / Color	Small	Medium	Large	Total
Blue	25	40	35	100
White	27	25	22	74
Black	8	23	15	46
Total	60	88	72	220

Suppose we want to find the conditional probability that a customer buys a black shirt (event A), given that the shirt he buys is size small (event B). From the table, the probability $P(A)$ that a customer buys a small shirt is $\frac{60}{220} = \frac{3}{11}$. The probability $P(A \cap B)$ that he buys a small, black shirt is $\frac{8}{220} = \frac{2}{55}$. The conditional probability $P(A|B)$ that he buys a black shirt, given that he buys a small shirt, is therefore $P(A|B) = \frac{2/55}{3/11} = \frac{2}{15}$.

Similarly, if we want to check whether the event a customer buys a blue shirt, A, is independent of the event that a customer buys a medium shirt, B. From the table, $P(A) = \frac{100}{220} = \frac{5}{11}$ and $P(B) = \frac{88}{220} = \frac{4}{10}$. Also, $P(A \cap B) = \frac{40}{220} = \frac{2}{11}$. Since $\left(\frac{5}{11}\right)\left(\frac{4}{10}\right) = \frac{20}{220} = \frac{2}{11}$, $P(A)P(B) = P(A \cap B)$ and these two events are indeed independent.

MULTIPLICATION RULE

The **multiplication rule** can be used to find the probability of two independent events occurring using the formula $P(A \text{ and } B) = P(A) \times P(B)$, where $P(A \text{ and } B)$ is the probability of two independent events occurring, $P(A)$ is the probability of the first event occurring, and $P(B)$ is the probability of the second event occurring.

The multiplication rule can also be used to find the probability of two dependent events occurring using the formula $P(A \text{ and } B) = P(A) \times P(B|A)$, where $P(A \text{ and } B)$ is the probability of two dependent events occurring and $P(B|A)$ is the probability of the second event occurring after the first event has already occurred. Before using the multiplication rule, you MUST first determine whether the two events are *dependent* or *independent*.

Use a **combination of the multiplication** rule and the rule of complements to find the probability that at least one outcome of the element will occur. This is given by the general formula $P(\text{at least one event occurring}) = 1 - P(\text{no outcomes occurring})$. For example, to find the probability that at least one even number will show when a pair of dice is rolled, find the probability that two odd numbers will be rolled (no even numbers) and subtract from one. You can always use a tree diagram or make a chart to list the possible outcomes when the sample space is small, such as in the dice-rolling example, but in most cases it will be much faster to use the multiplication and complement formulas.

EXPECTED VALUE

Expected value is a method of determining expected outcome in a random situation. It is really a sum of the weighted probabilities of the possible outcomes. Multiply the probability of an event occurring by the weight assigned to that probability (such as the amount of money won or lost). A practical application of the expected value is to determine whether a game of chance is really fair. If the sum of the weighted probabilities is equal to zero, the game is generally considered fair because the player has a fair chance to at least break even. If the expected value is less than zero, then players lose more than they win. For example, a lottery drawing might allow the player to choose any three-digit number, 000–999. The probability of choosing the winning number is 1:1000. If it costs \$1 to play, and a winning number receives \$500, the expected value is $\left(-\$1 \times \frac{999}{1,000}\right) + \left(\$499 \times \frac{1}{1,000}\right) = -\$0.50$. You can expect to lose on average 50 cents for every dollar you spend.

EXPECTED VALUE AND SIMULATORS

A die roll simulator will show the results of n rolls of a die. The result of each die roll may be recorded. For example, suppose a die is rolled 100 times. All results may be recorded. The numbers of 1s, 2s, 3s, 4s, 5s, and 6s, may be counted. The experimental probability of rolling each number will equal the ratio of the frequency of the rolled number to the total number of rolls. As the number of rolls increases, or approaches infinity, the experimental probability will approach the theoretical probability of 1/6. Thus, the expected value for the roll of a die is shown to be $(1 \times 1/6) + (2 \times 1/6) + (3 \times 1/6) + (4 \times 1/6) + (5 \times 1/6) + (6 \times 1/6)$, or 3.5.

PRACTICE

P1. Determine the theoretical probability of the following events:

(a) Rolling an even number on a regular 6-sided die.

(b) Not getting a red ball when selecting one from a bag of 3 red balls, 4 black balls, and 2 green balls.

(c) Rolling a standard die and then selecting a card from a standard deck that is less than the value rolled.

P2. There is a game of chance involving a standard deck of cards that has been shuffled and then laid on a table. The player wins \$10 if they can turn over 2 cards of matching color (black or red),

$50 for 2 cards with matching value (A-K), and $100 for 2 cards with both matching color and value. What is the expected value of playing this game?

P3. Today, there were two food options for lunch at a local college cafeteria. Given the following survey data, what is the probability that a junior selected at random from the sample had a sandwich?

	Freshman	Sophomore	Junior	Senior
Salad	15	12	27	36
Sandwich	24	40	43	35
Nothing	42	23	23	30

PRACTICE SOLUTIONS

P1. (a). The values on the faces of a regular die are 1, 2, 3, 4, 5, and 6. Since three of these are even numbers (2, 4, 6), The probability of rolling an even number is $\frac{3}{6} = \frac{1}{2} = 0.5 = 50\%$.

(b) The bag contains a total of 9 balls, 6 of which are not red, so the probability of selecting one non-red ball would be $\frac{6}{9} = \frac{2}{3} \cong 0.667 \cong 66.7\%$.

(c) In this scenario, we need to determine how many cards could satisfy the condition for each possible value of the die roll. If a one is rolled, there is no way to achieve the desired outcome, since no cards in a standard deck are less than 1. If a two is rolled, then any of the four aces would achieve the desired result. If a three is rolled, then either an ace or a two would satisfy the condition, and so on. Note that any value on the die is equally likely to occur, meaning that the probability of each roll is $\frac{1}{6}$. Putting all this in a table can help:

Roll	Cards < Roll	Probability of Card	Probability of Event
1	-	$\frac{0}{52} = 0$	$\frac{1}{6} \times 0 = 0$
2	1	$\frac{4}{52} = \frac{1}{13}$	$\frac{1}{6} \times \frac{1}{13} = \frac{1}{78}$
3	1,2	$\frac{8}{52} = \frac{2}{13}$	$\frac{1}{6} \times \frac{2}{13} = \frac{2}{78}$
4	1,2,3	$\frac{12}{52} = \frac{3}{13}$	$\frac{1}{6} \times \frac{3}{13} = \frac{3}{78}$
5	1,2,3,4	$\frac{16}{52} = \frac{4}{13}$	$\frac{1}{6} \times \frac{4}{13} = \frac{4}{78}$
6	1,2,3,4,5	$\frac{20}{52} = \frac{5}{13}$	$\frac{1}{6} \times \frac{5}{13} = \frac{5}{78}$

Assuming that each value of the die is equally likely, then the probability is the sum of the probabilities of each way to achieve the desired outcome: $\frac{0+1+2+3+4+5}{78} = \frac{15}{78} = \frac{5}{26} \cong 0.192 \cong$ 19.2%.

P2. First, determine the probability of each way of winning. In each case, the fist card simply determines which of the remaining 51 cards in the deck correspond to a win. For the color of the cards to match, there are 25 cards remaining in the deck that match the color of the first, but one of the 25 also matches the value, so only 24 are left in this category. For the value of the cards to match, there are 3 cards remaining in the deck that match the value of the first, but one of the three also matches the color, so only 2 are left in this category. There is only one card in the deck that will match both the color and value. Finally, there are 24 cards left that don't match at all.

Now we can find the expected value of playing the game, where we multiply the value of each event by the probability it will occur and sum over all of them:

$$\$10 \times \frac{24}{51} = \$4.71$$

$$\$50 \times \frac{2}{51} = \$1.96$$

$$\$100 \times \frac{1}{51} = \$1.96$$

$$\$0 \times \frac{24}{51} = \$0$$

$$\$4.71 + \$1.96 + \$1.96 = \$8.63$$

This game therefore has an expected value of $8.63 each time you play, which means if the cost to play is less than $8.63 then you would, on average, *gain* money. However, if the cost to play is more than $8.63, then you would, on average, *lose* money.

P3. With two-way tables it is often most helpful to start by totaling the rows and columns:

	Freshman	Sophomore	Junior	Senior	Total
Salad	15	12	27	36	90
Sandwich	24	40	43	35	142
Nothing	42	23	23	30	118
Total	81	75	93	101	350

Since the question is focused on juniors, we can focus on that column. There was a total of 93 juniors surveyed and 43 of them had a sandwich for lunch. Thus, the probability that a junior selected at random had a sandwich would be $\frac{43}{93} \cong 0.462 \cong 46.2\%$.

Iowa Core Practice Test #1

1. $f(x) = 5x + 10$. If $x = 10$, then what is the value of $f(x)$?

    a. 25
        b. 60
        c. 12
        d. 5

2. The table below lists values for x and $f(x)$.

x	$f(x)$
1	2
2	5
3	10
4	17
5	26

Which of the following equations describes the relationship between x and $f(x)$?

    a. $f(x) = x + 1$
        b. $f(x) = x^2$
        c. $f(x) = (-x)^2$
        d. $f(x) = x^2 + 1$

3. Mrs. Rose has 16 students in her class. Her class has three times as many girls as boys. How many girls and boys are in Mrs. Rose's class?

    a. 12 girls, 4 boys
        b. 4 girls, 12 boys
        c. 3 girls, 1 boy
        d. 9 girls, 7 boys

Question 4 – 8 pertain to the following bar graph:

Liz set a goal to lose 30 pounds in 12 months. The figure below contains a bar graph that describes her weight in months 1 – 12.

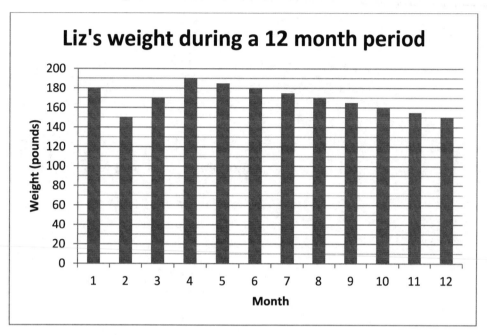

Figure: Bar graph for questions 4 – 8

4. What was Liz's initial weight?

a. 150 pounds
b. 170 pounds
c. 180 pounds
d. 195 pounds

5. How much weight did Liz lose by month 2?

a. 30 pounds
b. 20 pounds
c. 10 pounds
d. 0 pounds

6. Did Liz lose or gain weight from month 2 to month 4? How much weight did Liz lose or gain?

a. Liz lost 40 pounds
b. Liz gained 40 pounds
c. Liz lost 20 pounds
d. Liz gained 20 pounds

7. Which of the following statements is *not* supported by the weight loss data in Figure 1?

    a. Liz lost 30 pounds by the second month of her diet.

      b. Liz weighed more after the fourth month of her diet than she weighed at the beginning of her diet.

      c. Liz experienced slow but consistent weight loss after month 4 of her diet.

      d. Liz's rapid weight loss was sustainable for all 12 months of her diet.

8. Which of the following statements is most supported by the weight loss data in Figure 1?

    a. The most Liz weighed was 180 pounds over the entire course of her diet

      b. Liz lost weight every month during the entire 12 months of her diet

      c. Liz did not meet her weight loss goal

      d. Liz met her weight loss goal in month 12 through slow, consistent weight loss over time

9. Which of the following figures contains a graph of the function $y = 2x + 2$?

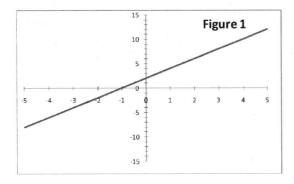
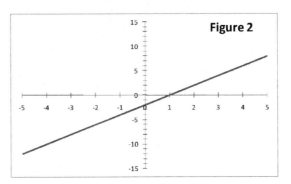
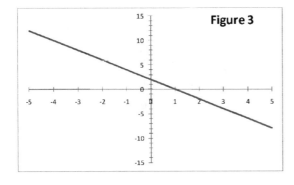
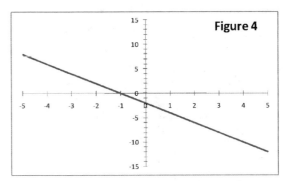

    a. Figure 1

      b. Figure 2

      c. Figure 3

      d. Figure 43

10. Which of the following figures contains a graph of the function $y = x^2 + 10$?

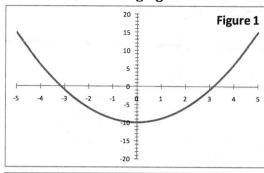

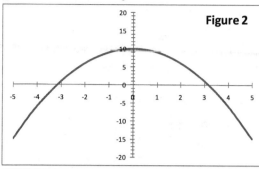

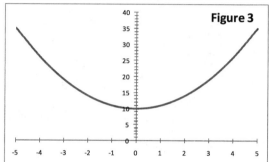

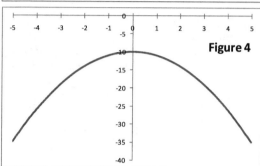

   a. Figure 1
     b. Figure 2
     c. Figure 3
     d. Figure 3

11. What is the domain of the function $f(x) = 3x + 1$?

   a. $x \geq -\frac{1}{3}$
     b. $x > 0$
     c. $x \geq \frac{1}{3}$
     d. All real numbers

12. What is the range of the function $g(x) = x + 4$?

   a. $g(x) \geq -8$
     b. $g(x) \geq 8$
     c. $g(x) > 0$
     d. All real number

13. The scatter plot below shows the heights and ages of various trees in New England. Which function best fits the data?

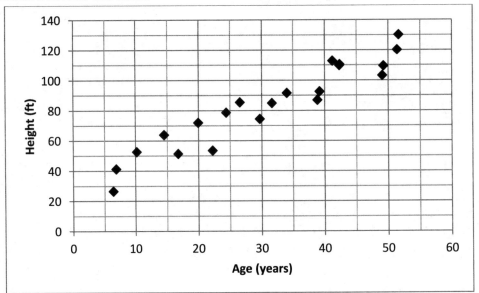

a. $h(a) = \frac{1}{8}a$

b. $h(a) = \frac{1}{8}a + 20$

c. $h(a) = a + 22$

d. $h(a) = 2a + 20$

14. Sketch a graph of the parent function $f(x) = log_2(x)$?

a.

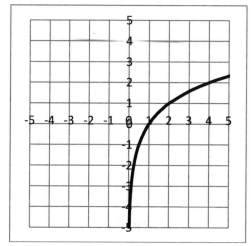

b.

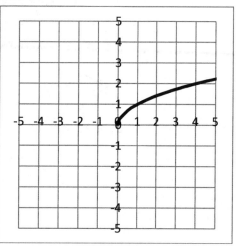

c.

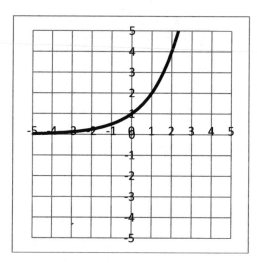

d.

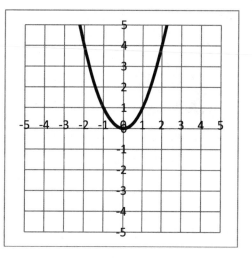

15. What transformation of the parent function $f(x) = x^2$ is needed to get the function $g(x) = (x - 2)^2 + 5$?

    a. Shift the parent function 5 units to the left and 2 units up
      b. Shift the parent function 2 units to the left and 5 units up
      c. Shift the parent function 5 units to the right and 2 units up
      d. Shift the parent function 2 units to the right and 5 units up

16. What transformation of the parent function $f(x) = |x|$ is needed to get the function $g(x) = -7|x|$?

    a. Stretch the parent function vertically
      b. Shift the parent function 7 units to the left
      c. Reflect the parent function over the x-axis and stretch it vertically
      d. Shift the parent function 7 units to the left and stretch it vertically

17. What is the inverse of the function $f(x) = \frac{15}{x}$?

    a. $f^{-1}(x) = \frac{1}{15x}$

        b. $f^{-1}(x) = \frac{15}{x}$

        c. $f^{-1}(x) = \frac{x}{15}$

        d. $f^{-1}(x) = 15x$

18. What is the inverse of the function $f(x) = 2 - 5x$?

    a. $f^{-1}(x) = \frac{x-2}{5}$

        b. $f^{-1}(x) = \frac{x+2}{5}$

        c. $f^{-1}(x) = \frac{2-x}{5}$

        d. $f^{-1}(x) = 2 - \frac{x}{5}$

19. Simplify the expression $\frac{x^2-3x-18}{5x-30}$.

    a. $\frac{x-6}{5}$

        b. $\frac{x+3}{5}$

        c. $\frac{(x-3)(x+6)}{5(x-6)}$

        d. $\frac{(x+3)(x+6)}{5(x-6)}$

20. Simplify the expression $x^5 \cdot (2x)^3$.

    a. $2x^8$

        b. $2x^{15}$

        c. $8x^8$

        d. $8x^{15}$

21. Which of the following boxplots correctly represents the data set shown below?

7, 8, 8, 11, 13, 14, 15, 15, 16, 17, 21, 23, 23, 24, 31, 35, 35, 35, 38, 38, 40, 45, 49, 50, 50

a.

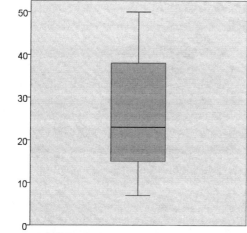

c.

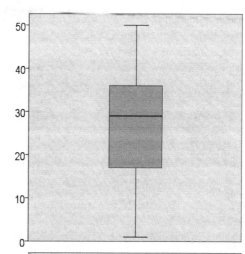

b.

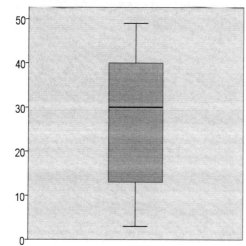

d.

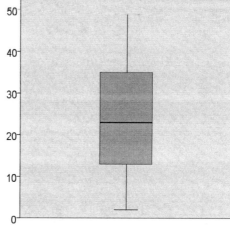

22. Given the parallel boxplots shown below, which of the following statements is true?

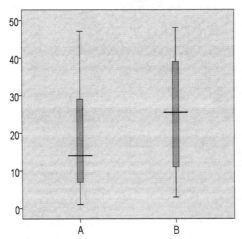

    a. The boxplot for data set A has a larger interquartile range and a larger median.
    b. The boxplot for data set B has a larger interquartile range and a larger median.
    c. The boxplot for data set A has a larger interquartile range and a smaller median.
    d. The boxplot for data set B has a larger interquartile range and a smaller median.

23. Given the double bar graph shown below, which of the following statements is true?

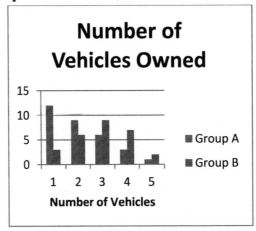

    a. Group A is negatively skewed, while Group B is approximately normal.
    b. Group A is positively skewed, while Group B is approximately normal.
    c. Group A is approximately normal, while Group B is negatively skewed.
    d. Group A is approximately normal, while Group B is positively skewed.

24. Which of the following data sets is represented by the histogram shown below?

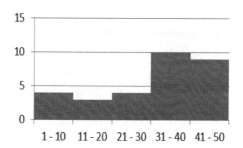

a. 6,7, 7, 8, 12, 13, 18, 22, 26, 27, 28, 31, 36, 36, 36,
36, 37, 38, 38, 38, 39, 41, 41, 41, 42, 42, 43, 43, 48, 49
b. 2, 3, 4, 4, 8, 9, 10, 10, 11, 15, 19, 21, 21, 21, 21,
22, 24, 24, 25, 29, 31, 33, 40, 43, 45, 46, 48, 48, 49, 50
c. 1, 2, 8, 8, 9, 9, 12, 13, 15, 15, 16, 17, 18, 19, 19,
21, 29, 31, 31, 35, 36, 38, 41, 42, 42, 45, 46, 47, 47, 49
d. 1, 4, 4, 5, 10, 10, 10, 12, 12, 16, 20, 22, 23, 23, 25,
27, 31, 31, 37, 39, 40, 41, 41, 43, 45, 46, 48, 49, 49, 50

25. The statistics scores for Sections 101 and 102 are shown below. Which of the following statements accurately compare the center and variability of the sets of scores?

Section 101	60	62	63	66	70	82	83	85	88	90	90	91	95	95	97
Section 102	65	65	67	69	69	70	73	76	77	79	86	90	95	98	98

a. The statistics scores for Section 101 show a greater center and variability.
b. he statistics scores for Section 101 show a greater center but smaller variability.
c. he statistics scores for Section 101 show a smaller center but greater variability.
d, The statistics scores for Section 101 show a smaller center and variability.

26. Given the histograms shown below, which of the following statements is true?

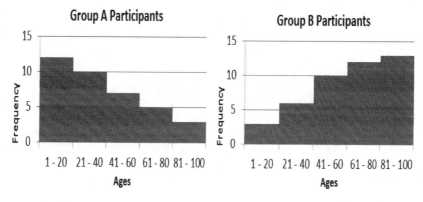

a. Group A is negatively skewed and has a mean that is less than the mean of Group B.
b. Group A is positively skewed and has a mean that is more than the mean of Group B.
c. Group B is negatively skewed and has a mean that is more than the mean of Group A.
d. Group B is positively skewed and has a mean that is less than the mean of Group A.

139

27. Given a normal distribution, which of the following best represents the area under the curve to the right of a z-score of 1.38?

    a. 0.03
      b. 0.08
      c. 0.12
      d. 0.15

28. Given $\mu = 18$ and $\sigma = 2$, which of the following best represents the proportion of scores falling above 19?

    a. 31%
      b. 18%
      c. 41%
      d. 22%

29. Which of the following best represents the area under the curve of a normal distribution, falling between the z-scores of −0.8 and 1.2?

    a. 62%
      b. 67%
      c. 72%
      d. 77%

30. Given the table below, which of the following best represents the probability that a student is enrolled at TAMU or prefers lattes?

	Latte	Cappuccino	Frappuccino	Total
TAMU	350	225	175	750
NMSU	325	300	275	900
Total	675	525	450	1650

    a. 55%
      b. 60%
      c. 65%
      d. 70%

31. What mathematician is generally considered the father of geometry?

    a. Descartes
      b. Euclid
      c. Plato
      d. Gauss

32. What postulate of Euclidean geometry distinguishes it from non-Euclidean geometry?

    a. The parallel postulate
      b. The right angle postulate
      c. Koch's postulate
      d. Euclid's third postulate

33. Which statement must be false in Euclidean geometry but can be true in non-Euclidean geometry?

a. Parallel lines never intersect

b. A circle is a two-dimensional figure

c. A quadrilateral has four sides of equal length

d. The sum of the angles in a triangle is less than 180°

34. Write the converse of the statement "If a bird is a penguin, then it cannot fly".

a. "If a bird is not a penguin, then it can fly"

b. "If a bird is not a penguin, then it cannot fly"

c. "If a bird can fly, then it is not a penguin"

d. "If a bird cannot fly, then it is a penguin"

35. Which statement is logically equivalent to "If John is 10 years old, then he is in the fifth grade"?

a. "If John is not 10 years old, then he is not in the fifth grade"

b. "If John is in the fifth grade, then he is 10 years old"

c. "If John is not in the fifth grade, then he is not 10 years old"

d. All of the above

36. Which of the following is a counterexample for the statement "If today is the weekend, then it is Saturday"?

a. It is before 6 pm on Saturday

b. Today is Sunday

c. Tomorrow is Sunday

d. It is Monday morning

37. Find a counterexample for the statement "All prime numbers are odd".

141

38. After seeing a list of the first 20 prime numbers, Tim conjectured that the difference between any two consecutive prime numbers is always less than 10. Which type of reasoning did he use?

    a. Indirect reasoning
        b. Deductive reasoning
        c. Inductive reasoning
        d. Circular reasoning

39. Use inductive reasoning to formulate a conjecture about the difference between the squares of consecutive positive integers.

    a. The differences are positive odd numbers
        b. The differences are prime numbers
        c. The differences are perfect squares
        d. The differences are divisible by positive prime numbers

40. Triangle *ABC* is isosceles. Every isosceles triangle has two congruent angles. What type of reasoning allows us to therefore conclude that triangle *ABC* has two congruent angles?

    a. Deductive reasoning
        b. Indirect reasoning
        c. Inductive reasoning
        d. Circular reasoning

41. Solve the equation $x^2 + 2x + 10 = 0$ for x.

    a. $x = -4$ and $x = 2$
        b. $x = -2$ and $x = 4$
        c. $x = -1 \pm 3i$
        d. $x = 1 \pm 3i$

42. Solve the equation $2x^2 - 2x + 14 = 0$ for x.

    a. $x = -\frac{1}{2} \pm \frac{3i}{2}\sqrt{3}$
        b. $x = \frac{1}{2} \pm \frac{3i}{2}\sqrt{3}$
        c. $x = -1 \pm 3i\sqrt{3}$
        d. $x = 1 \pm 3i\sqrt{3}$

43. Adam has $10 more than Betty. If Adam were to give $15 to Betty, then she would have twice as much money as Adam. Write this situation as a system of equations.

    a. $A = B + 10$
        $B + 15 = 2A$
        b. $B = A + 10$
        $B + 15 = 2A$
        c. $A = B + 10$
        $B + 15 = 2(A - 15)$
        d. $B = A + 10$
        $B + 15 = 2(A - 15)$

44. Solve the following system of equations.

$$y = -2x - 1$$
$$x + 3y = 7$$

a. $x = -2, y = -5$

b. $x = -2, y = 3$

c. $x = -1, y = -5$

d. $x = -1, y = 3$

45. Solve the following system of equations.

$$4x + y = 2$$
$$8y = 5 + x$$

a. $x = -1, y = 6$

b. $x = \frac{1}{3}, y = \frac{2}{3}$

c. $x = \frac{2}{3}, y = -\frac{2}{3}$

d. $x = 1, y = \frac{3}{4}$

46. Sophie has a total of twenty coins, dimes and quarters, together worth \$3.80. How many dimes does she have?

47. What is the domain of the function $f(x) = 2x^2 + 5x - 12$?

a. $x \geq \frac{3}{2}$

b. $x \leq -4$

c. $-4 \leq x \leq \frac{3}{2}$

d. All real numbers

48. What is the range of the function $g(x) = 2x^2 + 8x + 5$?

a. $g(x) \geq -3$

b. $g(x) > -2$

c. $g(x) \leq -2$

d. All real numbers

49. The quadratic function $h(x)$ is represented by the graph below. Find the roots of the function, and use them to write $h(x)$ as a function of x.

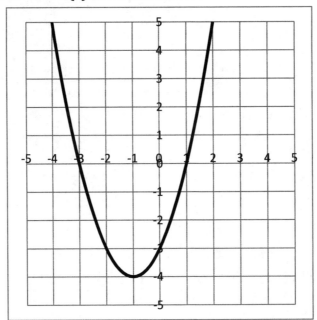

a. $h(x) = x^2 - 4x - 3$

   b. $h(x) = x^2 + 2x - 3$

   c. $h(x) = x^2 - 4x + 3$

   d. $h(x) = x^2 + 2x + 3$

50. If $f(x)$ is a quadratic function with roots at $x = -3$ and $x = 7$, what is $f(x)$?

a. $f(x) = x^2 - 21$

   b. $f(x) = x^2 - 10x + 21$

   c. $f(x) = x^2 - 4x - 21$

   d. $f(x) = x^2 + 4x - 21$

Answer Key and Explanations for Test #1

1. B: The equation describes a functional relationship between x and $f(x)$. To solve the equation, substitute 10 as the value of x, such that $f(10) = 5(10) + 10 = 50 + 10 = 60$.

2. D: For each value of x, $f(x) = x^2 + 1$,

$f(1) = (1)^2 + 1 = (1)(1) + 1 = 1 + 1 = 2$

$f(2) = (2)^2 + 1 = (2)(2) + 1 = 4 + 1 = 5$

$f(3) = (3)^2 + 1 = (3)(3) + 1 = 9 + 1 = 10$

$f(4) = (4)^2 + 1 = (4)(4) + 1 = 16 + 1 = 17$

$f(5) = (5)^2 + 1 = (5)(5) + 1 = 25 + 1 = 26$

3. A: Let x represent the number of boys in Mrs. Rose's class. Since Mrs. Rose has three times as many girls in her class as boys, 3x represents the number of girls in Mrs. Rose's class. The total number of students in the class is 16. Written as an equation and solved for x we get:

$$x + 3x = 16$$
$$4x = 16$$
$$x = 4$$

Hence $x = 4$ and $3x = 12$. Therefore, 4 is the number of boys and 12 is the number of girls. Also, $4 + 12 = 16$, the total number of students in the class.

4. C: According to the graph, in month 1, Liz weighed 180 pounds.

5. A: In month 1, Liz weighed 180 pounds. By month 2, Liz weighed 150 pounds. Since $180 - 150 = 30$, Liz lost 30 pounds by month 2.

6. B: In month 2, Liz weight 150 pounds but she weighed 190 pounds in month 4. Since $190 - 150 = 40$, Liz gained 40 pounds from month to month 4.

7. D: Liz experienced a rapid weight loss of 30 pounds by month 2; however she gained 40 pounds over the next 2 months, and her resulting weight was greater than her weight at the beginning of her diet. Therefore, her rapid weight loss was NOT sustainable for all 12 months of her diet.

8. D: Liz weighed 150 pounds by month 12, which was 30 pounds less than her initial 180 pounds. Thus Liz met her weight loss goal. Furthermore, from month 4 to month 12, Liz lost 5 pounds per month, which was means she met her goal through slow, consistent weight loss over time. Answer A is incorrect because Liz weight 190 pounds during month 4. Answer B is incorrect because Liz gained weight between month 2 and month 4. Answer C is incorrect because Liz did meet her 30 pound weight loss goal.

9. A: The equation is written in the form of the point slope formula: $y = mx + b$ where m is the slope of the line and b is the y-axis intercept. For the given equation $y = 2x + 2$, the slope of the line is positive 2 and the line intercepts the y-axis at positive 2. The graph in Figure 1 fits these criteria. The graph in Figure 2 intercepts the y-axis at negative 2. The graphs in Figure 3 and Figure 4 have slopes of negative 2.

10. C: The equation is written in the form $y = Ax^2 + B$ where A tells the concavity of the graph and B is the y- intercept. In this case, A equals positive 1. So the graph is concave up. B equals positive 10. So the graph intercepts the y-axis at positive 10. The graph in Figure 3 fits these criteria. The graph in Figure 1 intercepts the y-axis at negative 10. The graphs in Figure 2 and Figure 4 are concave down.

11. D: The domain of a function is the set of all possible input values for the function. In this case, the input for $f(x)$ is x. The easiest way to find the domain of $f(x)$ is to determine for which x-values the function is undefined. Then you can exclude those values from the domain.

Examine the given function. Notice that it does not contain a square root sign, a logarithm, or a fraction with x in the denominator. Therefore, the function is defined for all real numbers. You can see this visually by graphing the function. In the graph below, notice that the function can go to the left and right without end.

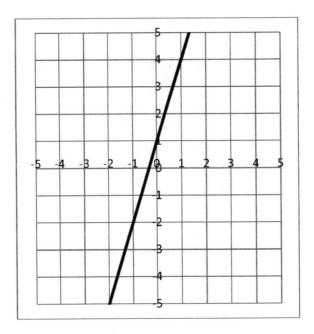

12. D: The range of a function is the set of all possible output values for the function. In this case, the output for $g(x)$ is the function itself, $g(x)$. Examine the given function. Let's say you choose some particular real number for $g(x)$. For any choice you make, you can find an x-value that will result in that choice by simply subtracting 4 from it. For example, say you choose $g(x) = -3$. Then you can use $x = -3 - 4 = -7$ to get your original value because $g(-7) = -7 + 4 = -3$. Since this will work for any real value for $g(x)$, the range of $g(x)$ is all real numbers. You can see this visually by graphing the function. In the graph below, notice that the function can go up and down without end.

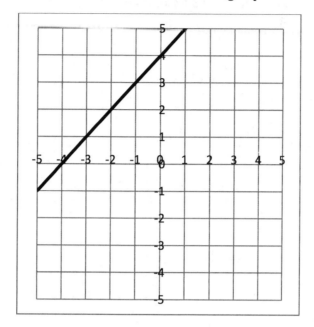

13. D: Examine the scatter plot. The function that best fits the data will be a line that goes through the middle of the data. Based on the leftmost points in the scatter plot, the height of the tree, $h(a)$, is about 25 when the age, a, is 6. Based on the rightmost points, $h(a)$ is about 120 when $a = 50$.

Now turn to the four answer choices for $h(a)$. As a test, substitute $a=6$ and $a=50$ into each to see how they compare to the data in the scatter plot.

Function	$h(6)$	$h(50)$
$h(a) = \dfrac{1}{8}a$	$h(6) = \dfrac{1}{8} \cdot 6 = 0.75$	$h(50) = \dfrac{1}{8} \cdot 50 = 6.25$
$h(a) = \dfrac{1}{8}a + 20$	$h(6) = \dfrac{1}{8} \cdot 6 + 20 = 20.75$	$h(50) = \dfrac{1}{8} \cdot 50 + 20 = 26.25$
$h(a) = a + 22$	$h(6) = 6 + 22 = 28$	$h(50) = 50 + 22 = 72$
$h(a) = 2a + 20$	$h(6) = 2 \cdot 6 + 20 = 32$	$h(50) = 2 \cdot 50 + 20 = 120$

Out of the four choices, the only function that approximates the leftmost and rightmost values from the scatter plot is $h(a) = 2a + 20$.

14. A: The logarithm of a number is the exponent to which the base must be raised in order to get that number. For example, since $2^3 = 8$, it is also true that $log_2(8) = 3$. To graph the given function, either use a graphing calculator or make a table of values. A table of values is shown below.

x	$\dfrac{1}{4}$	$\dfrac{1}{2}$	1	2	4
f(x)	-2	-1	0	1	2

From the table, the graph of $f(x)$ must pass through the points, $(\frac{1}{4}, -2)$, $(\frac{1}{2}, -1)$, $(1,0)$, $(2,1)$, and $(4,2)$. Graph these points on a coordinate plane, and then connect them with a smooth line. The resulting graph is shown below.

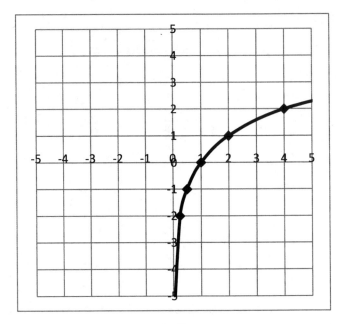

15. D: Transformations of a parent function include a translations, reflections, and dilations/compressions. In this case, the parent function is $f(x) = x^2$, which is a parabola.

Compare the two given function. There are two operations that must be done to $f(x)$ to get $g(x)$: first, you need to replace x with $(x - 2)$, and then you need to add 5 to the end. Both of these operations result in translations, or shifts, of the parent function horizontally and vertically. In particular, replacing x with $(x - 2)$ shifts the parent function 2 units to the right, while adding 5 to the end shifts it 5 units up. Thus, to get $g(x)$ from $f(x)$, you need to shift the graph of $f(x)$ 2 units to the right and 5 units up.

16. C: Transformations of a parent function include a translations, reflections, and dilations/compressions. In this case, the parent function is $f(x) = |x|$.

Compare the two given function. To get $g(x)$, you have to multiply the parent function $f(x)$ by -7. Multiplying a function by a negative number reflects it over the x-axis, while multiplying it by a number whose absolute value is greater than one (in this case, $|-7| = 7 > 1$) stretches it vertically. Thus, to get $g(x)$ from $f(x)$, you need to reflect the parent function over the x-axis and stretch it vertically.

17. A: The inverse of a function is a relation that *undoes* a function. The inverse of $f(x)$ is written $f^{-1}(x)$ by convention. To find the inverse of $f(x)$, first replace $f(x)$ with y. Then, swap the x and y values.

$$f(x) = \frac{15}{x}$$

$$y = \frac{15}{x}$$

$$x = \frac{15}{y}$$

Next solve the equation for y.

$$xy = 15$$

$$y = \frac{15}{x}$$

Finally, replace y with $f^{-1}(x)$ to get the inverse.

$$f^{-1}(x) = \frac{15}{x}$$

18. C: The inverse of a function is a relation that *undoes* a function. The inverse of $f(x)$ is written $f^{-1}(x)$ by convention. To find the inverse of $f(x)$, first replace $f(x)$ with y. Then, swap the x and y values.

$$f(x) = 2 - 5x$$

$$y = 2 - 5x$$

$$x = 2 - 5y$$

Next, solve the equation for y.

$$5y = 2 - x$$

$$y = \frac{2-x}{5}$$

Finally, replace y with $f^{-1}(x)$ to get the inverse.

$$f^{-1}(x) = \frac{2-x}{5}$$

19. B: To simplify the expression, first factor the numerator and the denominator. To factor the numerator, use trial-and-error to find two numbers whose sum is -3 and whose product is -18, and then put those numbers into the form $(x + \_)(x + \_)$. For the denominator, factor out the common factor, which is 5.

$$\frac{x^2-3x-18}{5x-30} = \frac{(x+3)(x-6)}{5(x-6)}$$

Now there is a common factor, $(x - 6)$, which is in both the numerator and the denominator. Therefore, you can further simplify the expression by cancelling it out.

$$\frac{(x+3)(x-6)}{5(x-6)} = \frac{x+3}{5}$$

20. C: To simplify the expression, first simplify the expression with parentheses. To raise $2x$ to the third power, raise both 2 and x to the third power separately.

$$x^5 \cdot (2x)^3 = x^5 \cdot 2^3 \cdot x^3$$

$$= x^5 \cdot 8x^3$$

Next, multiply the terms. Since they have the same base and are being multiplied together, add the exponents to the like base.

$$x^5 \cdot 8x^3 = 8x^{5+3}$$

$$= 8x^8$$

21. A: The minimum and maximum values are 7 and 50, respectively. The median is 23, while the first and third quartiles are 15 and 38. The boxplot for Choice A correctly represents these five values.

22. B: The boxplot for data set B shows a larger range between the first and third quartiles. In addition, its median is approximately 25, which is higher than the median of data set A.

23. B: Data is said to be positively skewed when there are a higher number of lower values, indicating data that is skewed right. An approximately normal distribution shows an increase in frequency, followed by a decrease in frequency, of approximately the same rate.

24. A: The data set, shown in Choice A, correctly represents a frequency of 4 for the interval 1 – 10, a frequency of 3 for 11 – 20, a frequency of 4 for 21 – 30, a frequency of 10 for 31 – 40, and a frequency of 9 for 41 – 50.

25. A: The scores for Section 101 have a mean of approximately 81.1, with a standard deviation of approximately 13.2. The scores for Section 102 have a mean of approximately 78.5, with a standard deviation of approximately 12.0. Thus, the center and variability of scores for Section 101 are greater.

26. C: Group B is negatively skewed since there are more high scores. With more high scores, the mean for Group B will be higher.

27. B: Using a standard z-table, the area from the mean to z is shown to be 0.4162. This area should be subtracted from 0.5 in order to show the area to the right of a z-score of 1.38. Thus, the area to the right of the z-score is 0.0838, or approximately 0.08. A z-table, including the smaller portion of area under a curve may also be used. This area is reported as 0.0838.

28. A: The z-score may be represented as $z = \frac{19-18}{2}$ or $z = \frac{1}{2}$. Using a standard z-table, the area from the mean to z is shown to be 0.1915. Subtraction of this area from 0.5 gives 0.3085. Thus, the proportion of scores falling above 19 is approximately 31%. A z-table, including the smaller portion of area under a curve may also be used. This area is reported as 0.3085.

29. B: A standard z-table shows an area of 0.2881 between a z-score of –0.8 and the mean. It also shows an area of 0.3849 between the mean and a z-score of 1.2. The sum of the two areas is 0.673. Thus, the area between the two z-scores is approximately 67%. Using a table that reports the mean to z, the two mean-to-z areas may be extracted and summed. You may also add the smaller portions and subtract the sum from 1.

30. C: The probability may be written as $P(A \text{ or } B) = \frac{750}{1650} + \frac{675}{1650} - \frac{350}{1650}$, which simplifies to $P(A \text{ or } B) = \frac{1075}{1650}$ or approximately 65%.

31. B: Euclid, a Greek mathematician who lived around 300 BC, is usually considered the father of geometry and an important figure in the development of the notion of mathematical rigor. His most famous work is *Elements*, a collection of geometric proofs, starting with definitions and axioms and proceeding to more complicated propositions. It was still a widely read work until the 20th century.

32. A: Euclid's famous treatise, *Elements*, contained five postulates. For centuries, it was generally agreed by mathematicians that the first four postulates were self-evident, whereas the fifth postulate, the so-called parallel postulate, was not as obvious because of its length and difficulty. In the nineteenth century, some mathematicians began to explore what would happen if the parallel postulate was assumed to be false. The resulting geometry came to be known as non-Euclidean geometry.

33. D: Non-Euclidean geometry is geometry in which the parallel postulate is assumed to be false. Pictorially, this means that Euclidean geometry is on a flat plane (it is the geometry we are most familiar with), whereas non-Euclidean geometry is on a curved surface. As a result, the angles of a triangle in Euclidean geometry always add up to exactly 180°. On the other hand, in non-Euclidean geometry, the angles can add up to either less than or more than 180° depending on whether the surface is curved like a saddle-shaped plane or an ellipsoid.

34. D: The converse of a statement "If p, then q" is "If q, then p", where p and q are any statement. In other words, to construct the converse, switch the two halves of the conditional. In the given expression, the p-statement is "a bird is a penguin" and the q-statement is "it [a bird] cannot fly". When you switch the two halves, the result is "If a bird cannot fly, then it is a penguin".

35. C: A conditional and its contrapositive always have the same truth table, so they are considered logically equivalent. On the other hand, the inverse and converse do not have the same truth table as the original statement, so they are not considered logically equivalent. Examine the choices A, B, and C and notice that choice A is the inverse of the original statement, choice B is the converse, and choice C is the contrapositive. Therefore, only the statement in choice C is logically equivalent to the original statement.

36. B: A counterexample is a specific example that violates a general statement. Since the given statement "If today is the weekend, then it is Saturday" is a conditional (i.e., it is in the form "If..., then..."), a counterexample will be an example in which the "if" part of the statement is true, but the "then" part is false. Therefore, for this problem, we need to find a day that is part of the weekend but is not Saturday. The only day that fits that description is Sunday.

37. 2: A counterexample is a specific example that violates a general statement. Since the statement is "All prime numbers are odd", a counterexample would be a prime number that is even. The only even prime number is 2 because any even number greater than it is divisible by 2.

38. C: Inductive reasoning involves making an observation, finding a pattern, and making a general conjecture based on that pattern. In this example, the pattern Tim found was that in the first 20 prime numbers, no two consecutive prime numbers are 10 or more apart. Using inductive reasoning, he generalized this pattern of the first 20 primes to apply to all prime numbers.

39. A: Inductive reasoning involves making an observation, finding a pattern, and making a general conjecture based on that pattern. The first four differences are:

$$1^2 - 0^2 = 1 - 0 = 1$$
$$2^2 - 1^2 = 4 - 1 = 3$$
$$3^2 - 2^2 = 9 - 4 = 5$$
$$4^2 - 3^2 = 16 - 9 = 7$$

Notice that these numbers are the first four positive odd numbers. Therefore, using inductive reasoning, we can make the conjecture that the difference between the squares of *any* consecutive positive integers is a positive odd number. Although this type of reasoning is not considered a valid method of mathematical proof, it is still useful for discovering possible theorems that can later be proved rigorously.

40. A: Deductive reasoning asserts conclusion that must necessarily be true based on a set of premises. In this problem, the premises are "Triangle ABC is an isosceles" and "Every isosceles triangle has two congruent angles". Since triangle ABC is an instance of an isosceles triangle, it must *necessarily* have two congruent angles. Therefore, this is an example of deductive reasoning.

41. C: The left side of the equation cannot be factored, so use the quadratic equation. Remember that the square root of a negative number is an imaginary number.

$$x = \frac{-b \pm \sqrt{b^2 - 4ac}}{2a}$$

$$= \frac{-2 \pm \sqrt{4 - 40}}{2}$$

$$= \frac{-2 \pm \sqrt{-36}}{2}$$

$$= \frac{-2 \pm 6i}{2}$$

$$= -\frac{2}{2} \pm \frac{6i}{2}$$

$$= -1 \pm 3i$$

42. B: The left side of the equation cannot be factored, so use the quadratic equation. Remember that the square root of a negative number is an imaginary number.

$$x = \frac{-b \pm \sqrt{b^2 - 4ac}}{2a}$$

$$= \frac{2 \pm \sqrt{4 - 112}}{4}$$

$$= \frac{2 \pm \sqrt{-108}}{4}$$

$$= \frac{2 \pm 6i\sqrt{3}}{4}$$

$$= \frac{2}{4} \pm \frac{6i\sqrt{3}}{4}$$

$$= \frac{1}{2} \pm \frac{3i}{2}\sqrt{3}$$

43. C: T the first sentence, "Adam has $10 more than Betty," can be written as $A = B + 10$, where A represents the amount of money Adam has and B represents the amount of money Betty has.

Next translate the second sentence "If Adam were to give $15 to Betty, then she would have twice as much money as Adam." This means that if Adam had $15 less (represented by the expression $A -$

15) and Betty had $15 more ($B + 15$), then Betty would have two times what Adam would have. So, the correct equation is $B + 15 = 2(A - 15)$.

44. B: Notice that the given system has two equations, and each equation has two variables, x and y. Therefore, the solution of the system of equations must have values for each of the two variables. To find the solution, you can use algebraic methods, graphs, tables, or matrices. For the purposes of this explanation, we will use an algebraic method called substitution.

To begin, notice that the first equation already has y isolated on the left side. Therefore, substitute the left side, $-2x - 1$, for y into the second equation, and then solve for x.

$$x + 3y = 7$$

$$x + 3(-2x - 1) = 7$$

$$x - 6x - 3 = 7$$

$$-5x = 10$$

$$x = -2$$

To find the value of y, substitute -2 for x in the first equation.

$$y = -2(-2) - 1$$

$$= 4 - 1$$

$$= 3$$

Therefore, the solution of the given system of equations is $x = -2, y = 3$. Check this solution on your own by substituting the values into the second equations to make sure that you get a true equality.

45. B: Notice that the given system has two equations, and each equation has two variables, x and y. Therefore, the solution of the system of equations must have values for each of the two variables. To find the solution, you can use algebraic methods, graphs, tables, or matrices. For the purposes of this explanation, we will use an algebraic method called elimination.

To begin, rewrite the first equation so it is in the form $Ax + By = C$. (The first equation is already in this form.)

$$4x + y = 2 \rightarrow \quad 4x + y = 2$$

$$8y = 5 + x \rightarrow -x + 8y = 5$$

Then, eliminate one of the variables. We will eliminate x. To do this, multiply the second equation by 4, and then add the equations together.

$$4x + y = 2 \quad \rightarrow \quad 4x + \quad y = 2$$

$$4(-x + 8y = 5) \rightarrow +(-4x + 32y = 20)$$

$$33y = 22$$

Solve the resulting equation by dividing both sides by 33. The result is $y = \frac{2}{3}$. To find the value of x, substitute $\frac{2}{3}$ for y in either equation, and then solve for x. We will use the first equation.

$$4x + \frac{2}{3} = 2$$

$$4x = \frac{4}{3}$$

$$x = \frac{1}{3}$$

Therefore, the solution of the given system of equations is $x = \frac{1}{3}, y = \frac{2}{3}$. Check this solution on your own by substituting the values into the second equation to make sure that you get a true equality.

46. 8. First translate the information in the word problem into two mathematical equations. In the problem, there are two unknowns: the number of dimes and the number of quarters. Let the variables d and q represent these quantities. In addition, we are given two separate pieces of information, namely that Sophie has twenty coins and that the coins are worth $3.80 altogether. We can translate these two statements into a system of equations.

$$d + q = 20$$

$$10d + 25q = 380$$

To solve this system of equations, you can use algebraic methods, graphs, tables, or matrices. For the purposes of this explanation, we will use an algebraic method called elimination. First eliminate one of the variables. We will eliminate q. Multiply the first equation by 25, and then subtract the second equation from the first.

$$25(d + q = 20) \qquad \rightarrow \qquad 25d + 25q = 500$$

$$10d + 25q = 380 \qquad -(10d + 25q = 380)$$

$$15d = 120$$

Next, solve the resulting equation by dividing both sides by 15. The result is $d = 8$. Therefore, Sophie has eight dimes. This answer makes sense; it tells us that she has 8 dimes and 12 quarters. Note that she has twelve quarters since the number of dimes and quarters together is twenty. The value of eight dimes ($0.80) and twelve quarters ($3.00) is indeed $3.80 all together.

47. D: The domain of a function is the set of all possible input values for the function. In this case, the input for $f(x)$ is x. The easiest way to find the domain of $f(x)$ is to determine for which values of x the function is undefined. Then you can exclude those values from the domain.

Examine the given function. Notice that it does not contain a square root sign, a logarithm, or a fraction with x in the denominator. Therefore, the function will be defined for all real numbers. You can see this visually by graphing the function. In the graph below, notice that the function can go to the left and right without end.

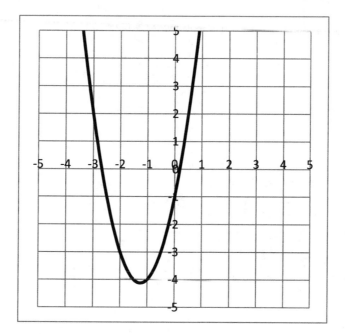

48. A: The range of a function is the set of all possible output values for the function. In this case, the output for $g(x)$ is the function itself, $g(x)$. To find the range, first graph the given function.

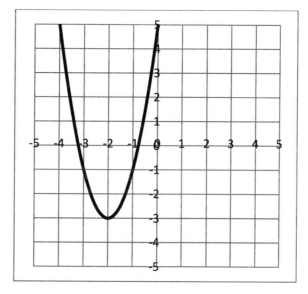

Notice that the graph is a U-shaped parabola, which means that its vertex is a minimum (rather than a maximum). Because of this, the range is the set of y-values above (and including) the minimum. In this case, the minimum is the point (-2,-3). Therefore, the range of $g(x)$ is $g(x) \geq -3$.

49. B: The roots of a quadratic function $f(x)$ are the values of x for which $f(x) = 0$. Graphically, the roots are the x-values where the graph of the quadratic function intercepts the x-axis. Based on the graph, $h(x)$ has x-intercepts at $x = -3$ and $x = 1$. Therefore, the roots of $h(x)$ are $x = -3$ and $x = 1$.

A quadratic function written in the form $h(x) = (x - a)(x - b)$ has roots at $x = a$ and $x = b$. Therefore, to find $h(x)$, substitute the roots, -3 and 1, for a and b and simplify the result.

$$h(x) = (x - a)(x - b)$$

$$= \left(x - (-3)\right)(x - 1)$$

$$= (x + 3)(x - 1)$$

$$= x^2 + 2x - 3$$

50. C: The roots of a quadratic function $f(x)$ are the values of x for which $f(x) = 0$. Quadratic functions may have two real roots, two imaginary roots, or one real double root. A quadratic function written in the form $f(x) = (x - a)(x - b)$ has roots at $x = a$ and $x = b$. Therefore, to find $f(x)$, substitute the given roots for a and b into $f(x) = (x - a)(x - b)$ and simplify.

$$f(x) = (x - a)(x - b)$$

$$= \left(x - (-3)\right)(x - 7)$$

$$= (x + 3)(x - 7)$$

$$= x^2 - 4x - 21$$

Iowa Core Practice Test #2

1. $p(y) = \frac{4y}{2} + 5$. If $y = 4$, then what is the value of $p(y)$?

    a. 9

      b. 7

      c. 13

      d. 37

2. The table below lists values for y and p(y).

y	p(y)
1	2
-1	2
2	5
-2	5
3	10
-3	10

Which of the following equations describes the relationship between y and p(y)?

    a. $p(y) = y + 1$

      b. $p(y) = 2y + 1$

      c. $p(y) = (y)^2$

      d. $p(y) = (y)^2 + 1$

3. Mr. Robinson has 20 students in his martial arts class. The ratio of boys to girls is 4:1. How many boys and girls are in Mr. Robinson's class?

    a. 15 boys, 5 girls

      b. 5 boys, 15 girls

      c. 16 boys, 4 girls

      d. 4 boys, 16 girls

Questions 4 – 6 pertain to the following passage:

Mrs. Langston owns an orchard with several different kinds of fruit trees. Half the trees are apple trees, one quarter are pear trees, approximately one eighth are orange trees and about one eighth are lemon trees.

4. Which of the pie graphs below best describes the percentage of trees in Mrs. Langston's orchard?

    a. Figure A

      b. Figure B

      c. Figure C

      d. Figure D

157

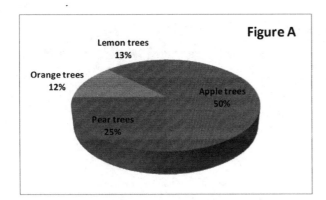

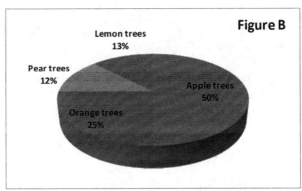

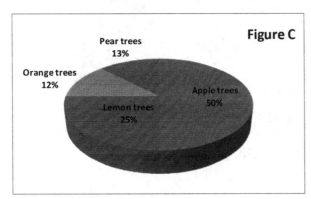

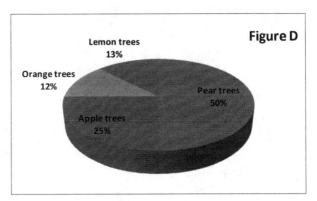

5. If Mrs. Langston has a total of 100 trees in her orchard, how many of each type of tree does she have?

a. 50 apple trees, 25 orange trees, 13 lemon trees, and 12 pear trees
b. 50 apple trees, 25 pear trees, 13 lemon trees, and 12 orange trees
c. 50 apple trees, 25 lemon trees, 13 pear trees, and 12 orange trees
d. 50 pear trees, 25 apple trees, 13 lemon trees, and 12 orange trees

6. Let y= the number of apple trees and let p(y) = the number of pear trees in Mrs. Langston's orchard. Which of the following equations best represents the relationship between apple trees and pear trees?

a. $p(y) = 2y$
b. $p(y) = \frac{y}{2}$
c. $p(y) = \frac{y}{4}$
d. $p(y) = \frac{y}{8}$

7. Based on the ratio of trees in Mrs. Langston's, she could probably produce the largest amount of which of the following products?

a. Lemonade
b. Orange juice
c. Apple sauce
d. Pear preserves

158

8. Based on the ratio of trees Mrs. Langston has in her orchard, which of the following statements is most likely false?

a. Mrs. Langston plants fewer lemon trees and orange trees because she earns the least amount of money from selling these fruits.

b. Mrs. Langston plants fewer pear trees than apple trees because pears are less profitable than apples.

c. Mrs. Langston plants more apple trees than any other kind of fruit because she earns the most money from selling apples.

d. Mrs. Langston plants more pear trees than any other kind of fruit because she earns the most money from selling pears.

9. Which of the following figures contains a graph of the function y = -3x – 3?

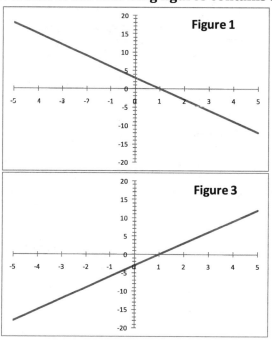
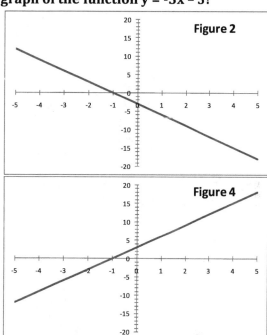

a. Figure 1

b. Figure 2

c. Figure 3

d. Figure 4

10. Which of the following figures contains a graph of the function y = -x² – 5?

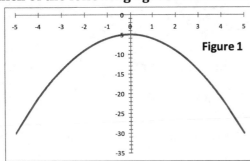

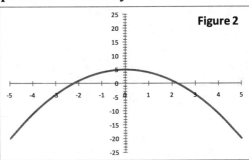

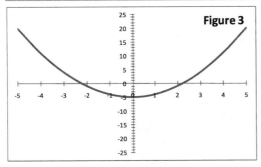

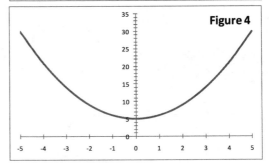

a. Figure 1
b. Figure 2
c. Figure 3
d. Figure 4

11. What is the domain of the function $f(x) = 2x + 3$?

a. $x \geq -\dfrac{3}{2}$
b. $x > 0$
c. $x \geq \dfrac{3}{2}$
d. All real numbers

22. What is the range of the function $g(x) = x - 2$?

a. $g(x) \geq -8$
b. $g(x) \geq 8$
c. $g(x) > 0$
d. All real numbers

13. The scatter plot below shows the heights and ages of various trees in New England. Which function best fits the data?

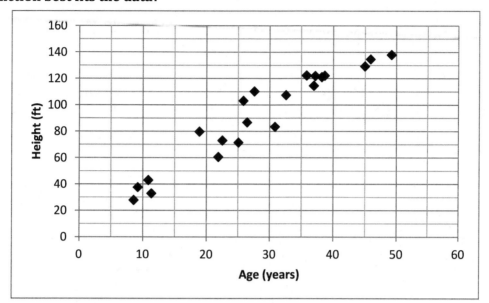

a. $h(a) = \left(\frac{1}{4}\right)a$

b. $h(a) = \left(\frac{1}{4}\right)a + 30$

c. $h(a) = a + 15$

d. $h(a) = 3a + 10$

14. Sketch a graph of the parent function $f(x) = log_3(x)$?

a.

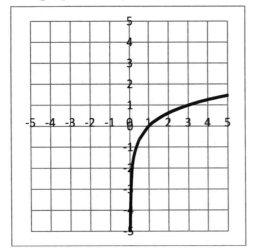

b.

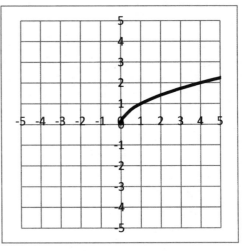

c.

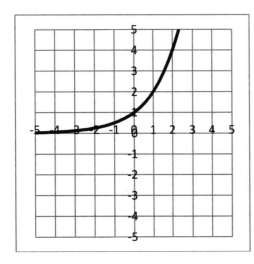

d.

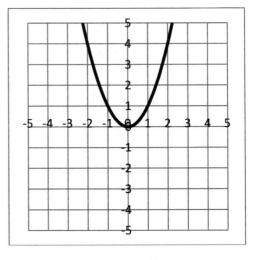

15. What transformation of the parent function $f(x) = x^2$ is needed to get the function $g(x) = (x + 1)^2 - 3$?

    a. Shift the parent function 1 unit to the left and 3 units down

      b. Shift the parent function 3 units to the left and 1 unit down

      c. Shift the parent function 1 unit to the right and 3 units down

      d. Shift the parent function 3 units to the right and 1 unit down

16. What transformation of the parent function $f(x) = |x|$ is needed to get the function $g(x) = 3|x|$?

    a. Stretch the parent function vertically

      b. Shift the parent function 3 units to the right

      c. Reflect the parent function over the x-axis and stretch it vertically

      d. Shift the parent function 3 units to the right and stretch it vertically

17. What is the inverse of the function $f(x) = 35/x$?

    a. $f^{-1}(x) = \frac{1}{35x}$

        b. $f^{-1}(x) = \frac{35}{x}$

        c. $f^{-1}(x) = \frac{x}{35}$

        d. $f^{-1}(x) = 35x$

18. What is the inverse of the function $f(x) = 6 + 2x$?

    a $f^{-1}(x) = \frac{x-6}{2}$

        b. $f^{-1}(x) = \frac{x+6}{2}$

        c. $f^{-1}(x) = \frac{6-x}{2}$

        d. $f^{-1}(x) = 6 + \frac{x}{2}$

19. Simplify the expression $\frac{x^2+2x-24}{5x-20}$.

    a. $\frac{x-4}{5}$

        b. $\frac{x+6}{5}$

        c. $\frac{(x-4)(x+6)}{5(x-4)}$

        d. $\frac{(x+4)(x+6)}{5(x-4)}$

20. Simplify the expression $x^6 \cdot (3x)^2$.

    a. $3x^8$

        b. $3x^{12}$

        c. $9x^8$

        d. $9x^{12}$

21. Which data set is represented by the boxplot shown below?

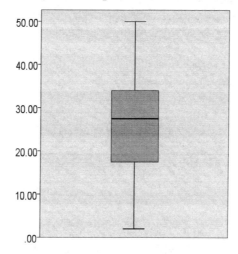

    a. 2, 3, 6, 9, 15, 20, 24, 25, 26, 27, 28, 29, 30, 30, 33, 35, 37, 39, 46, 50

        b. 1, 6, 6, 7, 10, 14, 14, 19, 20, 21, 24, 28, 35, 37, 38, 39, 41, 44, 44, 45

        c. 3, 3, 9, 10, 11, 12, 19, 20, 22, 23, 24, 24, 25, 28, 28, 30, 33, 36, 38, 45

        d. 3, 4, 4, 4, 5, 6, 10, 11, 15, 16, 18, 23, 25, 28, 28, 31, 35, 36, 37, 45

22. Given the stem-and-leaf plot shown below, which of the following statements is true?

Data Set A	Stem	Data Set B
1, 1, 8	0	2, 2, 4, 8, 9
4, 5, 5, 8, 9	1	3, 5
0, 1, 4, 7, 8, 9	2	3, 9
	3	1, 6
	4	0, 0, 2
0	5	0

a. Data set A shows a larger center and more variability.
   b. Data set A shows a larger center and less variability.
   c. Data set A shows a smaller center and more variability.
   d. Data set A shows a smaller center and less variability.

23. Given the double bar graph shown below, which of the following statements is true?

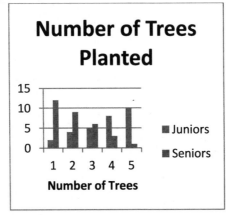

a. The number of trees planted by the Juniors is positively skewed, while the number of trees planted by the Seniors is approximately normal.
   b. The number of trees planted by the Juniors is negatively skewed, while the number of trees planted by the Seniors is positively skewed.
   c. The number of trees planted by the Juniors is positively skewed, while the number of trees planted by the Seniors is negatively skewed.
   d. The number of trees planted by the Juniors is approximately normal, while the number of trees planted by the Juniors is positively skewed.

24. Which frequency table is represented by the histogram shown below?

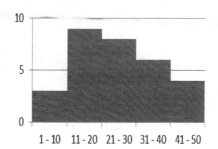

a.

Interval	Frequency
1 – 10	3
11 – 20	9
21 – 30	8
31 – 40	6
41 – 50	4

c.

Interval	Frequency
1 – 10	3
11 – 20	9
21 – 30	8
31 – 40	5
41 – 50	4

b.

Interval	Frequency
1 – 10	3
11 – 20	8
21 – 30	8
31 – 40	6
41 – 50	3

d.

Interval	Frequency
1 – 10	2
11 – 20	9
21 – 30	8
31 – 40	6
41 – 50	4

25. The numbers of volunteers in different states are shown in the table below. Which of the following statements is true?

Texas	8	17	18	19	20	21	21	21	22	28	29	31	41	45	48
New Mexico	7	11	15	29	30	30	31	33	34	36	37	42	44	44	45

a. The numbers of volunteers in Texas have a greater median and mean.
b. The numbers of volunteers in Texas have a greater median and a smaller mean.
c. The numbers of volunteers in Texas have a smaller median and mean.
d. The numbers of volunteers in Texas have a smaller median and a greater mean.

26. Which of the following measures is unaffected by a skewed distribution?

a. mean
b. median
c. standard deviation
d. range

27. Suppose data are normally distributed. Which of the following best represents the area under the curve, to the right of a z-score of 2.18?

    a. 0.01
      b. 0.03
      c. 0.04
      d. 0.06

28. Suppose data are normally distributed. Which of the following best represents the area under the curve, to the left of a z-score of 1.6?

    a. 0.87
      b. 0.90
      c. 0.92
      d. 0.95

29. Which of the following represents the area under the curve of a normal distribution, falling between the z-scores of 1.3 and 2.9?

    a. 0.09
      b. 0.21
      c. 0.63
      d. 0.90

30. Given the table shown below, what is the probability that a student is a Democrat or prefers math?

	History	Science	Math	Total
Democrat	13	30	37	80
Republican	20	38	12	70
Total	33	68	49	150

    a. $\dfrac{129}{150}$
      b. $\dfrac{46}{75}$
      c. $\dfrac{37}{150}$
      d. $\dfrac{37}{80}$

31. What is the name of Euclid's most famous work?

    a. Elements
      b. Principia Mathematica
      c. Treatise
      d. On the Equilibrium of Spheres

32. What is the name given to a statement that is not proved but is still considered true because it is thought to be self-evident?

    a. An axiom
      b. A corollary
      c. A definition
      d. A theorem

33. Which statement is true in Euclidean geometry but false in non-Euclidean geometry?

 a. A rectangle is a two-dimensional figure
  b. The sum of the angles of a triangle is always 360°
  c. The shortest line between two points is a great circle
  d. Parallel lines are a constant distance from one another

34. Write the inverse of the statement "If a man is unmarried, then he is a bachelor".

 a. "If a man is married, then he is not a bachelor"
  b. "If a man is married, then he is a bachelor"
  c. "If a man is not a bachelor, then he is married"
  d. "If a man is a bachelor, then he is unmarried"

35. Which statement is logically equivalent to "If Mary is 15 years old, then she is in the tenth grade"?

 a. "If Mary is not 15 years old, then she is not in the tenth grade"
  b. "If Mary is in the tenth grade, then she is 15 years old"
  c. "If Mary is not in the tenth grade, then she is not 15 years old"
  d. All of the above

36. Which of the following is a counterexample for the statement "If today is the weekend, then it is Sunday"?

 a. It is before 6 pm on Sunday
  b. Today is Saturday
  c. Tomorrow is Saturday
  d. It is Monday morning

37. Find a counterexample for the statement "Every number is either positive or negative".

38. A famous mathematician noted that when *n* is an integer between 0 and 40, the algebraic expression *n²+n+41* results in a prime number. He therefore conjectured that *n²+n+41* is a prime number for every positive integer *n*. Which type of reasoning did he use?

    a. Indirect reasoning
       b. Deductive reasoning
       c. Inductive reasoning
       d. Circular reasoning

39. Use inductive reasoning to formulate a conjecture about the sum of the first *n* powers of two (starting with *n=0*) added to one.

    a. It is a power of two
       b. It is perfect square
       c. It is prime number
       d. It is perfect number

40. Quadrilateral *ABCD* is a parallelogram. Every parallelogram has two pairs of congruent angles. What type of reasoning allows us to therefore conclude that quadrilateral *ABCD* has two pairs of congruent angles?

    a. Deductive reasoning
       b. Indirect reasoning
       c. Inductive reasoning
       d. Circular reasoning

41. Solve the equation $x^2 + 4x + 8 = 0$ for x.

    a. $x = -4$ and $x = 0$
       b. $x = 0$ and $x = 4$
       c. $x = -2 \pm 2i$
       d. $x = 2 \pm 2i$

42. Solve the equation $3x^2 - 3x + 7 = 0$ for x.

    a. $x = -\frac{1}{2} \pm \frac{5i}{6}\sqrt{3}$
       b. $x = \frac{1}{2} \pm \frac{5i}{6}\sqrt{3}$
       c. $x = -1 \pm 5i\sqrt{3}$
       d. $x = 1 \pm 5i\sqrt{3}$

43. Adam has $14 more than Betty. If Adam were to give $20 to Betty, then she would have twice as much money as Adam. Write this situation as a system of equations.

    a. $A = B + 14$
       $B + 20 = 2A$
       b. $B = A + 14$
       $B + 20 = 2A$
       c. $A = B + 14$
       $B + 20 = 2(A - 20)$
       d. $B = A + 14$
       $B + 20 = 2(A - 20)$

44. Solve the following system of equations.

$$y = 3x + 2$$
$$2x + y = 7$$

  a. $x = -1, y = 5$
     b. $x = -1, y = 9$
     c. $x = 1, y = 5$
     d. $x = 1, y = 9$

45. Solve the following system of equations.

$$3x + y = -4$$
$$5y = 4 + x$$

  a. $x = -\frac{7}{6}, y = -\frac{1}{2}$
     b. $x = -1, y = -1$
     c. $x = -\frac{3}{2}, y = \frac{1}{2}$
     d. $x = 1, y = 1$

46. Sophie has a total of fifteen dimes and quarters, together worth $2.85. How many dimes does she have?

47. What is the domain of the function $f(x) = 3x^2 + x - 2$?

  a. $x \geq \frac{2}{3}$
     b. $x \leq -1$
     c. $-1 \leq x \leq \frac{2}{3}$
     d. All real numbers

48. What is the range of the function $g(x) = 3x^2 - 6x + 1$?

  a. $g(x) \geq -2$
     b. $g(x) > 1$
     c. $g(x) \leq 1$
     d. All real numbers

49. The quadratic function $h(x)$ is represented by the graph below. Find the roots of the function, and use them to write $h(x)$ as a function of x.

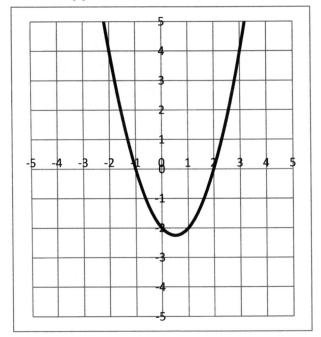

a. $h(x) = x^2 - x - 2$
b. $h(x) = x^2 - 2x - 2$
c. $h(x) = x^2 - x + 3$
d. $h(x) = x^2 + 2x + 3$

50. If $f(x)$ is a quadratic function with roots at $x = -4$ and $x = 6$, what is $f(x)$?

a. $f(x) = x^2 - 24$
b. $f(x) = x^2 - 10x + 24$
c. $f(x) = x^2 - 2x - 24$
d. $f(x) = x^2 + 2x - 24$

Answer Key and Explanations for Test #2

1. C: The equation describes a functional relationship between y and p(y). To solve the equation, substitute 4 as the value of y, such that

$$p(4) = \frac{4(4)}{2} + 5 = \frac{16}{2} + 5 = 8 + 5 = 13.$$

2. D: For each value of y, $p(y) = (y)^2 + 1$

$$p(1) = (1)^2 + 1 = (1)(1) + 1 = 1 + 1 = 2$$

$$p(-1) = (-1)^2 + 1 = (-1)(-1) + 1 = 1 + 1 = 2$$

$$p(2) = (2)^2 + 1 = (2)(2) + 1 = 4 + 1 = 5$$

$$p(-2) = (-2)^2 + 1 = (-2)(-2) + 1 = 4 + 1 = 5$$

$$p(3) = (3)^2 + 1 = (3)(3) + 1 = 9 + 1 = 10$$

$$p(-3) = (-3)^2 + 1 = (-3)(-3) + 1 = 9 + 1 = 10$$

3. C: Let y = the number of girls in Mr. Robinson's class. The ratio of boys to girls is 4:1. So for every 1 girl in the class, there are 4 boys in the class. Therefore, $4y$ equals the number of boys in Mr. Robinson's class. The total number of students in the class is 20. Therefore, the number of boys plus the number of girls equals 20 or

$$y + 4y = 20$$
$$5y = 20$$
$$y = 4$$

Hence y = 4 and 4y = 16. Therefore, 4 = the number of girls and 16 = the number of boys. Also, 4 + 16 = 20, the total number of students in the class.

4. A: Since half of the orchard contains apple trees, apple trees = 50%. In other words, $\frac{1}{2} = 0.5 =$ 50%. One quarter of the orchard contains pear trees. So pear trees = 25% or $\frac{1}{4} = 0.25 = 25\%$. Approximately one eighth of the orchard contains orange trees and one eighth contains lemon trees. One eighth is 12.5%, rounded to nearest whole number gives orange trees = 12% and lemon trees = 13%.

5. B: We know that apple trees = 50%, pear trees = 25%, lemon trees = 13%, and orange trees = 12%. Each percentage represents a portion of the total 100%. If the total number of trees is 100, then
apple trees = (50%) (100) = (0.5)(100) = 50 trees,
pear trees = (25%)(100) = (0.25)(100) = 25 trees,
lemon trees = (13%)(100) = (0.13)(100) = 13 trees,
orange trees = (12%)(100) = (0.12)(100) = 12 trees

171

6. B: Let y represent the number of apple trees. Then $p(y)$ represents the number of pear trees as a function of apple trees. Since Mrs. Langston has half as many pear trees as apple trees, the relationship can be represented as $p(y) = \frac{1}{2}y = \frac{y}{2}$.

7. C: Mrs. Langston has more apples in her orchard than any other fruit. Therefore, she could most likely produce the largest amount of a product that comes from apples, which in this case, is apple sauce.

8. D: The statement is false because Mrs. Langston did not plant more pear trees than any other kind of fruit. Instead, she planted the most *apple* trees.

9. B: The equation is written in the form of the point slope formula:
$y = mx + b$ where m is the slope of the line and b is the y-axis intercept. For the given equation, $y = -3x - 3$, the slope of the line is negative 3 and the line intercepts the y-axis at negative 3. The graph in Figure 2 fits these criteria. The graph in Figure 1 intercepts the y-axis at positive 3. The graphs in Figure 3 and Figure 4 have slopes of positive 3.

10. A: The equation is written in the form $y = Ax^2 + B$ where A tells the concavity of the graph and B is the y- intercept. In this case, A equals negative 1. So the graph is concave down. B equals negative 5. So the graph intercepts the y-axis at negative 5. The graph in Figure 1 fits these criteria. The graph in Figure 2 intercepts the y-axis at positive 5. The graphs in Figure 3 and Figure 4 are concave up.

11. D: The domain of a function is the set of all possible input values for the function. In this case, the input for $f(x)$ is x. The easiest way to find the domain of $f(x)$ is to determine for which x-values the function is undefined. Then you can exclude those values from the domain.

Examine the given function. Notice that it does not contain a square root sign, a logarithm, or a fraction with x in the denominator. Therefore, the function is defined for all real numbers. You can see this visually by graphing the function. In the graph below, notice that the function can go to the left and right without end.

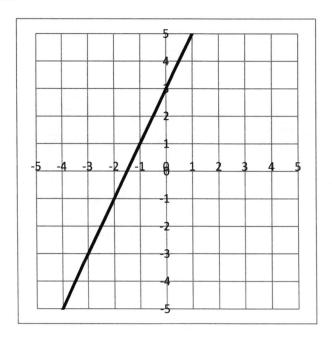

12. D: The range of a function is the set of all possible output values for the function. In this case, the output for $g(x)$ is the function itself, $g(x)$. Examine the given function. Let's say you choose some particular real number for $g(x)$. For any choice you make, you can find an x-value that will result in that choice by simply adding 2 to it. For example, say you choose $g(x) = -3$. Then you can use $x = -3 + 2 = -1$ to get your original value because $g(-1) = -1 - 2 = -3$. Since this will work for any real value for $g(x)$, the range of $g(x)$ is all real numbers. You can see this visually by graphing the function. In the graph below, notice that the function can go up and down without end.

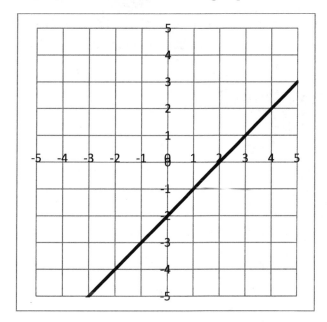

13. D: Examine the scatter plot. The function that best fits the data will be a line that goes through the middle of the data. Based on the leftmost points in the scatter plot, the height of the tree, $h(a)$, is about 23 when the age, a, is 8. Based on the rightmost points, $h(a)$ is about 139 when $a = 49$.

Now turn to the four answer choices for $h(a)$. As a test, substitute $a = 8$ and $a = 49$ into each to see how they compare to the data in the scatter plot.

Function	$h(8)$	$h(49)$
$h(a) = \dfrac{1}{4}a$	$h(6) = \dfrac{1}{4} \cdot 8 = 2$	$h(49) = \dfrac{1}{4} \cdot 49 = 12.25$
$h(a) = \dfrac{1}{4}a + 30$	$h(6) = \dfrac{1}{4} \cdot 8 + 30 = 32$	$h(49) = \dfrac{1}{4} \cdot 49 + 30$ $= 42.25$
$h(a) = a + 15$	$h(8) = 8 + 15 = 23$	$h(49) = 49 + 15 = 64$
$h(a) = 3a + 10$	$h(8) = 3 \cdot 8 + 10 = 34$	$h(49) = 3 \cdot 49 + 10$ $= 157$

Out of the four choices, the only function that approximates the leftmost and rightmost values from the scatter plot is $h(a) = 3a + 10$.

14. A: The logarithm of a number is the exponent to which the base must be raised in order to get that number. For example, since $3^2 = 9$, it is also true that $log_3(9) = 2$. To graph the given function, either use a graphing calculator or make a table of values. A table of values is shown below.

x	$\frac{1}{9}$	$\frac{1}{3}$	1	3	9
f(x)	-2	-1	0	1	2

From the table, the graph of $f(x)$ must pass through the points, $(\frac{1}{9}, -2)$, $(\frac{1}{3}, -1)$, $(1,0)$, $(3,1)$, and $(4,2)$. Graph these points on a coordinate plane, and then connect them with a smooth line. The resulting graph is shown below.

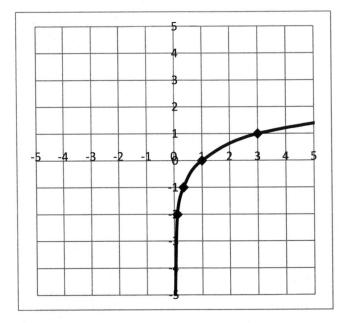

15. A: Transformations of a parent function include a translations, reflections, and dilations/compressions. In this case, the parent function is $f(x) = x^2$, which is a parabola.

Compare the two given function. There are two operations that must be done to $f(x)$ to get $g(x)$: first, you need to replace x with $(x + 1)$, and then you need to subtract 3 from the end. Both of these operations result in translations, or shifts, of the parent function horizontally and vertically. In particular, replacing x with $(x + 1)$ shifts the parent function 1 unit to the left, while subtracting 3 from the end shifts it 3 units down. Thus, to get the graph of $g(x)$ from the graph of $f(x)$, you need to shift the graph of $f(x)$ 1 unit to the left and 3 units down.

16. A: Transformations of a parent function include a translations, reflections, and dilations/compressions. In this case, the parent function is $f(x) = |x|$.

Compare the two given function. To get $g(x)$, you have to multiply the parent function $f(x)$ by 3. Multiplying a function by a positive number whose absolute value is greater than one (in this case, $|3| = 3 > 1$) stretches it vertically. Thus, to get $g(x)$ from $f(x)$, you need to stretch it vertically.

17. A: The inverse of a function is a relation that *undoes* a function. The inverse of $f(x)$ is written $f^{-1}(x)$ by convention. To find the inverse of $f(x)$, first replace $f(x)$ with y. Then, swap the x and y values.

$$f(x) = \frac{35}{x}$$

$$y = \frac{35}{x}$$

$$x = \frac{35}{y}$$

Next, solve the equation for y.

$$xy = 35$$

$$y = \frac{35}{x}$$

Finally, replace y with $f^{-1}(x)$ to get the inverse.

$$f^{-1}(x) = \frac{35}{x}$$

18. A: The inverse of a function is a relation that *undoes* a function. The inverse of $f(x)$ is written $f^{-1}(x)$ by convention. To find the inverse of $f(x)$, first replace $f(x)$ with y. Then, swap the x and y values.

$$f(x) = 6 + 2x$$

$$y = 6 + 2x$$

$$x = 6 + 2y$$

Next, solve the equation for y.

$$2y = x - 6$$

$$y = \frac{x-6}{2}$$

Finally, replace y with $f^{-1}(x)$ to get the inverse.

$$f^{-1}(x) = \frac{x-6}{2}$$

19. B: To simplify the expression, first factor the numerator and the denominator. To factor the numerator, use trial-and-error to find two numbers whose sum is 2 and whose product is -24, and then put those numbers into the form $(x + \_)(x + \_)$. For the denominator, factor out the common factor, which is 5.

$$\frac{x^2 + 2x - 24}{5x - 20} = \frac{(x+6)(x-4)}{5(x-4)}$$

Now there is a common factor, $(x - 4)$, in both the numerator and the denominator. Therefore, you can further simplify the expression by cancelling it out.

$$\frac{(x+6)(x-4)}{5(x-4)} = \frac{x+6}{5}$$

20. C: To simplify the expression, first simplify the expression with parentheses. To raise $3x$ to the third power, raise both 3 and x to the third power separately.

$$x^6 \cdot (3x)^2 = x^6 \cdot 3^2 \cdot x^2$$

$$= x^6 \cdot 9x^2$$

Next, multiply the two terms. Since they have the same base and are being multiplied together, add the exponents of the like base, x.

$$x^6 \cdot 9x^2 = 9x^{6+2}$$

$$= 9x^8$$

21. A: The data shown for Choice A has a minimum of 2, maximum of 50, median of 27.5, first quartile of 17.5, and third quartile of 34. The given boxplot represents each of these values.

22. D: Data set B has a larger center because there are more high scores. Data set A shows less variability, due to the clustering of scores between 1 and 29.

23. B: The number of trees planted by the Juniors is skewed left, with more higher numbers of trees planted. The number of trees planted by the Seniors is skewed right, with more lower numbers of trees planted.

24. A: The frequency table for Choice A correctly shows the frequencies represented by the histogram. The frequencies of values, falling between 1 and 10 is 3, between 11 and 20 is 9, between 21 and 30 is 8, between 31 and 40 is 6, and between 41 and 50 is 4.

25. C: The median number of volunteers in Texas is 21, with a mean of approximately 25.9. The median number of volunteers in New Mexico is 33, with a mean of approximately 31.2. Thus, the median and mean numbers of volunteers in Texas are smaller.

26. B: The median is unaffected by a skewed distribution, or data with extreme outliers. The median represents the value, at which 50% of the scores fall above and 50% of the scores fall below. The mean, standard deviation, and range are all impacted by non-normal data.

27. A: Using a standard z-table, the area from the mean to z is shown to be 0.4854. This area should be subtracted from 0.5 in order to show the area to the right of a z-score of 2.18. Thus, the area to the right of the z-score is 0.0146, or approximately 0.01. A z-table, including the smaller portion of area under a curve may also be used. This area is reported as 0.0146.

28. D: Using a standard z-table, the area from the mean to z is shown to be 0.4452. This area should be added to 0.5 in order to show the area to the left of a z-score of 1.6. Thus, the area to the left of the z-score is 0.9452, or approximately 0.95. A z-table, including the larger portion of area under a curve may also be used. This area is reported as 0.9452.

29. A: A standard z-table shows an area of 0.4032 between the mean and a z-score of 1.3. It also shows an area of 0.4981 between the mean and a z-score of 2.9. The difference of the two areas is

0.0949. Thus, the area between the two z-scores is approximately 9%. Using a table that reports the mean to z, the mean-to-z area for a z-score of 1.3 may be subtracted from the mean-to-z area for a z-score of 2.9.

30. B: The probability may be written as $P(A \text{ or } B) = P(A) + P(B) - P(A \text{ and } B) = \frac{80}{150} + \frac{49}{150} - \frac{37}{150}$, which simplifies to $P(A \text{ or } B) = \frac{46}{75}$.

31. A: Euclid, a Greek mathematician who lived around 300 BC, is usually considered the father of geometry and an important figure in the development of the notion of mathematical rigor. His most famous work is *Elements*, a collection of geometric proofs, starting with definitions and axioms and proceeding to more complicated propositions. It was still a widely read work until the 20th century.

32. A: Every branch of mathematics, including geometry, begins with basic definitions and unproven statements, called either axioms or postulates. New propositions, called theorems, are proved using deductive logic and previously established statements. Theorems that easily follow from another theorem are called corollaries.

33. D: Non-Euclidean geometry is geometry in which the parallel postulate is assumed to be false. Pictorially, this means that Euclidean geometry is on a flat plane (it is the geometry we are most familiar with), whereas non-Euclidean geometry is on a curved surface. As a result, parallel lines are a constant distance from one another in Euclidean geometry. On the other hand, in non-Euclidean geometry, parallel lines either curve away or toward one another depending on whether the surface is curved like a saddle-shaped plane or an ellipsoid.

34. A: The inverse of a statement "If p, then q" is "If $\sim p$, then $\sim q$", where p and q are any statement and the tilde ($\sim$) means "not" or "the opposite of". In other words, to construct the converse, negate (find the opposite of) both halves of the original statement. In the given expression, the p-statement is "a man is unmarried" and the q-statement is "he [a man] is a bachelor". Since being *not unmarried* is the same as being *married*, the inverse is "If a man married, then he is not a bachelor".

35. C: A conditional and its contrapositive always have the same truth table, so they are considered logically equivalent. On the other hand, the inverse and converse do not have the same truth table as the original statement, so they are not considered logically equivalent. Examine the choices A, B, and C and notice that choice A is the inverse of the original statement, choice B is the converse, and choice C is the contrapositive. Therefore, only the statement in choice C is logically equivalent to the original statement.

36. B: A counterexample is a specific example that violates a general statement. Since the given statement "If today is the weekend, then it is Sunday" is a conditional (i.e. it is in the form "If..., then..."), a counterexample will be an example in which the "if" part of the statement is true, but the "then" part is false. Therefore, for this problem, we need to find a day that is part of the weekend but is not Sunday. The only day that fits that description is Saturday.

37. 0: A counterexample is a specific example that violates a general statement. Since the statement is "Every number is either positive or negative", a counterexample would be a number that is neither positive nor negative. The only number that is neither positive nor negative is 0.

38. C: Inductive reasoning involves making an observation, finding a pattern, and making a general conjecture based on that pattern. In this example, the pattern the mathematician found was that, when n is an integer between 0 and 40, n^2+n+41 is a prime number. Using inductive reasoning, he generalized this pattern of 41 values of n to apply to all integer values of n.

39. A: Inductive reasoning involves making an observation, finding a pattern, and making a general conjecture based on that pattern. When n is between 0 and 4, the sum of the first n powers of two added to one are:

$$(2^0) + 1 = 1 + 1 = 2$$

$$(2^0 + 2^1) + 1 = (1 + 2) + 1 = 4$$

$$(2^0 + 2^1 + 2^2) + 1 = (1 + 2 + 4) + 1 = 8$$

$$(2^0 + 2^1 + 2^2 + 2^3) + 1 = (1 + 2 + 4 + 8) + 1 = 16$$

Notice that these numbers are all powers of two. Therefore, using inductive reasoning, we can make the conjecture the sum of the first n powers of two added to one is itself a power of two. Although this type of reasoning is not considered a valid method of mathematical proof, it is still useful for discovering possible theorems that can later be proved rigorously.

40. A: Deductive reasoning asserts conclusion that must necessarily be true based on a set of premises. In this problem, the premises are "Quadrilateral $ABCD$ is a parallelogram" and "Every parallelogram has two pairs of congruent angles". Since quadrilateral $ABCD$ is an instance of a parallelogram, it must *necessarily* have two pairs of congruent angles. Therefore, this is an example of deductive reasoning.

41. C: The left side of the equation cannot be factored, so use the quadratic equation. Remember that the square root of a negative number is an imaginary number.

$$x = \frac{-b \pm \sqrt{b^2 - 4ac}}{2a}$$

$$= \frac{-4 \pm \sqrt{16 - 32}}{2}$$

$$= \frac{-4 \pm \sqrt{-16}}{2}$$

$$= \frac{-4 \pm 4i}{2}$$

$$= -\frac{4}{2} \pm \frac{4i}{2}$$

$$= -2 \pm 2i$$

42. B: The left side of the equation cannot be factored, so use the quadratic equation. Remember that the square root of a negative number is an imaginary number.

$$x = \frac{-b \pm \sqrt{b^2 - 4ac}}{2a}$$

$$= \frac{3 \pm \sqrt{9 - 84}}{6}$$

$$= \frac{3 \pm \sqrt{-75}}{6}$$

$$= \frac{3 \pm 5i\sqrt{3}}{6}$$

$$= \tfrac{1}{2} \pm \tfrac{5i}{6}\sqrt{3}$$

43. C: Translate each sentence into a mathematical sentence. The first sentence, "Adam has $14 more than Betty,." can be written as $A = B + 14$, where A represents the amount of money Adam has and B represents the amount of money Betty has.

Next translate the second sentence "If Adam were to give $20 to Betty, then she would have twice as much money as Adam." This means that if Adam had $20 less (represented by the expression $A - 20$) and Betty had $20 more ($B + 20$), then Betty would have two times what Adam would have. So, the correct equation is $B + 20 = 2(A - 20)$.

44. B: Notice that the given system has two equations, and each equation has two variables, x and y. Therefore, the solution of the system of equations must have values for each of the two variables. To find the solution, you can use algebraic methods, graphs, tables, or matrices. For the purposes of this explanation, we will use an algebraic method called substitution.

To begin, notice that the first equation already has y isolated on the left side. Therefore, substitute the left side, $3x + 2$, for y into the second equation, and then solve for x.

$$2x + y = 7$$

$$2x + (3x + 2) = 7$$

$$5x = 5$$

$$x = 1$$

To find the value of y, substitute 1 for x in the first equation.

$$y = 3(1) + 2$$

$$= 3 + 2$$

$$= 5$$

Therefore, the solution of the given system of equations is $x = 1, y = 5$. Check this solution on your own by substituting the values into the second equations to make sure that you get a true equality.

45. C: Notice that the given system has two equations, and each equation has two variables, x and y. Therefore, the solution of the system of equations must have values for each of the two variables. To find the solution, you can use algebraic methods, graphs, tables, or matrices. For the purposes of this explanation, we will use an algebraic method called elimination.

To begin, rewrite the first equation so it is in the form $Ax + By = C$. (The first equation is already in this form.)

$$3x + y = -4 \rightarrow 3x + y = -4$$

$$5y = 4 + x \rightarrow -x + 5y = 4$$

179

Then, eliminate one of the variables. We will eliminate x. To do this, multiply the second equation by 3, and then add the equations together.

$$3x + y = -4 \quad \rightarrow \quad 3x + y = -4$$

$$3(-x + 5y = 4) \quad \rightarrow \quad -3x + 15y = 12$$

$$16y = 8$$

Solve the resulting equation by dividing both sides by 16. The result is $y = \frac{1}{2}$. To find the value of x, substitute ½ for y in either equation, and then solve for x. We will use the first equation.

$$3x + \frac{1}{2} = -4$$

$$3x = -\frac{9}{2}$$

$$x = -\frac{3}{2}$$

Therefore, the solution of the given system of equations is $x = -\frac{3}{2}, y = \frac{1}{2}$. Check this solution on your own by substituting the values into the second equation to make sure that you get a true equality.

46. 6: First translate the information in the word problem into two mathematical equations. In the problem, there are two unknowns: the number of dimes and the number of quarters. Let the variables d and q represent these quantities. In addition, we are given two separate pieces of information, namely that Sophie has fifteen coins and that the coins are worth \$2.85 altogether. We can translate these two statements into a system of equations.

$$d + q = 15$$

$$10d + 25q = 285$$

To solve this system of equations, you can use algebraic methods, graphs, tables, or matrices. For the purposes of this explanation, we will use an algebraic method called elimination. First, eliminate one of the variables. We will eliminate q. Multiply the first equation by 25, and then subtract the second equation from the first.

$$25(d + q = 15) \quad \rightarrow \quad 25d + 25q = 375$$

$$10d + 25q = 285 \quad \quad -(10d + 25q = 285)$$

$$15d = 90$$

Next, solve the resulting equation by dividing both sides by 15. The result is $d=6$. Therefore, Sophie has six dimes. Note that she has nine quarters since the number of dimes and quarters together is fifteen. The value of six dimes (\$0.60) and nine quarters (\$2.25) is indeed \$2.85 all together.

47. D: The domain of a function is the set of all possible input values for the function. In this case, the input for $f(x)$ is x. The easiest way to find the domain of $f(x)$ is to determine for which values of x the function is undefined. Then you can exclude those values from the domain.

180

Examine the given function. Notice that it does not contain a square root sign, a logarithm, or a fraction with *x* in the denominator. Therefore, the function will be defined for all real numbers. You can see this visually by graphing the function. In the graph below, notice that the function can go to the left and right without end.

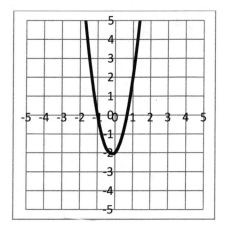

48. A: The range of a function is the set of all possible output values for the function. In this case, the output for $g(x)$ is the function itself, $g(x)$. To find the range, first graph the given function.

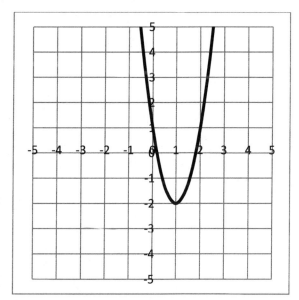

Notice that the graph is a U-shaped parabola, which means that its vertex is a minimum (rather than a maximum). Because of this, the range is the set of *y*-values above (and including) the minimum. In this case, the minimum is the point (1,-2). Therefore, the range of $g(x)$ is $g(x) \geq -2$.

49. A: The roots of a quadratic function $f(x)$ are the values of *x* for which $f(x) = 0$. Graphically, the roots are the *x*-values where the graph of the quadratic function intercepts the *x*-axis. Based on the graph, $h(x)$ has *x*-intercepts at $x = -1$ and $x = 2$. Therefore, the roots of $h(x)$ are $x = -1$ and $x = 2$.

A quadratic function written in the form $h(x) = (x - a)(x - b)$ has roots at $x = a$ and $x = b$. Therefore, to find $h(x)$, substitute the roots -1 and 2 for *a* and *b* and simplify the result.

$$h(x) = (x - a)(x - b)$$

$$= (x - (-1))(x - 2)$$

$$= (x + 1)(x - 2)$$

$$= x^2 - x - 2$$

50. C: The roots of a quadratic function *f*(x) are the values of *x* for which $f(x) = 0$. Quadratic functions may have two real roots, two imaginary roots, or one real double root. A quadratic function written in the form $f(x) = (x - a)(x - b)$ has roots at $x = a$ and $x = b$. Therefore, to find *f*(x), substitute the given roots for *a* and *b* into $f(x) = (x - a)(x - b)$ and simplify.

$$f(x) = (x - a)(x - b)$$

$$= (x - (-4))(x - 6)$$

$$= (x + 4)(x - 6)$$

$$= x^2 - 2x - 24$$

How to Overcome Your Fear of Math

The word *math* is enough to strike fear into most hearts. How many of us have memories of sitting through confusing lectures, wrestling over mind-numbing homework, or taking tests that still seem incomprehensible even after hours of study? Years after graduation, many still shudder at these memories.

The fact is, math is not just a classroom subject. It has real-world implications that you face every day, whether you realize it or not. This may be balancing your monthly budget, deciding how many supplies to buy for a project, or simply splitting a meal check with friends. The idea of daily confrontations with math can be so paralyzing that some develop a condition known as *math anxiety*.

But you do NOT need to be paralyzed by this anxiety! In fact, while you may have thought all your life that you're not good at math, or that your brain isn't wired to understand it, the truth is that you may have been conditioned to think this way. From your earliest school days, the way you were taught affected the way you viewed different subjects. And the way math has been taught has changed.

Several decades ago, there was a shift in American math classrooms. The focus changed from traditional problem-solving to a conceptual view of topics, de-emphasizing the importance of learning the basics and building on them. The solid foundation necessary for math progression and confidence was undermined. Math became more of a vague concept than a concrete idea. Today, it is common to think of math, not as a straightforward system, but as a mysterious, complicated method that can't be fully understood unless you're a genius.

This is why you may still have nightmares about being called on to answer a difficult problem in front of the class. Math anxiety is a very real, though unnecessary, fear.

Math anxiety may begin with a single class period. Let's say you missed a day in 6th grade math and never quite understood the concept that was taught while you were gone. Since math is cumulative, with each new concept building on past ones, this could very well affect the rest of your math career. Without that one day's knowledge, it will be difficult to understand any other concepts that link to it. Rather than realizing that you're just missing one key piece, you may begin to believe that you're simply not capable of understanding math.

This belief can change the way you approach other classes, career options, and everyday life experiences, if you become anxious at the thought that math might be required. A student who loves science may choose a different path of study upon realizing that multiple math classes will be required for a degree. An aspiring medical student may hesitate at the thought of going through the necessary math classes. For some this anxiety escalates into a more extreme state known as *math phobia*.

Math anxiety is challenging to address because it is rooted deeply and may come from a variety of causes: an embarrassing moment in class, a teacher who did not explain concepts well and contributed to a shaky foundation, or a failed test that contributed to the belief of math failure.

These causes add up over time, encouraged by society's popular view that math is hard and unpleasant. Eventually a person comes to firmly believe that he or she is simply bad at math. This belief makes it difficult to grasp new concepts or even remember old ones. Homework and test

183

grades begin to slip, which only confirms the belief. The poor performance is not due to lack of ability but is caused by math anxiety.

Math anxiety is an emotional issue, not a lack of intelligence. But when it becomes deeply rooted, it can become more than just an emotional problem. Physical symptoms appear. Blood pressure may rise and heartbeat may quicken at the sight of a math problem – or even the thought of math! This fear leads to a mental block. When someone with math anxiety is asked to perform a calculation, even a basic problem can seem overwhelming and impossible. The emotional and physical response to the thought of math prevents the brain from working through it logically.

The more this happens, the more a person's confidence drops, and the more math anxiety is generated. This vicious cycle must be broken!

The first step in breaking the cycle is to go back to very beginning and make sure you really understand the basics of how math works and why it works. It is not enough to memorize rules for multiplication and division. If you don't know WHY these rules work, your foundation will be shaky and you will be at risk of developing a phobia. Understanding mathematical concepts not only promotes confidence and security, but allows you to build on this understanding for new concepts. Additionally, you can solve unfamiliar problems using familiar concepts and processes.

Why is it that students in other countries regularly outperform American students in math? The answer likely boils down to a couple of things: the foundation of mathematical conceptual understanding and societal perception. While students in the US are not expected to *like* or *get* math, in many other nations, students are expected not only to understand math but also to excel at it.

Changing the American view of math that leads to math anxiety is a monumental task. It requires changing the training of teachers nationwide, from kindergarten through high school, so that they learn to teach the *why* behind math and to combat the wrong math views that students may develop. It also involves changing the stigma associated with math, so that it is no longer viewed as unpleasant and incomprehensible. While these are necessary changes, they are challenging and will take time. But in the meantime, math anxiety is not irreversible—it can be faced and defeated, one person at a time.

False Beliefs

One reason math anxiety has taken such hold is that several false beliefs have been created and shared until they became widely accepted. Some of these unhelpful beliefs include the following:

There is only one way to solve a math problem. In the same way that you can choose from different driving routes and still arrive at the same house, you can solve a math problem using different methods and still find the correct answer. A person who understands the reasoning behind math calculations may be able to look at an unfamiliar concept and find the right answer, just by applying logic to the knowledge they already have. This approach may be different than what is taught in the classroom, but it is still valid. Unfortunately, even many teachers view math as a subject where the best course of action is to memorize the rule or process for each problem rather than as a place for students to exercise logic and creativity in finding a solution.

Many people don't have a mind for math. A person who has struggled due to poor teaching or math anxiety may falsely believe that he or she doesn't have the mental capacity to grasp mathematical concepts. Most of the time, this is false. Many people find that when they are relieved of their math anxiety, they have more than enough brainpower to understand math.

Men are naturally better at math than women. Even though research has shown this to be false, many young women still avoid math careers and classes because of their belief that their math abilities are inferior. Many girls have come to believe that math is a male skill and have given up trying to understand or enjoy it.

Counting aids are bad. Something like counting on your fingers or drawing out a problem to visualize it may be frowned on as childish or a crutch, but these devices can help you get a tangible understanding of a problem or a concept.

Sadly, many students buy into these ideologies at an early age. A young girl who enjoys math class may be conditioned to think that she doesn't actually have the brain for it because math is for boys, and may turn her energies to other pursuits, permanently closing the door on a wide range of opportunities. A child who finds the right answer but doesn't follow the teacher's method may believe that he is doing it wrong and isn't good at math. A student who never had a problem with math before may have a poor teacher and become confused, yet believe that the problem is because she doesn't have a mathematical mind.

Students who have bought into these erroneous beliefs quickly begin to add their own anxieties, adapting them to their own personal situations:

I'll never use this in real life. A huge number of people wrongly believe that math is irrelevant outside the classroom. By adopting this mindset, they are handicapping themselves for a life in a mathematical world, as well as limiting their career choices. When they are inevitably faced with real-world math, they are conditioning themselves to respond with anxiety.

I'm not quick enough. While timed tests and quizzes, or even simply comparing yourself with other students in the class, can lead to this belief, speed is not an indicator of skill level. A person can work very slowly yet understand at a deep level.

If I can understand it, it's too easy. People with a low view of their own abilities tend to think that if they are able to grasp a concept, it must be simple. They cannot accept the idea that they are capable of understanding math. This belief will make it harder to learn, no matter how intelligent they are.

I just can't learn this. An overwhelming number of people think this, from young children to adults, and much of the time it is simply not true. But this mindset can turn into a self-fulfilling prophecy that keeps you from exercising and growing your math ability.

The good news is, each of these myths can be debunked. For most people, they are based on emotion and psychology, NOT on actual ability! It will take time, effort, and the desire to change, but change is possible. Even if you have spent years thinking that you don't have the capability to understand math, it is not too late to uncover your true ability and find relief from the anxiety that surrounds math.

Math Strategies

It is important to have a plan of attack to combat math anxiety. There are many useful strategies for pinpointing the fears or myths and eradicating them:

Go back to the basics. For most people, math anxiety stems from a poor foundation. You may think that you have a complete understanding of addition and subtraction, or even decimals and percentages, but make absolutely sure. Learning math is different from learning other subjects. For example, when you learn history, you study various time periods and places and events. It may be important to memorize dates or find out about the lives of famous people. When you move from US history to world history, there will be some overlap, but a large amount of the information will be new. Mathematical concepts, on the other hand, are very closely linked and highly dependent on each other. It's like climbing a ladder – if a rung is missing from your understanding, it may be difficult or impossible for you to climb any higher, no matter how hard you try. So go back and make sure your math foundation is strong. This may mean taking a remedial math course, going to a tutor to work through the shaky concepts, or just going through your old homework to make sure you really understand it.

Speak the language. Math has a large vocabulary of terms and phrases unique to working problems. Sometimes these are completely new terms, and sometimes they are common words, but are used differently in a math setting. If you can't speak the language, it will be very difficult to get a thorough understanding of the concepts. It's common for students to think that they don't understand math when they simply don't understand the vocabulary. The good news is that this is fairly easy to fix. Brushing up on any terms you aren't quite sure of can help bring the rest of the concepts into focus.

Check your anxiety level. When you think about math, do you feel nervous or uncomfortable? Do you struggle with feelings of inadequacy, even on concepts that you know you've already learned? It's important to understand your specific math anxieties, and what triggers them. When you catch yourself falling back on a false belief, mentally replace it with the truth. Don't let yourself believe that you can't learn, or that struggling with a concept means you'll never understand it. Instead, remind yourself of how much you've already learned and dwell on that past success. Visualize grasping the new concept, linking it to your old knowledge, and moving on to the next challenge. Also, learn how to manage anxiety when it arises. There are many techniques for coping with the irrational fears that rise to the surface when you enter the math classroom. This may include controlled breathing, replacing negative thoughts with positive ones, or visualizing success. Anxiety interferes with your ability to concentrate and absorb information, which in turn contributes to greater anxiety. If you can learn how to regain control of your thinking, you will be better able to pay attention, make progress, and succeed!

Don't go it alone. Like any deeply ingrained belief, math anxiety is not easy to eradicate. And there is no need for you to wrestle through it on your own. It will take time, and many people find that speaking with a counselor or psychiatrist helps. They can help you develop strategies for responding to anxiety and overcoming old ideas. Additionally, it can be very helpful to take a short course or seek out a math tutor to help you find and fix the missing rungs on your ladder and make sure that you're ready to progress to the next level. You can also find a number of math aids online: courses that will teach you mental devices for figuring out problems, how to get the most out of your math classes, etc.

Check your math attitude. No matter how much you want to learn and overcome your anxiety, you'll have trouble if you still have a negative attitude toward math. If you think it's too hard, or just have general feelings of dread about math, it will be hard to learn and to break through the anxiety. Work on cultivating a positive math attitude. Remind yourself that math is not just a hurdle to be cleared, but a valuable asset. When you view math with a positive attitude, you'll be much more likely to understand and even enjoy it. This is something you must do for yourself. You may find it helpful to visit with a counselor. Your tutor, friends, and family may cheer you on in your endeavors. But your greatest asset is yourself. You are inside your own mind – tell yourself what you need to hear. Relive past victories. Remind yourself that you are capable of understanding math. Root out any false beliefs that linger and replace them with positive truths. Even if it doesn't feel true at first, it will begin to affect your thinking and pave the way for a positive, anxiety-free mindset.

Aside from these general strategies, there are a number of specific practical things you can do to begin your journey toward overcoming math anxiety. Something as simple as learning a new note-taking strategy can change the way you approach math and give you more confidence and understanding. New study techniques can also make a huge difference.

Math anxiety leads to bad habits. If it causes you to be afraid of answering a question in class, you may gravitate toward the back row. You may be embarrassed to ask for help. And you may procrastinate on assignments, which leads to rushing through them at the last moment when it's too late to get a better understanding. It's important to identify your negative behaviors and replace them with positive ones:

Prepare ahead of time. Read the lesson before you go to class. Being exposed to the topics that will be covered in class ahead of time, even if you don't understand them perfectly, is extremely helpful in increasing what you retain from the lecture. Do your homework and, if you're still shaky, go over some extra problems. The key to a solid understanding of math is practice.

Sit front and center. When you can easily see and hear, you'll understand more, and you'll avoid the distractions of other students if no one is in front of you. Plus, you're more likely to be sitting with students who are positive and engaged, rather than others with math anxiety. Let their positive math attitude rub off on you.

Ask questions in class and out. If you don't understand something, just ask. If you need a more in-depth explanation, the teacher may need to work with you outside of class, but often it's a simple concept you don't quite understand, and a single question may clear it up. If you wait, you may not be able to follow the rest of the day's lesson. For extra help, most professors have office hours outside of class when you can go over concepts one-on-one to clear up any uncertainties. Additionally, there may be a *math lab* or study session you can attend for homework help. Take advantage of this.

Review. Even if you feel that you've fully mastered a concept, review it periodically to reinforce it. Going over an old lesson has several benefits: solidifying your understanding, giving you a confidence boost, and even giving some new insights into material that you're currently learning! Don't let yourself get rusty. That can lead to problems with learning later concepts.

Teaching Tips

While the math student's mindset is the most crucial to overcoming math anxiety, it is also important for others to adjust their math attitudes. Teachers and parents have an enormous influence on how students relate to math. They can either contribute to math confidence or math anxiety.

As a parent or teacher, it is very important to convey a positive math attitude. Retelling horror stories of your own bad experience with math will contribute to a new generation of math anxiety. Even if you don't share your experiences, others will be able to sense your fears and may begin to believe them.

Even a careless comment can have a big impact, so watch for phrases like *He's not good at math* or *I never liked math.* You are a crucial role model, and your children or students will unconsciously adopt your mindset. Give them a positive example to follow. Rather than teaching them to fear the math world before they even know it, teach them about all its potential and excitement.

Work to present math as an integral, beautiful, and understandable part of life. Encourage creativity in solving problems. Watch for false beliefs and dispel them. Cross the lines between subjects: integrate history, English, and music with math. Show students how math is used every day, and how the entire world is based on mathematical principles, from the pull of gravity to the shape of seashells. Instead of letting students see math as a necessary evil, direct them to view it as an imaginative, beautiful art form – an art form that they are capable of mastering and using.

Don't give too narrow a view of math. It is more than just numbers. Yes, working problems and learning formulas is a large part of classroom math. But don't let the teaching stop there. Teach students about the everyday implications of math. Show them how nature works according to the laws of mathematics, and take them outside to make discoveries of their own. Expose them to math-related careers by inviting visiting speakers, asking students to do research and presentations, and learning students' interests and aptitudes on a personal level.

Demonstrate the importance of math. Many people see math as nothing more than a required stepping stone to their degree, a nuisance with no real usefulness. Teach students that algebra is used every day in managing their bank accounts, in following recipes, and in scheduling the day's events. Show them how learning to do geometric proofs helps them to develop logical thinking, an invaluable life skill. Let them see that math surrounds them and is integrally linked to their daily lives: that weather predictions are based on math, that math was used to design cars and other machines, etc. Most of all, give them the tools to use math to enrich their lives.

Make math as tangible as possible. Use visual aids and objects that can be touched. It is much easier to grasp a concept when you can hold it in your hands and manipulate it, rather than just listening to the lecture. Encourage math outside of the classroom. The real world is full of measuring, counting, and calculating, so let students participate in this. Keep your eyes open for numbers and patterns to discuss. Talk about how scores are calculated in sports games and how far apart plants are placed in a garden row for maximum growth. Build the mindset that math is a normal and interesting part of daily life.

Finally, find math resources that help to build a positive math attitude. There are a number of books that show math as fascinating and exciting while teaching important concepts, for example: *The Math Curse; A Wrinkle in Time; The Phantom Tollbooth;* and *Fractals, Googols and Other Mathematical Tales.* You can also find a number of online resources: math puzzles and games, videos that show math in nature, and communities of math enthusiasts. On a local level, students can compete in a variety of math competitions with other schools or join a math club.

The student who experiences math as exciting and interesting is unlikely to suffer from math anxiety. Going through life without this handicap is an immense advantage and opens many doors that others have closed through their fear.

Self-Check

Whether you suffer from math anxiety or not, chances are that you have been exposed to some of the false beliefs mentioned above. Now is the time to check yourself for any errors you may have accepted. Do you think you're not wired for math? Or that you don't need to understand it since you're not planning on a math career? Do you think math is just too difficult for the average person?

Find the errors you've taken to heart and replace them with positive thinking. Are you capable of learning math? Yes! Can you control your anxiety? Yes! These errors will resurface from time to time, so be watchful. Don't let others with math anxiety influence you or sway your confidence. If you're having trouble with a concept, find help. Don't let it discourage you!

Create a plan of attack for defeating math anxiety and sharpening your skills. Do some research and decide if it would help you to take a class, get a tutor, or find some online resources to fine-tune your knowledge. Make the effort to get good nutrition, hydration, and sleep so that you are operating at full capacity. Remind yourself daily that you are skilled and that anxiety does not control you. Your mind is capable of so much more than you know. Give it the tools it needs to grow and thrive.

Thank You

We at Mometrix would like to extend our heartfelt thanks to you, our friend and patron, for allowing us to play a part in your journey. It is a privilege to serve people from all walks of life who are unified in their commitment to building the best future they can for themselves.

The preparation you devote to these important testing milestones may be the most valuable educational opportunity you have for making a real difference in your life. We encourage you to put your heart into it—that feeling of succeeding, overcoming, and yes, conquering will be well worth the hours you've invested.

We want to hear your story, your struggles and your successes, and if you see any opportunities for us to improve our materials so we can help others even more effectively in the future, please share that with us as well. **The team at Mometrix would be absolutely thrilled to hear from you!** So please, send us an email (support@mometrix.com) and let's stay in touch.

> **If you'd like some additional help, check out these other resources we offer for your exam:**
> **http://MometrixFlashcards.com/Iowa**